DRAWING DEPORTATION

Drawing Deportation

Art and Resistance among Immigrant Children

Silvia Rodriguez Vega

NEW YORK UNIVERSITY PRESS
New York

NEW YORK UNIVERSITY PRESS
New York
www.nyupress.org

References to Internet websites (URLs) were accurate at the time of writing. Neither the author nor New York University Press is responsible for URLs that may have expired or changed since the manuscript was prepared.

Library of Congress Cataloging-in-Publication Data
Names: Rodriguez Vega, Silvia author.
Title: Drawing deportation : art and resistance among immigrant children /
Silvia Rodriguez Vega.
Description: New York : New York University, 2023. |
Includes bibliographical references and index.
Identifiers: LCCN 2022006288 | ISBN 9781479810444 (hardback) |
ISBN 9781479810451 (paperback) | ISBN 9781479810468 (ebook other) |
ISBN 9781479810475 (ebook)
Subjects: LCSH: Immigrant children—Education—United States. | Immigrant children—
United States—Social conditions. | Immigrant children—Government policy—United
States. | Arts—Study and teaching—Psychological aspects. | Art therapy for children. |
Deportation—Psychological aspects.
Classification: LCC LC3731 .R63 2023 | DDC 371.826/912—dc23/eng/20220713
LC record available at https://lccn.loc.gov/2022006288

New York University Press books are printed on acid-free paper, and their binding materials are chosen for strength and durability. We strive to use environmentally responsible suppliers and materials to the greatest extent possible in publishing our books.

Manufactured in the United States of America

10 9 8 7 6 5 4 3 2 1

Also available as an ebook

To all children of immigrants serving as bridges between worlds.

If I could draw a crane poem now
I would paint us blue
shivering in this cell
and Fernanda with a crowbar
knocking down guards
breaking open the lock
that keeps us trapped.

    Aida Salazar, "Crowbar Blue"

CONTENTS

Color illustrations appear as inserts following pages 62 and 126.

Introduction

From Caged Childhoods to Caged Children

Daniela was 9 years old when she started coming into the community center in Phoenix, Arizona, to do homework. Sometimes we would play sports or do arts and crafts. She loved volunteering to pass out peanut-butter-and-jelly sandwiches during snack time. Daniela always wore a high ponytail that at the end of the day would be low after a full day of playing. One afternoon in 2007, Daniela rushed into the center without her backpack and with no ponytail. I knew something was wrong; her face had a look of desperation. Crying and distraught, Dani told me that the sheriffs had taken her father. She sobbed and could not take full breaths as she tried to tell us what happened. "The sheriffs took him!" she cried. She was unsure if her father would be deported to Mexico and feared she would never see him again.

Sadly, this was not an uncommon occurrence at the center. For months, Maricopa County sheriff's deputies would carry out immigration raids in this neighborhood, specifically in the mobile homes in front of our community center where Daniela and many immigrant families lived. After this incident, Daniela did not return as often. She lost focus at school and once confessed that she wanted to stop going as she feared that when she returned, her mother might be missing, too. Unfortunately, Daniela was not the only student who came into the center sharing similar stories of separation and fear.

Almost 10 years later, in 2016, Elisa—a 12-year-old who lives in Los Angeles—was feeling the same pain and distraction at school because of losing one of her family members and being far from loved ones. "We saw on the news that his body [Elisa's cousin] was found on the border," she recounted with tears in her eyes as she explained the term "immigrant" during our theater-arts class. Elisa had made the journey herself from El Salvador, alone, when she was only 10. Her mother's wish was for Elisa to reunite with her aunt in Los Angeles. It had now been two years since she last saw her mother. She missed her very much but was terrified of her migrating because she did not want anything to happen to her. Now Elisa lived with her aunt's family, including her other cousin, Julio, who attended the same school and participated in the same theater class. When Elisa shared what had happened to their cousin Alex, Julio also cried and told us how painful it was that they could never see Alex again. The topic is so devastating for the family that no one ever talks about it. So, when Elisa and Julio shared with the class, we all cried with them.

Although there is scholarship about undocumented youth, little is known about preadolescent children of immigrants or migrant children, who are the fastest-growing segment of the US child population.[1] This book aims to understand legal violence from the perspective and experience of young children. This can be difficult to do given that traditional research methods like surveys may be biased to best serve adults, and because stigma, language barriers, and age can be factors that make interviewing children difficult. For this reason, few studies document the impact of detention and deportation directly from children's accounts. Art is a powerful tool that can help us to understand children's complex thoughts while allowing them to process their feelings, which has prompted an increasing interest in recent years in art methodologies.[2] This book utilizes drawings and theater to shed light on the lives of children of immigrants during this anti-immigrant political era.

In this book I argue that young immigrant children[3] are not passive in the face of the challenges presented by US anti-immigrant policies of the last two decades. Through an analysis of preadolescents' drawings, theater performances, and family interviews, we can gain key insight into both the impact of the "deportation machine" on children's lives and well-being, and how the use of art helps them develop personal agency to respond creatively, manage their emotions, and reimagine the dilemmas presented by legal violence.

History of Family Separation

Under former president Donald Trump's administration, a handful of appallingly anti-immigrant policies, such as family separation under the zero-tolerance[4] policy, made the headlines and shocked the public. Images of children in cages with metallic blankets and audio recordings of children crying hysterically for their parents surfaced in the media. Things continued to worsen. Investigative reports revealed the physical, emotional, and sexual abuse of children in detention centers by guards and service providers.[5] Additionally, health and educational measures were completely ignored and abandoned.[6] Soon after followed stories of Central American children who died while detained.[7] Deaths along the journey also took the lives of other children and parents as increasingly restrictive asylum policies made journeying to the United States more dangerous than ever before. Although the zero-tolerance policy was terminated, the country seemed irremediably polarized by anti-immigrant rhetoric and impossible choices. In 2020, nearly three years after the zero-tolerance policy, lawyers reported that over 600 children had still not been reunited with their families after the federal government deported parents without their children—without keeping track of any family records.[8]

The practice of family separation as a tactic of control is not new. In fact, it is a very American practice developed across time during many presidential administrations, perfected and institutionalized since the colonial invasion. While the United Nations has stated that "forcibly transferring children of one group to another" is part of international law's definition of genocide,[9] historians have documented how in the US, separating families became a profitable business model during slavery and later was used as a war tactic for surveillance and coercion. Some believe that child-protective services and agencies were used to destroy the Black family.[10] In *Taking Children*, Briggs demonstrated how the US effectively kidnapped Black children and sold them to White families, and abducted Native American children from their families and tribal communities to assimilate them in boarding schools.[11] In some ways the tactic of child abduction by the state crosses racial and class lines. Even as early as the 1900s, poor White parents and children were terrified that agents of the state would "snatch" their children.[12] Indeed, in 1904 when Irish immigrant children were deemed uncared for because of the dire poverty they experienced and were thought not to acclimate well to elite adoptive families in New York, the Catholic Church of New York placed the children in the homes of Catholic Mexican families in Arizona. Even though the religion was the same, this was considered an act of "racial transgression" and sparked violence by Anglo vigilante groups, who abducted the children from their Mexican homes and nearly lynched the nuns who had placed them there. The legal system via the Supreme Court was so entrenched in upholding whiteness that it ruled in favor of the vigilantes when the Catholic Church sued, ultimately demonstrating the historical lineage of family separation by way of White supremacy.[13]

Keeping children away from their parents is not the only tactic the US has implemented to control groups of people deemed an unwanted threat. Several times in the nation's history detention protocols have been altered to detain parents *with* their children, holding them in detention *together*, as, for instance, in the case of the detention of Japanese American families in internment camps during World War II. Decades later President Obama would call centers like these "family residential centers," where underage Central American children could be kept together with their parents. The legacy of White supremacy created a blueprint that Obama institutionalized and Trump perfected as they continued to pursue family-separation polices. Policies like zero tolerance took the next step of not only detaining families, but separating children from parents once families were apprehended and detained. Indeed, family separation is a "counterinsurgency tactic used to bring hopelessness, despair, grief, and shame."[14] In this way American systems are responsible for continued genocide and crimes against humanity, utilizing enforcement to generate such dire circumstances that migrant families would not dare to make the journey north or would leave the US of their own volition through what the US government called "self-deportation" or "attrition through enforcement."[15] However, despite the harsh deterrence measures by Obama, Trump, and Biden, record numbers of families and unaccompanied minors have continued to come to the US border.

Anti-immigrant Policy and Childhood Trauma

Legal Violence

Drawing from scholarship on symbolic and structural violence, Menjívar and Abrego[16] developed the term "legal violence" to refer to the various forms of structural injustices in society that directly or indirectly harm people through the rule of law. They maintain that when positive intentions motivate violence or when it is a by-product of larger goals, violence becomes socially acceptable. Legal violence can function as a lens that captures the destructive consequences of otherwise socially "accepted" legal outcomes. For example, structural violence is exemplified in the way undocumented immigrants may become separated from their families, be denied access to resources and upward mobility, or experience inhumane punishment for their precarious legal status.[17] This punishment is acceptable to the status quo because it is in the name of the country's larger goals—in the case of immigration, in the name of national security. With this foundational understanding of legal violence, this book illuminates the impact of legal violence on the lives of children of immigrants and their well-being.

Effects of Detention and Deportation on Children

Children of immigrants are the fastest-growing segment of the US child population, accounting for one-fourth of the nation's 75 million children, yet they do not receive equal protection under the law.[18] For example, many of the anti-immigrant policies targeting undocumented adults at the national and local levels ultimately and sometimes unintentionally affect children in harmful ways that range from developmental to social to educational harm.[19] Approximately 5.3 million children in the US have at least one undocumented parent.[20] Demographers predict that by 2040, one in three children will live in an immigrant household.[21] Coupling the number of children of immigrants with the circumstances of today's anti-immigrant society has resulted in immigrant communities feeling the overwhelming effects of deportation enforcement. The Obama administration deported more immigrants than any other administration before his presidency.[22] Building on this strategy, in 2016 during Trump's first year, his administration managed to increase immigrant detention by 43%.[23] Indeed, despite the enforcement excesses and deportations of the Obama administration, the effect of the Trump administration's policy to end all documented and undocumented immigration has been judged to be much worse. The Migration Policy Institute found that from 2017 to 2020 the Trump administration dismantled and reconstructed the US immigration system with over 400 executive orders.[24] Some estimates of policy alterations to immigration law put the range at 400 to 1,000 policy changes during these four years.[25]

Coupled with these high rates of deportation, children of immigrants found themselves separated from their families, adopted by family members, or waiting for adoption in foster care.[26] In Trump's first year in office, his administration controversially instituted the zero-tolerance approach, separating asylum-seeking families at the border and establishing more child-detention facilities. In the month of November 2017 alone, state authorities apprehended seven thousand "family units" in addition to 4,000 unaccompanied minors or children traveling without an adult.[27] Although a court order demanded the reunification of these children with their parents, this process has proven to be long and arduous as the Trump administration admitted to not knowing the exact number of children they had separated from their parents.[28] It was through this zero-tolerance approach to immigration policy that the Trump administration used family separation and criminalization as purposeful tactics to deter future immigrants from coming to or staying in the US.[29] Moreover, a report by the *Washington Examiner* found that the number of children separated from their parents grew to 250 per day during President Trump's tenure.[30]

Detention and deportation create detrimental outcomes for all children in mixed-status families because of the fear of familial disintegration. Some argue that the trauma was magnified for children separated from parents and detained apart from them, as opposed to the minors who came alone seeking to find parents or relatives already in the US. Even when children do not experience deportation, they fear for the security of their family.[31] Additionally, children often conflate immigration agents with local law enforcement, resulting in fear of any public official. Likewise, children in mixed-status families tend to assume that all immigrants are undocumented, often seeing themselves as undocumented even when they have US citizenship.[32] Consequently, the psychological and practical effects on children include fear, distrust, depression, anxiety, and financial instability.[33] In fact, caregivers have reported frequent crying, loss of appetite, sleeplessness, clingy behavior, and increased levels of fear and anxiety in these children.[34]

Impact on Schooling and Educational Well-Being

When it comes to school settings, teachers report that children exposed to immigration raids often missed school and were seldom able to concentrate when they attended, resulting in the slipping of grades.[35] The consequences of detention and deportation can thus affect children's abilities to transition into a healthy adolescence.[36] For instance, as children, undocumented immigrants experience inclusive access to public education, but as adults they are denied participation in jobs, higher education, and other privileges like driving, traveling, and voting.[37] Legal status affects every aspect of the ecological development of young people, from health, cognitive, educational, and socio-emotional development to their engagement with the labor market.[38]

As children in immigrant families come of age they receive a series of societal messages about their cultural, ethnic, and racial group. Even when these messages can be seemingly positive, they still may be detrimental to students. For example, Asian students are often perceived as "smart" and "hard-working," perpetuating the "model minority myth."[39] While they can be interpreted as neutral or benign, these messages tend to overtly or covertly advance ideologies of White supremacy. For others they can be overtly negative, such as the racist perceptions of all Latinx[40] people being "illegal." Through societal treatment, media representations, and political sentiments, social mirroring can influence children's identities in detrimental ways.[41] Because of these negative messages, "adolescents may find it difficult to develop a flexible and adaptive sense of self."[42] Hence, being undocumented can cause serious risks to any person's well-being, particularly during a time of high anti-immigrant sentiment and police violence.

The Psychological Impact of Stress on Youth

Legal violence as represented by the policy contexts described above is experienced as a climate of fear and uncertainty in the daily lives of the children discussed in this book. This fear relates to the possibility that their parents might be ripped out of their household and sent to another country. Experiencing this fear every day constitutes trauma over time.

For those who hear about a direct family member or someone their family knows being deported, the trauma is heightened.[43] The effects of trauma on children can be detrimental across their lifetime.

Trauma is defined as a lasting, substantial negative psychological impact.[44] It may result from a single occurrence, such as an accident, or it may stem from several experiences that happen over time. It may also be due to progressive exposure to neglect, abuse, or severe events of violence or war. Loss of possessions or family members can also cause chronic stress.[45] This chronic stress does not affect all children in the same way. Some young people can develop emotional, cognitive, or developmental issues due to long-term exposure to chronic stress. In the 1980s trauma scholar Terr identified two forms of traumatic events: acute trauma (type 1), which involves one single event, and chronic trauma (type 2), which happens multiple times as the result of various events.[46] When children are traumatized, there are many feelings they may experience, including helplessness, confusion, and shame. These feelings create fear and lack of trust for others or their environment.[47]

There are various factors that contribute to the impact of trauma in the lives of children. Depending on the developmental stage, development aspects, temperament, resiliency, attachment to parents/caregivers, and other factors may influence the kinds of reactions children have to trauma. Some children react and behave differently depending on their age and situation. Some of the most common symptoms for school-age children range from feeling helpless or uncertain in preschool to becoming anxious in elementary school or feeling depressed and alone in middle and high school.[48]

Understanding Stress

Since the Immigration Reform and Control Act (IRCA) of 1986 there has been no pathway to citizenship for the undocumented. Policy has therefore created the conditions for chronic stress for millions of children in immigrant families. The threat to children is a significant one—of parental loss. Parental loss is one of the most traumatic events that a child can face.[49] Children in urban areas experience stress[50] that, coupled with fears of deportation, can become chronic or toxic. Sociological demographer Landale and colleagues found higher internalizing (depression, anxiety, withdrawal) and externalizing (aggressive and acting out) behavioral problems in a sample of Mexican-origin, primary-school-age children with undocumented parents relative to their counterparts with documented or US-citizen parents.[51] By adolescence, having an undocumented parent, relative to one who is documented, was associated with higher levels of self-reported anxiety and depressive symptoms in a North Carolina study.[52]

Sometimes toxic stress—the form of bodily stress response associated with long-term health and mental-health consequences—can persist when the child is no longer in physical danger, but through recall of the stress-causing event or situation. Stress in a young child can lead to changes in the brain such as "hypertrophy and overactivity in the amygdala and orbitofrontal cortex, whereas comparable levels of adversity can lead to loss of neurons and neural connections in the hippocampus and medial PFC."[53] Moreover, the consequences of these changes can include anxiety as well as impaired memory and mood control.[54] In other words, the developing architecture of the brain can be impaired in numerous ways that create a weak foundation for later learning, behavior, and health. Effectively this can hinder a person's quality of life.

Understanding that issues concerning decision-making, mood, behavior, cognitive problems, self-regulation, impulse control, and working memory are all consequences of chronic toxic stress, exposure to the chronic threat of parental loss and family separation in children should be alarming for educators and parents. We know that often children who are exhibiting these signs are reprimanded, suspended, and expelled, contributing to the school-to-prison pipeline.[55] Scholars at the nexus of schooling and prison studies have drawn the parallels that exist between third- and fourth-grade reading levels and high school dropout rates as data predictors of prison beds needed in the future.[56] Considering that stress and trauma can hinder learning and behavior in schools, it is troubling that children are essentially tracked toward incarceration in adulthood because of structural and legal violence in their childhoods. Moreover, in a study of children in urban areas, Mallett (2017) found that young people affected by harsh school-discipline protocols and involved formally with the juvenile courts share several common vulnerabilities.[57] Most often, these children and adolescents are impoverished, of color, maltreatment victims, students with special-education needs, and lesbian, gay, "bisexual, transgender, or queer." All these circumstances can create a great deal of stress for young people when they are shamed and marginalized by the school system and society at large.

Now Let Us Heal

Markers of the body's attempts to prevent overstress include decrease in heart rate, lowering of metabolism, decrease in the rate of breathing, and restoring a healthy biochemical balance. Together, this is called the body's "relaxation response."[58] When a person is experiencing high stress, it is imperative that the bodily system gain an opportunity to recover and relax again. To begin the relaxation response, mind-body researcher Herbert Benson created a four-step process: first, to be in a quiet environment; second, to use a mental device such as a word or a phrase that can be repeated over and over; third, to adopt a passive attitude; and fourth, to be in a comfortable position. These various steps can be achieved through different techniques, including biofeedback, meditation, yoga, hypnosis, systematic desensitization, autogenic training, music, imagery, and progressive muscle relaxation.[59] The most effective way to reduce the dangerous levels of stress immigrant youth experience is, of course, to change the societal structures that prey on young people's lives and well-being. Since this is a long-term challenge, faster solutions are necessary.

A *praxis of art and healing* through the art-making process can include all the four phases of relaxation: quiet, repetition, passivity, and comfort. For children living under stress from poverty, violence, and uncertainty of well-being due to possible family deportation, relaxation techniques can help mitigate the effects of stress on the mind and body.[60] In my work I draw on theater, storytelling, and drawing as artistic mediums where children can experience some quiet, repetition, passivity, and comfort as a way of relaxing and creating opportunities for healing by processing real-life events though art making.

Art is central to the process of relief and recovery and the externalization of traumatic memories and experiences. Creative interventions can encourage this process of externalization, such as through various modalities of art. There are many kinds of art activities children can engage in to externalize traumatic experiences, but what makes them effective is that during the process of creating, children can emotionally process, resolve conflict, and gain a sense of well-being.[61] For this healing process, children may not be able to rely on words to describe traumatic events, memories, or feelings. Art thus becomes an important alternative to facilitate communication or nonverbal expression. The visual becomes essential as it introduces "iconic symbolization" as a way of giving trauma a visual identity. Through art, the trauma is externalized and identified in symbolic form.[62] Thus, the use of metaphor and symbolism becomes important for children.

Specific art forms like drama and theater can enable children to use their bodies in particular ways that otherwise would be too difficult in regular communication. For example, the kinesis and bodily rhythm in theater can create trust and safety in storytelling with a physical form that is not threatening or dangerous for the child.[63] Similarly, when a child is acting out a role during a theater exercise, the child gains distance from the real-life scenario and thus processes the information cognitively and views the situation with more clarity.[64] Acting grants children the distance and opportunity to develop trust with the facilitator and peers, and most importantly, in themselves. Often children will choose to embody perpetrators or agents of abuse to overcome them and regain control—an approach that, as we will see, children in my work adopted. Theater activities are important in that they create community through group collaboration. For children who have experienced trauma, this support network can be essential.[65] Through theater, children are exposed to important factors for healing, such as validation, laughter, empathy, universality, community, and connection.

Resilience

It is important to note that resilience is not the antidote to stress and trauma in children; rather, eradicating the structures that create harm and disparities would be the most sensible long-term solution needed to effectuate lasting change. However, in the absence of that type of dismantling of legally sanctioned violence, there are several important factors that can affect the resilience of children. Resilience refers to "the process of, capacity for, or outcome of successful adaptation despite challenging or threatening circumstances."[66] When studying resilience development in children, researchers pay specific attention to three resilience phenomena: good outcomes in high-risk children, sustained competence in children under stress, and recovery from trauma.[67] According to Cloitre et al., Rice and Groves, and Malchiodi, the following factors influence resilience in children: positive beliefs about self and the future; talents, hobbies, and/or special skills; and strong cultural connections and cultural identity, among others.[68]

Children who have experienced chronic adversity fare better or recover more successfully when "they have a positive relationship with a competent adult, they are good learners and problem-solvers, they are engaging with other people, and they have areas of competence and perceived efficacy valued by self or society."[69] Protective factors are resources or promotive processes that foster resilience and lessen the impact of adverse social environments on children.[70] Scholars also refer to these protective factors as "assets." Moreover, there are a common set of counteracting factors that help children overcome obstacles and develop resilience. These include facilitating supportive adult-child relationships; building a sense of self-efficacy and perceived control; providing opportunities to strengthen adaptive skills and self-regulatory capacities; and mobilizing sources of faith, hope, and cultural traditions.[71] For the reasons mentioned above, it is imperative to consider how art, specifically theater, offers children the opportunity to recreate difficult and violent realities that often lead to trauma. Choosing an alternative reality gives children power and shows them how to problem-solve in their day-to-day life.

The Power of Art

As children's drawings serve to make meaning out of the world around them, it is important to understand that children's art is based on physical movement and visual awareness.[72] Some scholars have seen the value of art in research and have incorporated it into their scientific methodology. These include visual-arts methods like PhotoVoice—a participatory method of research where participants use cameras/phones to take photographs that correspond to the topic of study; similarly, drawings and performance have been especially useful for children who have experienced traumatic events in their lives such as illnesses, war, and abandonment.[73] By conducting mixed-methods studies that incorporate drawings into longer family interviews and ethnographic work, some scholars have used art therapy to understand views on immigration and family formation. However, most have not centered on the art created by their participants.[74]

For example, Smokowski and Bacallao use "cultural maps"—drawings with roots in spatial studies—to complement the interview data they gathered from bicultural children in the US.[75] The drawings and interviews expressed the confusion and dilemmas that children face in navigating two worlds, with the maps helping the young people to communicate how they can coexist in two locations at once. Similarly, Dreby and Adkins use children's drawings as complementary components of a mixed-methods study. Children in this study drew family members, and how they imagined their parents' lives in the US.[76] Recent studies have highlighted the importance of making music, particularly for immigrant children and refugees in Australia. Marsh posits that art activities for marginalized children are important in enabling social inclusion, identity construction, and cultural maintenance for bicultural kids.[77] We know that art education is crucial in schools, particularly for its positive effects on healthy development and rich educational experiences otherwise not readily available to marginalized children.[78]

Boal, creator of the Theater of the Oppressed methods, believes that we are all "spect-actors" rather than just spectators or actors. We are all performing on the stage that is everyday life. Some perform theater of cruelty, while others rehearse resistance. I use the term resistance in this book to exemplify the ways children and youth speak back to power. Education scholars Solorzano and Delgado-Bernal define and theorize resistance through the concept of transformational resistance—a consciousness and agency that seeks to transform, rupture, and dismantle the conditions causing harm.[79] Hannegan-Martinez and colleagues later advance the concept of transformational resistance to highlight the ways youth resist in a myriad of ways even through what are perceived to be negative oppositional behaviors like righteous indignation as described in this book.[80] Like a mirror, theater gives us humans the ability to observe ourselves. In this way, children's theater performances and other artistic expressions like drawings provide us with the unique ability to witness society through the experiences of the most vulnerable. Yet given this research that shows the benefits of art for disenfranchised youth, it is concerning that there have been massive cuts to arts funding, particularly in public inner-city schools that serve most disenfranchised young people.[81]

The Research Project and Methodology

This book makes a clear case about the implied disposability of children's lives when the political strategy for immigration policy relies on family separation. This work also demonstrates the specific ways family separation happens and is normalized through everyday acts of legal violence—acts that I have personally experienced. Some academic traditions value objectivity, seeing it as a goal. I concur with Ewing, who argues that the experiential knowledge of people of color is not only a legitimate source of evidence but is, in fact, critical to understanding the function of racism as a fundamental American social structure. Furthermore, I agree that the myth of objectivity "serves as a camouflage for the self-interest, power, and privilege of dominant groups in US society."[82] By challenging notions of "neutral" or "objective" research, scholars expose research that silences, ignores, and distorts epistemologies of people of color.[83]

Growing up in Arizona as an undocumented person, and later working with immigrant communities and children for over 16 years, I came to understand the complexities of navigating an undocumented existence. At the age of 14, I joined a street theater group in Arizona that tackled important topics in the Mexican American community such as education, teenage pregnancy, and peer pressure. Years later, I cofounded a theater group called Teatro Nopalero for undocumented students in Phoenix. This was a grassroots group that used theater as an educational tool to fight anti-immigration policies. These early experiences, coupled with my subsequent academic training, have enabled me to harness the *rasquachismo* (an underdog perspective as a means of empowerment and resistance) and resilience I learned and apply it to my work with children in the borderlands.[84]

This book draws on research from two border states, at two different political moments. The first part of the book is based on work conducted at an after-school program in Phoenix, Arizona, from 2008 to 2010 with immigrant children who had experienced a family deportation or lived with the fear of familial separation. I collected over 200 drawings from children and youth aged 8 to 17 and analyzed them for their content about immigration. I also conducted two years of ethnographic field-work in Maricopa County, the county in which Phoenix sits. The second study took place from 2015 to 2017 in Los Angeles, where two cohorts of students participated in a theater class that I designed and taught. It is important to note that during this time, the country was going through the 2016 US presidential elections, and by the second year of the study, Donald Trump was in his first year in office. All this context contributed insight about children's perceptions, pre- and post-Trump's election. This second project incorporated three years of fieldwork; interviews with parents, children, teachers, and administrators; class and home ob-servations; recorded theater performances and practices; visual analy-sis of drawings; student journal entries; and pre/post-surveys. When it comes to the stress the young people experience, I focused in the Los Angeles project on the keen signals of middle-school-age students rang-ing from 11 to 13 years old.

As noted earlier, trauma affects the brain and behavior in a variety of ways; however, this book does not center on the fields of psychology, art therapy, or medical anthropology. Rather, it takes an interdisciplin-ary approach in which I focus on the lived experiences of children who may have experienced violence or trauma vis-á-vis political structures. Although there are built-in protective factors that help the body prevent overstress, these factors have not advanced fast enough to mitigate the toxic and chronic stress that so many children experience because of trauma-inducing social structures.[85]

First Site of Study: After-School Community Centers in Arizona

As mentioned above, during the highly politicized time in Arizona for immigrants of 2008 to 2010, I collected more than 200 drawings from children in the city of Phoenix. The drawings came from children who participated in a summer arts program created by a local not-for-profit organization with three community centers that offered students after-school mentoring and extracurricular programming. All three community centers are in Maricopa County. The first, Centro de Apoyo (names of the organization and community centers have been changed to protect their identity), is in the downtown area; Comunidad Unida is in South Phoenix; and Empowering Community is in North Phoenix. Centro de Apoyo mainly serves younger children; its goal is to integrate mothers and children in gang-prevention programs. This center is located across the street from a local high school and in the center of a Mexican immigrant community facing gentrification. Comunidad Unida is located across the street from a community of mobile homes where Maricopa County sheriffs conducted multiple immigration raids from 2006 to 2008. Most of the children in this area qualify for a free or reduced lunch, and in 2010, during the time of this study, Arizona had the second-highest poverty rate in the country.[86] Empowering Community was located next to a day-labor center that closed in 2010. This center faced daily harassment from anti-immigrant protesters and sheriff's deputies who intimidated the day laborers and immigrant residents. Occasionally, members of the group United for Sovereign America—an anti-immigrant biker group—would camp outside the day-labor center to yell and harass people while recording and intimidating potential employers. The hostility of the community context deeply shaped the experiences of the immigrant residents and children in the three different communities.

I gained access to the nonprofit that runs the three community centers when I worked as an after-school mentor for the South Phoenix center in 2008.[87] There I helped students with homework and organized extracurricular activities. Later, the organization asked me to create a two-month summer arts program for all three centers. Each week's curriculum was themed after an art form, and students participated in several activities including field trips, conversations with guest artists, and hands-on art making. The program's curriculum was scheduled to conclude with a community art exhibit and an uncovering of the mural created by the youth.

Most of the children felt that peace was important in the community and that the mural should portray that. I then asked the children to describe what peace looked like to them. A 9-year-old boy asserted, "Peace looks like the sheriff shaking hands with a Mexican"; then someone replied, "Yes!" The children went on to talk about when sheriffs detained their parents in the community, or when the police impounded the car of a family member because that person did not have a driver's license. Others spoke about their older siblings not being able to go to college because they did not have "papers." Most kids stated that they were fearful that Immigration and Customs Enforcement (ICE) could take away their parents while they were at school.

The youth developed the sketch of the mural collaboratively. Everyone was ambitious in designing a 35ft x 30ft mural that would depict the experiences of immigrant families, including undocumented students in cap and gowns, children without their parents, and incarcerated immigrants. In the center would be the sheriff and the Mexican shaking hands as a symbol of peace, and on the left side of the wall would be the result of the peace offering, symbolized by the handshake as families united, youth were graduating, and children were playing. The location of the mural would be on a wall behind the Comunidad Unida center. This location was important because gangs and graffiti crews constantly tagged the wall as the nearby basketball courts made it a popular location.

However, despite the approval of the first sketch by the organization's staff, some of the board members stopped the mural project the day the outlining started because of their concerns about the controversy the mural could spark in a conservative state like Arizona. They also feared losing funders or grants. When the youth found out the mural was not going to happen, they were visibly distressed. Seeing their reactions, I first prompted them to write or draw a picture about why this mural was important to them. The response was overwhelming and revealed that the experience of drawing the issues the youth faced was cathartic for them. Using crayons, colored pencils, and markers, they shared stories of their families' fears about ICE raids. They addressed letters to President Obama asking him to intervene in Arizona. Others pleaded with Sheriff Joe Arpaio to stop separating families. As they drew their pictures, they began to share with each other and to listen to the experiences of their friends. Children later approached me and said that their cousin or friend also wanted to make a drawing "about the mural." Overall, the youth wrote poems, letters, or made drawings about their identity, growing up in Arizona, and their reflections on immigration policies, which later became the basis for this research.

Many of the children in this study are second-generation Mexican Americans. The age range is large (6 to 18), spanning elementary, middle, and high school. Some of the children had just arrived in the US a few years earlier and felt more comfortable speaking and writing in Spanish. However, most of the children at all centers navigated their community and relationships in Spanglish (a Spanish-English hybrid language). Many of the children attended schools near the community centers and lived in the vicinity. Consequently the children shared similar challenges, including repeated cycles of poverty, attending less-than-optimal schools, and facing developmental issues stemming from parents' lack of access to early childhood educational programs because of anti-immigrant legislation.[88] They also faced a lack of access to educational resources and limited college options because of undocumented status and being at risk for poor health outcomes owing to a lack of access to healthcare.[89]

Second Site of Study: School Arts Program in Los Angeles

In Los Angeles I designed a second arts curriculum, specifically building on the previous work done in Arizona. This time the work would be research-focused with an attempt to answer the questions: How do current anti-immigrant policies affect children in immigrant families? How can the art-making process mediate children's experiences with the law? And, how can artistic methods serve researchers and educators who work with children or other vulnerable populations?

One of the main goals of this work was to bring art into the school. Guided by research and lived experiences indicating the power of art, I believe that the drawings themselves merit special attention in the form of analysis and epistemological development that can become a tool to work with children or other vulnerable populations. This work attempts to understand how art could be a possible tool to mitigate these stressors and even heal the emotional and/or mental trauma they cause. The contributions of this work are threefold: (1) to provide insight into the understudied population of preadolescent children of immigrants; (2) to center the art made by the children as visual testimonies and material representations of their lives; and (3) to position children as active agents of their own lives, not only as victims.

This study took place in the neighborhood of Watts, located in South Central Los Angeles. This was an important site for this research. Watts has a history of poverty, police brutality, job scarcity, and inadequate food and housing options.[90] Contemporary scholars call this lack of fresh foods a "food desert."[91] Children growing up in Watts confront the same issues their predecessors faced in the 1960s and '90s during the uprisings sparked by police brutality and marginalization. Given these realities, children in the area experience housing, food, and educational insecurities in their daily lives. Coupled with overpolicing, violence, and immigration issues, these stressors can have detrimental consequences for their development.

Currently, Watts[92] is a Mexican and Central American immigrant-receiving neighborhood, but this was not always the case. In the 1980s Watts experienced a demographic shift.[93] Historically, Watts has been predominantly an African American community. Overtime, Watts's population grew to approximately 41,000 residents. Of those people, about 61% were Latinx (mainly Mexican), 37% Black, 0.5% White, 0.5% other, and 0.3% Asian, according to a report in the *Los Angeles Times* based on US census information (Mapping L.A. 2000). The median household income is $25,161 per family, yet most families make less than $20,000 a year.[94] Only 2.9% of Watts residents have a four-year degree and only 3,009 have a high school diploma. Much of this population is young. Watts has 17,346 people per square mile, making the population density one of the highest in Los Angeles County.

Coordinated under the leadership of Chicana artist and professor Judith F. Baca of the Social and Public Art Resource Center (SPARC) and the University of California, Los Angeles (UCLA), where the California-based portion of this project was conducted, the SPARC team partnered with the Los Angeles Unified School District (LAUSD) to bring muralism/self-portraiture, choral poetry, dance, music, photography, and theater classes to Liberating Our Dreams Academy in Watts. Although considered an arts academy, Liberating Our Dreams Academy did not have art classes for many years previously. In fact, the only creative component offered to students came from parent-led workshops in knitting and crafts. As a new elementary school in its sixth year, the school had faced some challenges, including community violence, change in administration, a steady increase in the number of foster-care youth, and mothers dying prematurely from cancer. The school is 95% Latinx, many of whom are recently arrived immigrants from Mexico, Guatemala, El Salvador, and Honduras.

After discussing the purpose of the class with the principal, we decided that it would be best for me to partner with the sixth-grade English Language Learners (ELL)/Emergent Bilingual Learner (EBL) class since it was predominantly comprised of newly arrived students, children of immigrants, and second- and third-generation students who were struggling to pass the state's English exam. This class was often labeled as the "difficult" one by their full-time teacher. The school administrators also wanted to place me in this class because they agreed that the (difficult) children in this class would benefit from my contemplative approach to art instruction. In a preparatory meeting, the school principal shared that many students had a hard time knowing how to communicate properly, and the teacher mentioned to me during one of my observations that their "bad behavior" was the main challenge she faced in the class. Since her large class struggled to stay on task, the teacher chose to run a highly structured class where every single minute was accounted for with a stopwatch and the tone of instruction and communication was authoritative and firm—a pattern of social control that contributes to racialized inequities in education.[95]

In working with this class of students, I understood why they struggled to learn English and pass the English exam. There were a great deal of external, complex factors affecting the lives of these students that were similar to the dilemmas the children in Arizona faced. These included repeated cycles of poverty, less-than-optimal schools, and developmental issues due to parents' lack of access to early childhood educational programs.[96] Moreover, as these young children transition into adulthood, they often lack access to educational resources and college options because of their undocumented status and being "at risk" for poor health outcomes because of a lack of access to healthcare.[97] Thus, developing a curriculum that provided a healing space for these students was an important element of this work.

Overview of the Book

In this book I argue that young children of immigrants resist the legal violence and anti-immigrant sentiments they experience in daily life. Through an analysis of children's drawings, theater performances, and family interviews, we can learn both the impact of the "deportation machine" on children's lives and how they develop personal agency to respond creatively and reimagine the dilemmas presented by structural violence coalescing with their families' legal status. Children can resist in ways that reimagine reality because they navigate interstitiality and in-between spaces. Scholars including W. E. B. Du Bois, Gloria Anzaldúa, Leo Chavez, Pat Zavella, and Lynn Stephen have called this a double consciousness, liminal space, or *nepantla*.[98] In this liminality, children of immigrants may or may not have citizenship, but in neither case have membership in American society. As people, and in this case, children, are shaped by two cultures, they feel as though they do not belong neither here nor there; they feel excluded from both worlds.[99]

Chapter 1 presents a general overview of the policies that have led to where we are. It highlights the impact of the Obama presidency and Sheriff Joe Arpaio's deportation raids on immigrant families in Arizona, and it documents the shift to the Trump administration, tracing the evolution of restrictive national immigration and border policies. The chapter describes the context of Phoenix, Arizona, and the way in which it foreshadowed draconian anti-immigrant sentiment at a national level. This chapter also lays out the unique legal landscapes of Arizona and California and how they create worrisome conditions for mixed-status families and their children.

Chapter 2 highlights how fear of the previously outlined policies manifests at school, home, and in community contexts. Through an analysis of children's drawings and theater performances in Arizona and California, this chapter demonstrates how art allowed children to express fears around familial disintegration, violence, and racism. It makes visible the worries that children feel as they go to and from school, particularly centering on their fears of the construction of the border wall. It also demonstrates how lines are blurred between police officers, sheriffs, and highway or Border Patrol agents, and the fear of family members being apprehended in their homes or during their drives to work.

Chapter 3 discusses the tools that children in Arizona harness to respond to and navigate racism. This chapter offers serious consideration of the detrimental impact of anti-immigrant politicians and policies on children of immigrants, with a specific focus on the children in Arizona.

Chapter 4 explores the resistance of children in California to anti-immigration policies. Ultimately, both chapters 3 and 4 posit that as acts of desperation, these responses mirror and mimic the elimination, the ridicule, or the dehumanization of Trump in the Los Angeles case or of Sheriff Arpaio in the Phoenix case as a way of rebelling and resisting. In this way, children demonstrate their will to survive and assert the dignity and humanity of themselves and their families. This chapter also makes the case that the art-making process is instrumental in helping children to cope in positive ways.

Chapter 5 describes how the art-making process, or what I describe here as a *praxis of art and healing*, helps us to discern the ways children in Arizona were able to express solutions, and how the youth in California embodied alternatives. Rather than just reacting with righteous indignation, this creative praxis allows children to process their emotions and reimagine destructive situations with creative solutions. This chapter describes how the responses to legal violence that children created in both Arizona and California, particularly through comedy, satire, hope, friendship, and the *re*humanization of themselves and those around them, can help us reimagine educational, arts-based, and societal responses to legal violence.

The conclusion briefly reiterates the book's overarching argument and how it has been developed across the volume. I emphasize the need for a praxis of art and healing that highlights the ways legal violence affects children, especially by explaining children's response to the fears of familial separation. I also recap the possibilities for coping and healing through art. The volume ends with an explanation of how this approach can be useful for other researchers and educators who work with vulnerable populations like children and immigrants.

1

Policies

The Constricted Lives of Immigrant Children

A large cage surrounds the home of 15-year-old Gabriel's family. The cage is thoughtfully drawn as a three-dimensional object that holds the home and each of the family members left in Gabriel's life. His father was deported back to Mexico during one of the routine immigration raids in Phoenix, Arizona, by Sheriff Joe Arpaio. At one of the windows with green curtains are Gabriel, his mother, and younger sister pictured with frowns on their faces. Outside of the caged home, the mood is also depressed as the sun, flowers, and trees are all frowning and dry. The gray skies color the sadness in Gabriel's life. On the bottom, the sub-title of the image describes the theme of the drawing—"Immigration is making everything fall apart" (plate 1.1). The family feels trapped by the fear of leaving the home as going outside could mean that the mother could also be deported. Gabriel's feelings are also included in the find-ings of the "Facing Our Future" report issued by the Urban Institute in 2010. Published at the time when massive workplace raids shocked the nation, it describes the anxiety and fear experienced by children whose undocumented parents could be chained, arrested, and removed from the country at any moment.[1] Children affected by these locally imple-mented, nationally broadcast immigration raids felt a pervasive sense of insecurity, which can lead to problems with anxiety.[2] This type of insecurity is a prime example of how legal violence fosters an unstable and unpredictable environment that aims to become normalized over time in order to serve the goal of "attrition through enforcement," such that life is so unbearable that people "choose" to self-deport.[3] Gabriel's drawing seems to foreshadow the insidious "family reception/day care centers and tender-age facilities" where immigrant and Central Ameri-can families and children would be detained following the institution of the zero-tolerance policy in the summer of 2018.

Carla is a sixth grader who drew what she called "A mom and dad at the border distracting a security guard to get the kids through." This drawing (plate 1.2) was created just before the 2018 zero-tolerance policy that Trump championed during his presidency. It illustrates the constricted and arduous path that Central American children endure in their attempt to reach the US. Carla made the drawing when two classmates shared the story of their cousin who attempted to migrate from El Salvador to the US. Two years earlier, one of her classmates had made the same journey when she was only 10 years old. In this scene, the mother and father who are in the US use any possible tool to help their children arrive safely, even if they must go to the border themselves and get their children through the fenced wall. Parents are often helpless to free their children from detention as they are also captive in detention centers across the border and in the US. However, through art, children can challenge current realities and create scenarios in which parents are powerful enough to free their children from detention centers which Carla depicts as cages.

For policies and practices that separate children from their parents to be within the law, the humanity of those affected must be negated. De Genova and Peutz posit that deportation "is not an account of what [migrants] have *done*, but merely an account of what they *are*."[4] Even in the face of international law and human rights discourses, people are considered disposable vis-à-vis their deportability.[5] They are framed in this way through the creation of an "us vs. them" mentality; it is through the idea of citizenry that the "illegal, undocumented, alien, criminal, and other" is created.[6] As this chapter will demonstrate, this way of thinking about people is one that Arizona politicians and legislators mastered and the Trump administration exacerbated at a national level.

National and Historical Context of Migration to the United States

Migrant labor has been crucial throughout the history of the US. In fact, some argue that the US economy is one that is addicted to immigrant labor.[7] Before the construction of the southern wall in California in 1904, Mexican workers referred to as "birds of passage" would easily migrate seasonally to the US and return to their homes in Mexico during the cold winter months when crops decreased.[8] Migration only became a major issue to US politicians when the racist goal of deterring Chinese immigrants from entering the US through Mexico prompted the construction of the US-Mexico border.[9] It was during this time that Mexican migrants were constructed as either the needed laborer or the unwanted "illegal alien."[10] With the establishment of the Bracero Program in 1942, which involved a bilateral agreement between the US and Mexico where Mexican workers entered the US to work in agricultural jobs across the southwest, Mexicans were given access to jobs but not incorporation into American society. Moreover, the creation of the Mexican farmworker was the modern solution to the colonial problem of labor shortage.[11] From 1948 to 1964 the US imported about 200,000 workers per year, many of whom were underpaid and some of whom are still owed wages until this day.[12] During this time the construction of the wall and the Bracero Program put an end to the open-door policy whereby seasonal Mexican migrants had entered and exited the country with ease.[13] In 1947 the General Agreement on Tariffs and Trade (GATT) was ratified—a multilateral agreement that regulated international trade, setting the stage for further policies that opened the borders to commerce but not to people. Although the Bracero Program was meant to be a solution to "illegal" immigration, instead it generated more undocumented migrants, especially in states like Arkansas, Texas, and Missouri that did not want to admit Mexicans (non-Whites) into White-only public spaces.[14] This exacerbated the narrative of Mexicans as "wetbacks" and criminals, sparking public hysteria about them as "dangerous and criminal social pathogens."[15] The result was Operation Wetback of 1954, a massive enforcement effort to apprehend and deport undocumented farmworkers to Mexico.[16] As the country focused on civil rights and war, the Hart-Celler Act or Immigration and Nationality Act of 1965 was a welcome change that eliminated the origins formula, which favored White Northern and Western Europeans, and established new quotas.[17] These new quotas attempted to put immigrants on an equal footing and opened migration to parts of the world previously excluded, namely Asia, Southern, and Eastern Europe.[18] However, as Massey and Pren note, "as a result of shifts in US immigration policy between the late 1950s and the late 1970s, Mexico went from annual access to around 450,000 guestworker visas and a theoretically unlimited number of resident visas in the United States (in practice averaging around 50,000 per year), to further cementing a restricted immigration pathway" inevitably leading to further criminalization.[19]

Legislation would continue to be restrictive until the Immigration Reform and Control Act (IRCA) of 1986, which provided amnesty for 2.7 million undocumented immigrants and established sanctions against employers who hired undocumented people.[20] From that point on, immigration resources would be heavily applied to enforcement rather than services. Then, in 1994, through the North American Free Trade Agreement (NAFTA), the US and Mexican markets (except labor) were fused together, creating a situation in which the US increasingly relied on undocumented labor while simultaneously attempting to restrict its flow.[21] Post-NAFTA, undocumented migration into the US increased despite becoming highly restricted, dangerous, and criminalized.

Historically, apart from the Great Depression era, the number of undocumented immigrants has steadily increased since the founding of the border. In response, immigration policy has grown more exclusionary.[22] First, in 1993, the Clinton administration began a series of programs aimed to "get serious" about border enforcement.[23] In 1994 Immigration and Naturalization Services (INS)—now known as Immigration and Customs Enforcement (ICE)[24]—implemented Operation Gatekeeper in three phases. With the goal of constricting geographic access to the US, the first phase of Operation Gatekeeper focused on the Imperial Beach area of the Pacific Ocean. The second phase targeted the San Diego area, and the third sought to end migration through the eastern part of the border. By the implementation of the final phase in 1998, Operation Gatekeeper had already forced most undocumented migrants to traverse desolate areas of the Sonoran Desert in Arizona. The Clinton administration believed that they would deter immigrants by cutting off access through California and Texas; nonetheless, migrants continued to risk their lives by crossing through the dangerous conditions of the Sonoran Desert. Since then thousands of bodies have been found; two-thirds of them remain unidentified.[25]

Such deterrents to migration take the form of structural violence, which is embedded in the fabric of the country. Another way such legal violence occurs is through the convergence of immigration and criminal law that undocumented families face in the form of more severe legal repercussions stemming from their lack of protected status. Structural violence treats immigrants as possible threats to society as opposed to "Americans in waiting."[26] This criminalization of immigrants paves the way for a seemingly logical transition from immigration law to criminal law and thus surveillance and enforcement.[27] The pattern of increased immigrant criminalization began at the end of the Clinton presidency and continued in George W. Bush's presidency.[28] Since then ICE has taken an aggressive posture on enforcement of the 1996 Illegal Immigration Reform and Immigrant Responsibility Act (IIRIRA), which set the stage for the growth of the vast immigration-enforcement system through the authorization of significant funding for border and interior enforcement and through the establishment of an interwoven set of enforcement partnerships and programs.[29] In fact, IIRIRA eroded the rule of law by "eliminating due process from the overwhelming majority of removal cases, curtailing equitable relief from removal, mandating detention (without individualized custody determinations) for broad swaths of those facing deportation, and erecting insurmountable, technical roadblocks to asylum."[30] The implementation of IIRIRA allowed for "the concept of 'criminal alienhood,'" which has "slowly, but purposefully" conflated criminality and lack of immigration status.[31]

Indicative of this process is the 2002 transition from INS to ICE, which coincided with the Department of Homeland Security (DHS) consolidating national security and immigration through ICE and Customs and Border Protection (CBP). This change marked another turning point in the cyclical history of the US, where immigrants are thought of as "others" and even "dirty" and "deviant," thereby leading to a wave of criminalization policies. Moreover, as immigration-related offenses become criminalized as federal felonies, immigrants "catch" criminal records at expedited rates, making noncitizens the (new) face of federal prisons.[32] The effects of detention on mixed-status families are devastating. This sort of legal violence is inflicted not only on undocumented immigrants but also, through a spillover effect, on the lives of non-immigrant community members. As such, US-citizen children, extended-family members, and individuals in the countries of origin feel the brunt of legal violence. This type of violence is structural because it comes from exploitative labor markets and discriminatory legal systems that play out through legal issues when immigrants try to access education, immigration-status, housing, and other services. It is maintained through the "uncertainty of everyday life caused by the insecurity of wage or income, a chronic deficit of food, dress, housing, and healthcare, and uncertainty about the future which is translated into hunger."[33] Lack of access to these services perpetuates inequalities, which are later normalized. As society normalizes the perpetual legal barriers and social stigmas immigrants face, immigrants begin to internalize these forms of disdain and bias.

In 2001 the perceived threat of foreigners became ever present in the wake of 9/11. Coupled with the Great Recession, Brown immigrants became the targets of legislative repression all over the country. Even though the 9/11 hijackers entered the US through the northern border with Canada, the militarization of the southern US-Mexico border became a top priority as this historical moment extended an opportunity to curtail immigration from undesirable destinations where predominantly Brown immigrants originate, such as south of the US. Immigration enforcement in the US and at the southern border increased significantly. Notably, the same level of military focus did not materialize along the Canadian border.[34] This is important to highlight because the racialization of the *Brown* immigrant body has a lasting effect on children of immigrants in the US.[35] US-citizen children hold fears of deportation and feel the effects of heavy-handed anti-immigrant rhetoric because of their and their families' ethnicity, culture, skin color, and language.[36]

As with every new immigrant group that has entered the US, the varying categories of exclusion and inclusion become heightened depending on the economic, social, and political factors of the time. The Obama and Trump administrations are often perceived to have been at opposite political poles, both ideologically and in practice. Yet, as we will see, children and adolescents in immigrant families experienced similar levels of concern about their family unity and safety during both administrations. Although it might be simpler to claim that immigration is a political issue constricted and expanded by either Democrats or Republicans, it is more accurately understood as a larger structural tool for the logics of White supremacy birthed through slavery and colonization and maintained by a racially motivated legal system.

Why Arizona's Immigration Context Matters

As the country deported more immigrants than ever before beginning in the mid-2000s, Arizona earned the notorious identity of the "laboratory" and "ground zero" for anti-immigrant policies. Aligned with the national goal of the Department of Homeland Security (DHS) to bring about "attrition through enforcement," Arizona has passed measures that make immigrant life unbearable and impossible.[37] Multiple punitive measures have been ratified in the last two decades, starting in 2004 when Arizona lawmakers made already-restricted opportunities like voting unavailable to undocumented immigrants. In 2005 the "Coyote Law" was passed, making the federal felony of smuggling someone across the border (including smuggling of oneself) a local felony.[38] The political climate intensified in 2006 when six propositions that directly targeted the livelihood of undocumented individuals were passed. Included in the state's ballot were laws that denied bail to people accused of a crime and made undocumented children and youth ineligible for Head Start programs and in-state tuition. Another law made English the official language, and another prohibited undocumented immigrants from taking English or General Education Development (GED) classes that were subsidized by the state. In 2008 the "Employer Sanction Law," Proposition 208, was passed, penalizing any business that knowingly hired undocumented workers.[39]

However, rather than punishing businesses, worksite raids became the norm as local law enforcement took the place of federal immigration officers by raiding businesses, detaining undocumented workers, and handing them to ICE. This happened through the 287(g) agreements, which generally allowed and funded state and local law enforcement to enter in agreement with ICE under a joint Memorandum of Agreement (MOA). Under the 287(g) agreements, state and local entities received authority to act as federal immigration enforcement within a local jurisdiction (e.g., to start the detention process and to contact ICE). Then, in 2009, House Bill 2008 required that if an undocumented person applied for services through any state public program the state employee must report such a person to ICE, even when the individual's children legally qualified for those programs. Lastly, and perhaps most infamously, in

2010 lawmakers passed Senate Bill 1070, which aimed to legalize racial profiling of anyone suspected of being undocumented.[40]

From 2002 until the present, immigration raids have continued in Arizona on a daily basis.[41] Arizona is also home to the self-proclaimed "America's Toughest Sheriff" (now ex-sheriff of Maricopa County) Joe Arpaio, who first became sheriff in 1993. In 2014 Arpaio was elected for a sixth term and boasted about detaining and deporting undocumented immigrants by the thousands. With support from the DHS and federally funded programs like 287(g), Secure Communities, and the Criminal Alien Program (CAP), immigrants in Arizona of various legal statuses lived in fear of being taken away and separated from their family members.[42] Secure Communities or "S-Comm" was designed as a database shared between ICE, the FBI, and local law enforcement, meant to capture the biometric information of any immigrant whom any of those entities encountered. Importantly, if at any time an undocumented immigrant was questioned as a victim of a crime, or was detained because of a broken taillight, that person's information would be sent to federal authorities. Similarly, the Criminal Alien Program (CAP) allows ICE to use and fund local facilities to interview, investigate, and hold undocumented people. In 2016, after 24 years in office, in the wake of numerous investigations as well as lawsuits relating to human torture and wrongful deaths in his jails and detention centers, Joseph Arpaio was voted out of office. In fact, five years earlier, the Justice Department found him guilty of unconstitutionally targeting and racially profiling people in Mexican communities and retaliating against those who criticized him, including the media.[43] After Arpaio was found guilty, he was held in contempt when he knowingly objected to ending his racial-profiling program targeting the Latinx community. However, a month before he was sentenced for this offense, President Trump pardoned Arpaio in what turned out to be the first of several constitutionally suspicious uses of his pardoning powers.[44] In 2020 the Ninth Circuit Court of Appeals ruled that Arpaio's petition to have his guilty verdict wiped from his record was unfounded.[45]

Through the organizing of immigrant communities after this anti-immigrant period, the author of SB1070, Russell Pearce, was also removed from power. Pearce, a Republican member of the Arizona State Senate known as the "Arizona anti-immigrant champion," was voted out of office in large part owing to a well-organized campaign of community members and activists.[46] As of 2019 Pearce was a chief deputy for the Treasury Office in Arizona, and during a rally that year he announced that he was willing to shed blood to protect the country after long-standing laws were repealed, including one that prohibited teachers from discussing LGBTQ topics in the classroom.[47]

The palpable anti-immigrant sentiment in Arizona made its way to other parts of the country through dissemination of anti-immigrant rhetoric and policies at the national and local levels. From 2010 to 2012, more than 31 states proposed similar policies to Arizona's SB1070 or more severe measures, such as Alabama's House Bill 56, which makes "harboring" (i.e., living or driving with) undocumented people a crime.[48] In 2010 then-entrepreneur and television personality Donald Trump went on national TV on Larry King's show and was asked about Arizona's law. Trump praised the work being done in Arizona; when asked if he was in favor of stopping people on the street, he replied that it made sense to him that it was not necessary to stop blond people, because "there are not many blonds in Mexico." Six years later Trump would use this same logic when announcing his campaign for presidency, galvanizing the same anti-immigrant rhetoric about Mexicans that had made Arpaio and Pearce infamous.[49] Particularly with regard to lives of immigrant communities, Arizona is vital for understanding how policies like these affect such communities and young children of immigrants in the rest of the nation.

"YES, WE CAN . . .": Obama's Federal "Deportation Machine" and Local Campaigns

Instead of keeping the promise of legalization for the 12 million undocumented people in the country after 9/11, the Obama administration deported over three million people during its tenure (2008–16)—more than any other administration in US history including Trump's.[50] One of the leaders of the deportation efforts was Janet Napolitano. During her time as the head of DHS, nearly two-thirds of the people deported had no criminal record and were deported for only minor infractions, such as traffic violations.[51] This reality was counter to the narrative explained to the public. The Obama administration had claimed that only the "worst criminals" would be deported. The truth is that through police-ICE collaborations, nearly every immigrant who was stopped for a traffic violation or encountered police presence entered the criminal justice system, regardless of criminal background, when they could not prove they were legally present in the US.

The Obama administration repeatedly claimed that they were tough on immigrants and border enforcement because they believed that if they first "secured the border," Republicans and independents would reach an agreement and help pass the highly controversial Comprehensive Immigration Reform Bill, which would provide a path toward legalization for the 12 million undocumented people already in the US. Yet rather than creating opportunities for legalization, Obama gave the Trump administration a blueprint for immigration enforcement and further border militarization.[52] However, the anti-immigrant sentiment that fueled this "deportation machinery" was not new.[53] The pattern of increased deportations began during the end of George W. Bush's presidency.[54] Since then ICE has taken an aggressive posture toward the enforcement of the 1996 Illegal Immigration Reform and Immigrant Responsibility Act (IIRIRA). Only five months after ICE's establishment in March 2003, the strategic plan titled Operation Endgame was formulated.[55] Implemented in 2003 by the Office of Detention and Removal within ICE, Endgame's prime goal was to deport every "removable alien" within a 10-year period. This was a strategic and purposeful 10-year plan, which came to fruition during Obama's second term.[56] With this plan came a 200% increase in ICE's budget. DHS allocated $1.6 billion to enforcement both within the US interior and along the border while allocating only $161 million to immigration services, such as naturalization services.

The unequal distribution of funds was due, in large part, to intense lobbying by private prison contractors and county jailers.[57] Two of the main lobbyists and policy formulators were Correction Corporation of America (CCA), which changed its name to CoreCivic, and the GEO Group. These groups helped to establish the for-profit immigration system that criminalized undocumented immigrants and made detention centers a profitable business model. In 2013 these corporations received 10% of ICE's budget.[58] In 2019 DHS allocated $2.7 billion to detain 51,379 migrants, double the 2015 budget of $1.3 billion.[59] This for-profit model applied to immigrant detention has generated "the creation of a detention industry totally divorced from public safety," where making a profit from each immigrant is the main priority.[60] The construction of detention centers has boomed since Endgame began. Since then immigration detention has become the fastest form of incarceration in the US, and in 2021 approximately 25,162 people were detained in detention centers nationwide; that number continues to grow steadily.[61]

One situation that the developers of Endgame lamented was that their detention practices were not compliant with the Flores Settlement of 1993, which requires that DHS transfer unaccompanied children to the custody of the Division of Children's Services within 72 hours of identification, except in some very limited circumstances.[62] An investigation found that children in Border Patrol custody were held in stark and wholly inappropriate conditions, sometimes for longer than is permitted under the Flores Settlement.[63] In a statement, the secretary of homeland security declared: "There are certain housing needs that are required when you have children. We're working . . . to find a way to solve those housing needs so that when family groups come across, we have the ability to detain them as well, until we can remove them. And, we don't release them into the community where, more likely than not, they're going to abscond."[64]

Although proponents of Endgame did not think it was a complete success because of the challenges they faced in detaining children, the damages this plan wreaked on undocumented immigrant communities were catastrophic. It set forth a new approach to immigration law and criminal law in which the two became intertwined, thus criminalizing immigration. Ultimately, the detention and deportation of unaccompanied minors began to rise in 2012 and spiraled by the time the Trump administration took office.[65] Although the Obama administration deported more people than any previous presidential administration, there were certain protections extended to undocumented youth who met certain requirements.

Deferred Action for Childhood Arrivals (DACA)

Thanks to years of organizing by undocumented youth all over the country, President Obama issued Deferred Action for Childhood Arrivals (DACA) as an executive order to provide temporary relief to youth who had been brought to the US as children. Enrollees needed to have entered the US before the age of 16, to have been born after 1981, to have lived in the US since 2007, to be enrolled in school or to have completed high school, and to meet the qualifications of "good moral character," which include no prior felony or misdemeanor convictions and passing a background check.[66] After meeting these requirements and paying the $495 fee, young people have temporary protection and a work permit for a period of two years, after which they are able to reapply for renewal as long as the applicant still meets the guidelines.

Research on DACA has provided evidence that enrollment increased young people's short-term financial stability and upward mobility.[67] DACA recipients and their families also developed a sense of belonging in the US and experienced cumulative benefits that fostered major shifts in their lives such as securing employment and being able to support their families financially.[68] Although Trump attempted to end DACA, in the summer of 2020 the Supreme Court blocked this initiative.[69] Thus, the over 640,000 DACA enrollees as of 2020 were no longer at risk of detention and deportation. But after the Supreme Court decision, the Trump administration rejected all new applications.[70] Although the Biden administration has indicated its intention to support DACA's conversion from executive order to permanent legislation, this had not occurred by the end of his first year in office.

Trump's Policy Impacts

From the beginning of Donald Trump's presidential campaign, one of the promises that most galvanized a broad base of support for his election was to build a wall between the US and Mexico. Within five days of his inauguration, he signed an executive order to immediately construct a physical wall on the southern border measuring between 18 and 30 feet high.[71] Although he proposed to build 1,000 miles of this wall, only 452 miles were built; in its first year in office, the Biden administration had neither taken down nor added to any sections of the border wall.[72]

Restricted Access to Asylum

The asylum process in the US has historically provided refuge for people fleeing persecution, war, and violence.[73] Trump's change of the asylum process included two executive orders that set the tone for the country's reception of immigrants already in the US and those seeking entry. In early 2017 Trump signed Executive Order 13769, which prohibited entry to visitors, immigrants, or refugees from Muslim-majority countries.[74] In the midst of the massive protests in response, this order was enjoined in court by a federal judge. Eventually, the Supreme Court upheld Trump's Muslim ban by a five-to-four vote in June 2018.[75] At that time Trump also announced a plan to end Temporary Protected Status (TPS) for over 300,000 people from Central American countries like El Salvador, Honduras, Nicaragua, and others like Syria, Haiti, Nepal, Sudan, South Sudan, Yemen, and Somalia.[76] TPS is extended to nationals of other countries who have experienced ongoing armed conflict such as war, natural disasters like hurricanes and earthquakes, and other significant events that do not allow them to live in their home country.[77] TPS provides work permits and protection from deportation for an extended period of time, and since taking office, the Biden administration has postponed the ending of TPS for citizens of these countries and explicitly established a new TPS period for those from Haiti.

Detention Facilities: Expansion, Conditions, and Duration of Detention

The Trump administration's restrictive asylum policies were in part a reaction to an increase in asylum petitions in 2018 and 2019 stemming from the historical and contemporary destabilization of Central American counties in large part influenced and funded by the US.[78] This surge in cases created a longer backlog of people waiting for their applications to be processed, with some waiting several years. The limits on asylum were an integral part of the anti-immigrant approach espoused by Stephen Miller under Trump.[79] One of the most damaging developments was Attorney General Sessions's binding opinion in Matter of A-B- that excluded domestic abuse and gang violence from the types of persecution that US asylum law had previously recognized as circumstances for seeking asylum.[80] These are the very forms of violence that impelled many Central American families and children to migrate.

This in combination with other policies that increased criminalization of immigration has resulted in a greatly expanded network of detention centers that ICE contracts private prison companies to run. This neoliberal privatization has made shareholders in private prison companies rich while simultaneously damaging the lives of many immigrants whose freedom has been sacrificed for profits. For example, since 2017, 40 new detention centers were added to the system, and the numbers of immigrants held increased from under 40,000 at the beginning of the Trump administration to over 50,000 in 2020.[81] These detention centers lack attention to the health and well-being of those detained, as evidenced by frigid temperatures, overcrowding, illness, sexual abuse, and death. During the 2019–20 fiscal year, 17 migrants died while in custody.[82] At the local level, when it comes to adult detention centers, states like California and New York have responded by refusing to implement some key federal policies such as the detention of undocumented immigrants and by breaking agreements with federal agencies such as ICE.[83]

Detention centers and makeshift detention camps that house minors have been reported to hold children in filthy conditions without access to basic hygiene items, including soap and toothbrushes.[84] Doctors were barred from giving flu vaccines to children and families detained in virus-stricken facilities.[85] During the initial onset of the COVID-19 pandemic, there were 5,300 cases of the virus in detention centers based on over 26,000 tests—indicating a positivity rate of over 20%, over three times that of the US as a whole.[86] This likely indicated inadequate procedures for preventing virus transmission and protecting detainees from the virus. In recent years immigrant detainees have also faced greater obstacles in gaining access to lawyers and legal materials than previously. For instance, starting in 2020, nongovernmental organizations were no longer guaranteed access to detention centers, with increased restrictions on access, visitation, and legal education. Each facility also eliminated law books that had previously been required by law to be kept in detention-center libraries.[87] Under the Biden administration, detention centers were expanded. Two facilities—the Irwin County Detention Center in Georgia and the C. Carlos Carreiro Immigration Detention Center in Bristol County, Massachusetts—were investigated by journalists who documented poor conditions that led to their closing, suggesting that the problems with this form of detention continued into the new administration.[88] Despite the closing of the two centers, the number of immigrant detainees soared in Biden's first year in office.[89]

The duration of detention was also a target of policy during the Trump administration. The Flores Settlement noted above was the outcome of a federal court decision that limited child detention to a maximum of 20 days; after that children must be released to a childcare agency or relative.[90] This settlement also required that children be detained in the least restrictive way possible. As a response, the Obama administration built detention facilities for parents and children to be held together in what the administration called "childcare centers" or "family reception centers." Later Trump sought to end protections put in place since the 1997 Flores case.[91] In late 2019 a judge ruled against Trump's attempt to detain children for an indefinite period.[92] The provision violated the United Nations' Convention on the Rights of the Child, which stipulates that children should not be detained indefinitely and that above all, the best interest of the child should be the main priority.[93]

Border Enforcement: Criminalization, Family Separation, and Remain-in-Mexico Policies

Several policies have resulted in changes in the experiences of migrants, including children and youth, at the border. Together these policies have created conditions that placed more immigrants in the criminal justice system, separated parents from children, and made asylum requests substantially more costly and difficult. Criminalization of immigration increased most notably with the zero-tolerance policy implemented in May 2018. Based on this policy, anyone who entered the country without documentation faced criminal prosecution even if they were seeking asylum. As a legal strategy to discourage other migrants from coming, zero-tolerance aimed to use the threat of family separation to deter migration. This strategy led to the establishment of child and toddler detention centers where children were detained together in fenced, cage-like structures along the US border.[94] During the time the policy was implemented, upward of 5,400 children under 18 were separated from their parents, yet accurate files and records were never maintained by state authorities.[95] Because of the backlash that this policy prompted, Trump issued an executive order on June 22, 2018, that separated children from their parents only when adults had criminal records; days later a federal judge ruled that children and parents must be reunited in no fewer than 30 days.[96] However, since there had been no clear, systematic way of tracking which children belonged with which parents, at the end of the Trump administration over 500 families still remained separated. Other children and youth entered the foster-care system while their parents were deported, and some children were released to individuals suspected of human trafficking.[97]

Aside from criminalization, the Trump administration set a record for the lowest asylum-acceptance rate since the refugee program began with the Displaced Persons Act of 1948.[98] For example, with the "Remain in Mexico" policy, also known as the Migrant Protection Protocols (MPP), instituted in January 2019, migrants could no longer have their asylum applications considered at the ports of entry but were required to return to Mexico pending a hearing with an immigration judge. During this time over 65,000 migrants applied for asylum and were moved to Mexico; and even two years later, many are still waiting to see a judge.[99] Towns on the border like Ciudad Juárez, Matamoros, and Tijuana were converted into makeshift detention camps. Medical doctors, lawyers, and a United Nations human rights commissioner visited the camps and expressed concerns about the degrading and dangerously overcrowded conditions that families and children faced.[100] Doctors Without Borders spoke with over 500 migrants in Nuevo Laredo and found that the longer migrants wait in these camps, the more at risk they are for physical and mental harm.[101] During the Biden administration's first year, these makeshift camps at the US-Mexico border within Mexico have actually increased, and as of 2022 the "Remain in Mexico" or MPP policy remains in effect.[102] The Supreme Court is set to hear the MPP policy case by the end of 2022.[103]

While many waited in camps at the border, others were deported back to their countries to wait for their asylum cases to be decided. According to a report on asylum-seekers sent back to El Salvador, 138 were killed and many others were tortured.[104] From the US, migrants were sent to designated "safe third-party countries" to await their asylum decision. For example, more than 800 Mexican, Honduran, and Salvadoran asylum seekers (most commonly fleeing violence or persecution in their countries) were sent in 2020 to Guatemala, which has one of the highest rates of violence in the Western Hemisphere.[105]

Twitter, Trump, and Trauma

Twitter served as one of the main ways Trump was able to shape anti-immigrant rhetoric in the US. From his candidacy, throughout his presidency, and up until the January 6, 2021, insurrection, Twitter was the primary tool he used to mobilize his supporters.[106] Ultimately, because of the ways they "glorified violence," Trump's tweets were deemed too egregious and in violation of Twitter's rules and conduct, resulting in a permanent ban from Twitter and Facebook.[107] However, despite social media platforms finally taking a stance on violent hate speech, much of the damage to vulnerable communities had already been done.[108] Studies indicate that Trump's narratives may have promoted hate crimes that targeted select communities.[109] In 2020 crimes against Asian Americans increased by 150% after Trump weaponized inflammatory language that blamed China for COVID-19.[110] Similarly, 2019 marked the year of the highest incidence of hate crimes reported to the FBI in the last decade, most of which targeted Black people, Jewish people, gay men, and the Latinx community.[111] Outside of Twitter and social media, Trump's claims were far-reaching and broadcasted daily on local and national news channels, making the exposure to children inevitable and constant.

Social Media Representation of Latinx Immigrants

As we have seen, the 2016 US presidential campaign was infamous for its negative rhetoric directed at Mexicans, Muslims, undocumented immigrants, asylum seekers, and refugees.[112] Scholars have documented the ways in which media narratives about Trump's policies erased the nuanced and complex identities of immigrants and "reproduce[d] the daily demonization of Latinos as criminals."[113] This approach is one the US media had long perfected, relying on political narratives in which migrants were described as "illegal" and their migration as "dangerous waters" rushing across the border to overwhelm the nation.[114]

The impact of attaching a criminal identity to Latinx immigrants is to propagate fear and stress about crime, terror, and threats to the nation, affecting the everyday lives of immigrants and nonimmigrants alike, despite the fact that studies have found that immigrants are less likely to commit crimes than US-born populations of the same demographic.[115]

Alarmingly, the record-high number of immigrant apprehensions and deportations has perpetuated negative stereotypes of Latinx people in the media. For example, in their study of media representation in Kansas, Menjívar et al. (2018) found that after decades of policies and media narratives promoting images of Latinx people as criminals, the perceptions and social relations between immigrants and nonimmigrants have suffered. Moreover, the rampant "rhetoric of securitization, criminalization, and terrorism during a presidential campaign that placed anti-immigrant sentiment center stage is the result of a long history of laws and media narratives targeting Latino/as, linking their physical appearance, identities, values, and behaviors to crime."[116] The social construction of the "Brown Threat" continues to be reproduced and amplified, leading to fear, surveillance, and dehumanization of immigrant communities, but particularly of undocumented people.[117] The media's role in fostering the narrative of the "Latino threat" is clear.[118] The way Latinx immigrants are portrayed in the media also demonstrates a general tendency to frame immigrants in a negative light, which is consistent with a "threat" narrative but inconsistent with actual immigrant demographics.[119] This negative representation has been found to be exceptionally detrimental to young college-age Latinx immigrants. In a quantitative psychological study, Chavez et al. found that negative emotional responses to media portrayals were associated with participants' higher perceived stress, lower subjective health, and lower subjective well-being. Consequently, it is inferable that children of immigrants also experience negative emotions and health outcomes when media outlets position immigrants as criminals and threats.[120]

It is difficult to talk about immigrant children and the last decade of increased border enforcement and restrictive immigration policies without the topic of fear. Fear is what gives laws, people, situations, and places power. It is what drove the Obama era's "attrition through enforcement" and what reproduced concepts like illegality and legal violence during the Trump administration. Creating fear was the motivator for Sheriff Arpaio's immigration raids and deportation campaigns. This emotional cloud of fear is experienced by different family members in mixed-status families in varying ways. Undocumented adults or parents in these families undergo what Cacho calls a social death, where the fear of possible separation continually constrains a person's life until they feel they have none.[121] Songs have been written about this lack of freedom experienced by immigrant communities, as described by the popular *norteño* song by Los Tigres del Norte, "La jaula de oro" or "The Golden Cage," where they are able to work in the country but not truly live or be free.[122] This is also the title of a documentary about adolescent Central American migrants and their journey north.[123]

The next chapter centers the impact of these polices on the lives of children, looking at how these narratives of fear manifest at school, home, and in the community. Through an analysis of children's drawings and theater performances in Arizona and California, we will see how art allowed children to express fears around familial disintegration, violence, and racism. This chapter makes visible the worries that children feel as they go to and from school, particularly the fear of the border-wall construction. It also demonstrates how lines are blurred between enforcement entities of the state, such as police officers, sheriffs, highway, or Border Patrol agents. The fears of enforcement officers highlight children's fear that their family members will be detained or deported.

2

Fear

"We Are Trapped, Like in a Cage"

When children have witnessed or experienced family separation, they frequently report having nightmares, tantrums, and trouble concentrating at school.[1] Even if their families are united and the children have US citizenship, they often fear for their own lives as if they were undocumented, often confusing their parents' immigration status for their own.[2] This chapter demonstrates how immigration policies come to affect children in border states like Arizona and California through the theme of fear. By highlighting children's expressions of fear through topics of family separation, state violence, and racism, we gain key insights into the impact of laws on their lives.

Fear of Family Separation in Arizona

Considering all the ways the law affects immigrant families, and puts those who are undocumented at risk for deportation, it is understandable that children of immigrants would be fearful of family separation. During my time with children in Arizona, detention and deportation were the most commonly recurring topics among children of all ages. Over one-third of children from Phoenix were preoccupied with thoughts about family separation in various forms. This chapter analyzes the drawings that young people created with narratives related to being taken away, incarceration, separation at the border, and being left alone, prompted by their visions of what a mural about peace in their community meant.

Fear of Being Taken

At the time he made his drawing (figure 2.1) in 2008, Alex was a 7-year-old boy in elementary school living in South Phoenix. I saw him daily in his school uniform, a white polo shirt and navy-blue pants. Alex was born in Phoenix, but his parents were undocumented immigrants from Sonora, Mexico. Sonora is located on the other side of the border, just a few hours by car. However, Alex had never been there because, as he said, his family "don't have papers." Like many of the children who were involved in developing a mural about peace at the community center, Alex drew images that were the opposite of peace, in which he depicted authority figures taking someone away, as exemplified in figure 2.1. Children expressed the fear that sheriffs would take away not only their parents or loved ones but them as well. Alex's drawing took up very little space on the 11 x 8.5 sheet of paper. Although the children had access to multiple pieces of paper, markers, crayons, and colored pencils, some drew only in pencil and on the bottom left corner of the paper. Despite the small scale of Alex's drawing, the content of the image

Figure 2.1. Alex (Elementary School).

Figure 2.2. Alex (Elementary School).

is powerful. Zooming in (figure 2.2) we can see three stick figures and a vehicle with lights on top, like a police car with the sirens wailing. Two of the individuals are shackled together and have long streams of what resemble tears running down their faces, along with big frowns. The third figure closest to the car is wearing some kind of headset with wires. On one side, the figure with the headset is holding one person by the arm and with the other hand is touching the car. It is unclear if Alex drew himself in this picture or someone he knows, but researchers affirm that if children live within a mixed-status family, they too internalize the fear of being undocumented, even if they are citizens and legally cannot be deported.[3]

Alex's drawing informs readers about the everyday lives of immigrant communities, especially in highly surveilled places like Maricopa County in Phoenix. This image and many like it warn viewers about the dangers of color-blind thinking when it comes to interactions between communities of color and police officers.[4] They demonstrate that in some communities, enforcement officers represent a threat rather than a source of safety.[5] In particular, Alex's drawing illustrates how authorities exercise legal violence in immigrant communities, where children often talked about "seeing sheriffs take immigrants away." Policies like the 287(g) agreements, which authorize state and local entities to act as federal immigration enforcement within a local jurisdiction, rupture family cohesion, creating lasting consequences for children. Reports from 2007, 2010, and 2018 argue that children's academic, emotional, and physical well-being decreases when a parent is detained.[6] Unfortunately, arrests, detention, and raids were common themes in these children's drawings.

The next two images, plate 2.1 and plate 2.2, are similar examples of children's fears related to being taken away or the arrest of a parent. In the first, drawn by Cynthia, age 10, the image looks like a comic where there is interaction between two characters on what looks like a bright and sunny day. Word bubbles indicate dialogue between the two individuals. One says, "Don't take me, I have a family to take care of," and the other responds, "I don't care!!!!!!!!!" The figure who does not care is much larger and taller than the other. He is presumably a sheriff's deputy, as indicated by the vehicle on the left side with the word "sheriff" drawn with a gray marker. This figure of authority has very white skin, which becomes especially apparent when looking at the dark complexion of the much smaller character who is being taken away in what appear to be handcuffs, with blue tears running down his face. Not only does this image make clear the troublesome thoughts about parents with families waiting for them getting arrested, but also how race and phenotype play a part in the power dynamics of who is getting arrested, detained, and deported. When I asked Cynthia about her drawing, she said, "They are deporting a Mexican family." We know now that Arizona's sheriff deputies were found guilty by the Department of Justice of unfairly targeting immigrant communities and organizing raids by racially profiling immigrant drivers coming home from work.[7] Cynthia makes the connection between racial profiling and arrests clear in her drawing.

In the next drawing, plate 2.2, Luisa, age 9, depicts what looks like a dark and stormy night out of a children's picture book. Strong lightning is shooting from the cloudy sky and there is a huge moon on the horizon. It seems that the image is almost drawn based on a memory of a real-life event, as Luisa intends to make sure the viewer knows it's night with the labeling and underlining of the word. This nighttime arrest by a grinning Sheriff Joe Arpaio shows how he is specifically taking a Mexican dad and a Mexican mom. Then, on the bottom right corner, a son and daughter are crying and left alone. The arrest is also viewed by people waiting at the bus stop and witnessing on the bottom left; witnesses are saying "OMG" and they are surrounded by hearts within their word bubble, demonstrating feelings of sending love to the fam-

ily being arrested and separated. To Luisa, labeling the ethnicity or nationality of those getting arrested is important. In the consciousness of
this 9-year-old, sheriffs who target and take Mexicans in the thick of
the night is a scary thing. Multiple children including Luisa often told
me about the *redadas* or raids in their neighborhood. Children's parents
warned each other via text and phone calls about the raids currently
happening, something kids like Luisa also knew.

Fear of Incarceration

Isela and her entire family are undocumented, her mother told me
during one of the drop-offs she made at the community center every
day. She mentioned that she was unsure if Isela knew about the family's legal status. "Esta muy chiquita," she said. "She is too little." But the
next image makes clear that there is a certain level of understanding as
Isela highlights the fear of being incarcerated from the point of view of
a child who anticipates being arrested or detained by the authorities.
Plate 2.3 is set during the day, as indicated by a large sun and a blue sky.
Most of the action in this image is near a house, where a large character
labeled "Sheriff" holds a girl in each arm. Not far from them is another
unlabeled character, and on the bottom left are three other kids playing
near a pool with a slide. As in the previous image, the sheriff exhibits a
large smile as the two little girls—identified as "niñas"—cry and frown.
Isela drew a police car instead of a sheriff's deputy's car, a common point
of confusion by the kids. Research by Sarah Rendón-García echoes the
experience of Isela's mom in negotiations about how, when, and what to
tell her children about their immigration status.[8]

The ubiquity of structural violence can be seen in the police and sheriff being an all-too-familiar presence in the lives of these youth. These
findings coincide with a study indicating that middle-school Latino
boys may be at risk for academic-adjustment problems resulting from
the constant presence of law enforcement and strict immigration laws.[9]
Scholars of symbolic violence[10] state that individuals see the legal structures as normalized and natural and often internalize the negative perceptions believed about them, such as, "I am/We are criminals," notions
expressed in the drawings in this section.

Separation on Two Sides of the Border

Children in Arizona also drew images expressing the fear of being separated from their family members by the US-Mexico border. Some of the youth shared stories of their family members attempting to cross back into the US or about ICE taking their mom or dad away from the community of mobile homes where they lived. One example is Vicente's drawing (see figure 2.3). Vicente, 17, was a high school senior who drew an image about a family of five with a line between them. The striking aspect of the drawing that makes it so personal is that the image includes the names of people who are living on the other side of the border, or what Vicente refers to as *la linea*, or "the line." Here, three of the stick figures have names, invoking the common situation of binational families who live straddling the two sides of the border, at times described as "familias transfronterizas."[11] The three people on the left who have a home and a car appear to be frowning. The two individuals on the right seem to be near yet far away, as depicted by the small cloud that could be

Figure 2.3. Vicente (High School).

part of the larger cloud on the left. Data by migration scholars has documented how at times, young children feel abandoned in the country of origin when their parents migrate to the US.[12]

Similarly, when a sudden separation occurs following a deportation, children also express feelings of abandonment, post-traumatic stress disorder, and depression. Elementary-school student Fernando created plate 2.4, which is set along the border as well. On the left is Mexico and on the right is the US. Between the walls or fence of the border are bodies drawn in a brown marker and labeled "hide." Along the center of the drawing, there is a red car labeled "cop" with the sirens on. Although these diagonal brown bodies are on both sides of the border, only the one on the US side is labeled with the verb "hide." Logically, there would be no reason for "cops" or police officers to be out of their jurisdiction, but in these children's minds, police officers can be anywhere. The next drawing is similar in that it depicts cops on the border rather than Border Patrol agents or ICE officers. The blurred lines between agencies like Customs and Border Protection (CBP or Border Patrol) and police officers foster the feelings of constant surveillance and never-ending fear of being pulled over, with that interaction potentially resulting in family separation.

The obsessive emphasis on the border is not difficult to understand when one considers the geographic proximity of Phoenix to the Sonoran Desert, which spans the US-Mexico line and extends into the interior of both countries. Communities in Arizona constantly migrate to and from neighboring Mexican cities. Following are examples of drawings related to the theme of separation along the two sides of the border. These images also make clear the connection of fear and state officials. Plate 2.5, by elementary-school student Angel, depicts a cop near a border fence with barbed wire at the top. As in the previous image, the presence of police officers on the border stands out, as police officers are more commonly found in cities and urban areas. To children who live in a city like Phoenix, however, police presence is not unusual as they are seen as the ultimate authority. Although police presence is evident, the trust in these institutions has deteriorated to the point that victims of crimes who are undocumented are unwilling to report those crimes for fear of deportation.[13] Overpolicing in low-income communities does not translate into more safety and security in these neighborhoods.

Middle-schooler Mario drew plate 2.6, which also depicts a large border fence with very spiky and dangerous barbed wire on top on the left side of the image. We know the setting is at night by the bright yellow-orange light coming from the helicopter, which casts its spotlight on someone below who is squatting down or emerging from the ground. Below the helicopter is a bus full of detainees crossing the border, as depicted by the bars on the windows of the bus. The sighting of a bus taking people who have been detained and are being deported is commonplace in Arizona. These buses can be spotted along the highway at various hours of the day. Since the establishment of the Border Patrol in the early 1900s, buses have been the main source of transportation when deporting people en masse.[14] Thus, in a place like Arizona it is common to see buses with migrants being taken from detention centers across the border. Already the border is a hypermilitarized zone where cars and pedestrians can wait for hours to cross into the US after being questioned and having their documents and belongings inspected. In places like Tijuana and San Diego or Sonora and Tucson, the presence of US military, Border Patrol, and other types of police is one around which people must negotiate every day.

Expanding on the theme of border enforcement, in plate 2.7, elementary-school student Julian depicts a SWAT-team helicopter, police car, and bus or tank headed toward the "border of Mex[ico]." This image seems to convey the most action-packed scene of a film, where authorities dramatically chase suspects. Julian draws the border as a single webbed panel with barbed wire along the top. Many scholars and demographers have noted that most children in mixed-status families are US citizens by birthright and because of the legal status of the parents, they rarely come across the border.[15] This is the experience of millions of children growing up in the US, who, like Julian, have never visited their family's country of origin and may grow up without having contact with extended-family members.

In the minds of these children, the entities that enforce the separation made by the US-Mexico border are cops/police officers and not Border- or highway-patrol officers, who are more likely to be found in border regions. These images demonstrate some of the ways state-sponsored legal violence in the form of IIRIRA at the national level and through SB1070 and Secure Communities at the local level makes the transition from

Highway Patrol officer to police officer to ICE agent almost seamless. Children often confuse types of law enforcement by drawing a sheriff's-deputy car but including a police officer in the same drawing, nodding to the legal marriage between criminal and immigration law, which systematically criminalizes immigration and migrants. This criminalization of immigrants paves the way for a seemingly logical transition from immigration law to criminal law and thus surveillance and enforcement.[16]

Fear of Abandonment

Children in this study also drew pictures centered on loneliness and abandonment caused by family separation or the fear of it. The images represented in this subsection demonstrate a range of emotions like sadness, anger, and fear. For example, Pedro, a middle-school student, made the drawing in plate 2.8 of a boy sitting at the bottom left corner of the paper with his hands on his face in a position often taken by children as they cry. "This is how I feel" was the only thing Pedro was able to say when I asked about his drawing. Visually and symbolically, there is nothing else in the drawing except for this boy at the corner of a blank page. As with Alex's image, Pedro feels there is no need to draw anything on the rest of the sheet of paper. Just this simple image is enough to express what he is experiencing and feeling. However, unlike the image drawn by Alex in figure 2.1, this one is in color. The color contrasted with the white page highlights the skin tone of the little boy in the drawing, the brown hair on his head and his brown skin, illuminating the phenotype of this specific immigrant community and their suffering. The image portrays feelings of sadness and desperation, emotions that are cited in reports about children who have been separated from their families. Indeed, some of the children in Arizona reported feeling afraid to go to school, because when they get back home, they might not find their parents there. This image transmits a sense of loneliness and isolation, and perhaps of hopelessness or entrapment. Often it is difficult to understand what children think and how they feel. But with one simple drawing and a simple sentence, Pedro makes it abundantly clear how immigration issues are affecting him.

Figure 2.4 aligns with Pedro's drawing. Maria, too, is a middle-school student. Her parents and two eldest siblings are undocumented; she and

Figure 2.4. Maria (Middle School).

her sister are the only ones who have citizenship. When I asked her how she was feeling one day, she drew a picture instead of telling me about it verbally. Using three colors, she drew a girl in the center of the page with three word bubbles coming from her head. Each bubble has one word in it: "mad," "sad," and "angry." The person in the drawing was made with expressive eyebrows but no mouth, indicative of feeling voiceless and unable to express oneself. The rest of the page is colored in a blue hue, which resonates with the popular expression "feeling blue." The voicelessness was reiterated by the fact that she did not verbally tell me how she was doing; instead she let this drawing speak for her. Many of the children I met preferred to express their ideas and feelings with drawings rather than verbally or with text.

Children's Fears in California

Deportation and family separation were the main preoccupations of the children with whom I worked in Arizona. As the following sections demonstrate, these children were not the only ones with these preoccupations. Deportations in Arizona or California do not exist in a vacuum and children are aware of the various systems that operate in the criminalization of immigrants and of the efforts at mass deportation stemming from the nation-state in general. The policies we have discussed have serious consequences for the lives of affected families. As we have seen, children in Arizona respond to these policies with deep-seated fears about being separated from their parents because of detention, deportation, imprisonment, or being abandoned on the other side of the border. Although children in California have a different political reality, during the time of the study in Los Angeles anti-immigrant rhetoric and legislation had already spread to conservative and liberal states alike, and the children in Los Angeles demonstrated a similar fear of immigration policies to those of the children in Arizona. However, their fear was expressed as more directly related to the US president at the time of the study, Donald Trump.

Fear of Borders

To children of immigrants, the border seems to be familiar like a distant family member who is often talked about, remembered, contemplated, and problematized. This is especially the case for children who live in places along the border and in cities that are less than a two-hour drive from Mexico. Even when trips to the border or Mexico do not happen because of undocumented status or scant available funds, the border is ever present in the imaginary of an immigrant family. Even more so, for the Central American migrant children I met in Los Angeles, the border is a recent memory—often a painful one. The sixth graders I worked with in South Central Los Angeles had a lot to say about the border since there was an integration of interviews and theater performance that children in Arizona did not experience. Some wanted to share stories of their own family's migration; others, stories involving meeting a "coyote"[17] or crossing with strangers and meeting their family members at places like McDonald's as soon as they stepped foot on the US side of the border. Other children had radical new ideas about what to do with the border or when one was separated from one's family. Children were constantly preoccupied with the concept of separation, particularly given Trump's campaign promises to build a wall between the US and

Mexico. The children's drawings shed light on what they thought and felt about the highly contested space between the US and Mexico and what separation meant for them and their families.

In Luis's drawing (plate 2.9), he presents what he remembers or thinks the border is like. Luis, 11, arrived with his family when he was 9. He shared the story of how he had to ride in a car with another family and say he was a stranger's son. He came with someone else's passport and when he made it to the US, he met up with his real parents at a nearby McDonald's. Luis recalls that he did not want to leave his friends in Mexico, but his parents needed to come to the US "for a better life."

In Luis's rendition, the US-Mexico border is a very busy place. On the US side, there is a big city with many tall buildings, including a casino, a McDonald's where one can "have fun and get a happy meal," and a hospital identifiable only by the large billboard with a cross that in Mexico is known as the Cruz Roja, or Red Cross. On the Mexican side, there are no buildings, only some cacti and gravestones. In between the two is a border made up of two pillars and an electric fence in between. The fence is labeled with two signs on either side that read, "Danger is a Electrical Fence" [sic]. On top of the two towers are "border agents"; one looks angry and the other is sleeping. Although Luis, like other children, had full access to color pencils, markers, and crayons, the entire image is in gray tones and pencil. The only colorful objects are the cacti, the cars and lines on the road, and the red siren lights on top of the border with lightning symbols in dark blue. When I asked Luis how he knew what the border looked like, he explained, "Cuz I remember and cuz my parents." When I asked him what he meant, or to elaborate, he shared that he wanted to draw the desert where people die and the *linea* (the line, border, or checkpoint) where people cross. What is clear from Luis's drawing is that the border is a contested space with dangerous situations that could cost someone their life.

Another way fear made its way into children's perceptions of the border was in our plays and skits. Plate 2.10 shows what students made during one of the improvisational image exercises of Theater of the Oppressed,[18] I asked students to create the image of "what is a border." I had five volunteers to start the image. This time only boys wanted to volunteer; I accepted that and told them they had to work together—without planning it out—to create a frozen image using their bodies, like a photograph. When I counted down students from five to one, everyone was to freeze in their final image. The counting from five, to four, to three, all the way to one allowed students to quickly improvise roles, negotiate positions, and generate emotion. No matter what, when I got to zero students had to freeze and commit to the image.

When I reached zero, I noticed that students quickly divided themselves into what appeared to be two categories of people: those in danger and those with guns. There was one more person who appeared to be working with the gunmen. On the top right, he was holding one of the two people who had their hands raised in the air as that person gazed at one of the guns closest to him. The person he is holding has a surprised or fearful look on his face. The second student with his hands in the air looks as if he is balancing precariously on a tightrope. The two with the guns have different expressions on their faces; one of them has a mischievous smile while the other is more assertive and serious. I asked students looking at the image from the outside to identify what was going on and what characters were present. It was not difficult for them to interpret this image as the two with the guns and the one apprehending an immigrant are playing the role of Border Patrol agents, while the two with their hands in the air are migrants who have just been caught attempting to cross the border. Students who participated in constructing the image agreed with the guesses of the classmates; they had created a scene where CBP apprehended immigrants crossing the border.

Plate 2.11 also highlights the vulnerability of migrants while crossing, this time in a drawing by Ernesto, a 12-year-old who was born in Los Angeles. His dad came to the US from Michoacán, Mexico, to work but was deported. Ernesto shared his father's story of crossing the border. In this picture we see a large desert that is drawn only on the top corner of the paper. For visibility purposes, plate 2.11 zooms into this corner. Ernesto's image is small yet contains a complex story. He draws a vast desert with mountains and cacti, but we see a big, bright, and presumably hot sun behind one of the desert mountains. In Ernesto's drawing, much is happening; there is an office of sorts and a large car with sirens and the Mexican flag. On the right, one figure looks more passive while the second is actively using a megaphone toward a lone stick figure that is also running.

Like plate 2.12, this drawing also demonstrates a hypervigilance not only toward the US but also toward Mexico. There is also a representation of another danger that many people face when crossing the border. Under the office-like building, we see a snake in motion, slithering back and forth. Thus the dangers of crossing are multiple. In addition to the border agents or enforcement officers both in Mexico and the US, there is also a great danger represented by the natural elements, symbolized by the cacti that are colored in both drawings, and in the portrayal of the desert with the heat that many people must endure to make it across, some falling tragically short in the excruciating conditions, not least a lack of water.

Fear of borders also comes through in Julio's drawing (plate 2.12). At age 11, Julio is able to represent the dangers of crossing the border. Two children are concerned about the lack of water, a reality many people face and even die from. On the left of the image, we see a large cactus with many thorns and spikes. For those who live in or near deserts, it may be commonly known that cacti like this saguaro contain water inside. Yet for those migrating from faraway places where the weather might not be so arid, the fear of severe thirst may be one of the reasons people pay thousands of dollars to be guided through the desert and helped to survive the difficult journey. At the top of this picture is a large cloud with a big yellow sun in the upper right corner. As the two children look at the cactus, one says to the other, "We can get water from the cactus"; the girl on the right replies, "Yea but how do we open it?" The figure with the idea has a slight smile on his face, while the figure on the right has a little frown as she is concerned about how they will persevere.

Children are well aware of the dangers on the border. Here Julio knows about the scarcity of water and how it affects migrants' ability to survive while crossing. Ironically, Julio chose a blue backdrop for the image, in which the most important task is finding water. Generally, when preparing to migrate and cross the desert on foot, immigrants are told to bring two gallons of water, but it is difficult to carry that much. Even when someone can carry two gallons, it is far from enough water to survive the extreme heat of the desert. According to centers that keep data on deaths along the border, most people who die while crossing succumb to dehydration, heatstroke, and drowning in places near the Rio Grande.[19]

During our class time, students shared stories about their parents or grandparents crossing the border. It was uncommon to hear students talk about their own crossings since most could not remember them. However, some had crossed more than once because of their US-citizenship or other legal status. During one of our class conversations, Julio shared his experience of crossing the border. He vividly described how he heard the gunshots that killed one of his older brothers: "After my dad died, I went to his *entierro* [funeral], in Mexico. When we crossed back people were shooting towards the *frontera* [border]. . . . I went in the grass, slowly, and then they saw my two brothers; big brothers. . . . They got one of them. I didn't know what happened. . . . I went running with the others, but they got my brother. I lost my dad and brother at the same time."

When Julio and his brothers were going to mourn their father's death, another tragedy happened. He was not sure who fired the shots at first—there had been two coyotes who were accompanying him, his brothers, and a larger group of people, but a little farther along he saw "US police officers in green," which signified the US Border Patrol. Julio's eyes filled with tears when he told the story, and he said he did not think of it often even though it had occurred just two years earlier. Julio told me after class that it was painful when TV or a song prompted him to think about the border because he then remembered it all over again.

Similarly, Fernando had also been to the border. He told the class that his dad had papers that he passed down to him, meaning that he adjusted his immigration status through his father. Once they went to Mexico to see a doctor, something that is common with transborder (*transfronterizo*) families as medical assistance and medicine are much more affordable in Mexico than in the US.[20] He remembered that the journey back to the US was difficult because they could not get on an airplane. Although Fernando had indicated that he and his dad were documented, the experience he described seems to match many anecdotes of people crossing the border with the help of a coyote because they do not have proper documentation. Fernando told the class, "I remembered a strange place, an old man that knows my dad. I went there. In the middle of *la frontera*, my dad would visit him, and so I went with him, and he said that he was going to take me to the end of the *frontera*." I asked Fernando where his mom was, and he replied, "Here in the US." Fernando made it across the border with the help of the old man his dad knew. However, he did not think his family would be going back to Mexico for a long time.

Like families in Arizona that straddle the border, Santiago's family is divided, living on both sides. At 12 years old, Santiago was always getting in trouble in class with his teacher Ms. Solano. When he came to theater class, he initially became shy, but he liked to volunteer regularly to play the role of a bully, CIA agent, Border Patrol agent, or any parental or other older roles. In one of the exercises, Santiago mentioned in passing that he did not know much English because he had gone to school in Mexico. His friends asked him, "But weren't you born here?" Santiago said he was, but he had to leave Los Angeles because his mom was deported, and he and his sister had to follow her while his dad stayed behind with his oldest brother. The dad would stay in the US trying to make a living for the family and the older son, who was in high school, would also stay to finish school.

Santiago and his older sister, Laura, went to live with their mother in Mexico when he was 8 years old. This went on for three years until the family was able to reunite in Los Angeles. During those three years the children would take turns crossing the border to see their parent on either side. Because of the difficult transition between countries, Santiago's older brother did not finish high school. Laura met someone in Mexico and fell in love, having her first child there and dropping out of school. When Santiago returned to the US with his family including Laura, he had trouble keeping up in school as he had gotten used to teachers speaking Spanish.

Santiago and Laura's parents were still undocumented. When Trump became president, Laura said that fear enveloped her family, especially because her husband was undocumented and she was concerned that the same thing, family separation, would happen again. Her younger siblings also lived in fear of having their parents deported. That prospect was not far from reality, as just the year before their uncle had been deported and now their cousins were going through the same thing. Santiago and Laura's uncle had 12 daughters, all of whom had been born in the US and had not been able to see their dad. Since the dad was the main source of income for the family, the family was not only suffering from the separation between them and their father but also from the economic impact of his absence and overall uncertainty. Laura and her two children were separated from the children's father; since he did not have legal documents to enter the US, he remained in Mexico. Laura told me, "I wanted to come sooner because my daughter, I want her to go to school and start here and not struggle like my brothers." Laura intended to start the process of getting papers for her husband soon so they could all be reunited in the US. Santiago and his sister Laura's family continued to live fragmented by deportation and anti-immigrant measures that aimed to keep his family in Mexico. Although many of the family members were US citizens, they could not use many of the benefits to which they were entitled because they lived in another country. Years later Santiago's mom continued to tell her kids that if she was deported (again), she would take them with her because she could not stand to be without them. The children objected, saying that they would want to stay in the US with their older sister and brother; their expressions indicated that it was hard having to negotiate one's existence and to live every day with the fear and uncertainty of possible separation.

For children in mixed-status families in South Central Los Angeles, the border is not only something talked about on the news or fought about in Congress. The *frontera* is incredibly important to them. Some of these kids have recently arrived to reunite with their family members. Other children remember having lost very close family members who attempted to face the heat and other dangers of crossing without documentation. Although most of the students have never been across the border, they remain acutely aware of its presence.

Fear of Trump's Border Wall

As we have seen, the literature on children of immigrants indicates that children often confuse their own immigration status; even when they are US citizens, they believe that they could be deported as if they, too, were undocumented.[21] Similarly, during my time with this group of sixth graders in South Central Los Angeles, "the wall" was extraordinarily salient as a certainty, and they believed it had already been constructed. Sometimes children had creative ideas on how to solve the issue of the wall's construction. Compared to the Arizona context, the wall was a much more prevalent theme in the California context because the data was collected around the time of Trump's obsession with the subject. For instance, children in California also believed various figures could solve the problem, like former president Obama or El Chapo (Joaquin Loera) Guzmán, one of the most powerful and influential Mexican drug lords infamous for his control of the Sinaloa Cartel; at the time of this data collection he had just been captured by the US Drug Enforcement Administration (DEA). Children also included themselves or their parents in their drawings as efficacious change makers. The following are examples of children's anecdotes during the two years I spent at the middle school, reflecting their fear and their mocking and satire of the wall's construction and its proponents.

The importance of the border wall was apparent from the first day of class at Liberating Our Dreams Academy. After playing an icebreaker game and doing student introductions, I asked students to reflect on what was happening around the world and in the country. The task was to think about what they believed to be the biggest problem at present. I asked them to raise their hand if they wanted to share; twelve students shared and some added other issues or agreed about the problems others had shared. Some of the issues children raised included (in the following order): the drought in California, the border fence or wall, Donald Trump (or as called by students, DT or Donald Trompas),[22] deportations, the greenhouse effect, global warming, lack of jobs, "gang banging," and robberies. I will discuss the use of "Trompas" later; here I focus on the awareness of multiple social problems. This list made clear that children are not passive in society; rather, they acutely listen to what is happening around them, are aware of issues, and can think in complex ways about how society's problems affect their families and communities.

As we continued this brainstorming activity, at least five other students said something in relation to Trump. I asked if the students could pick one issue of all those mentioned to create an image.[23] Sifting through the list of issues shared by them and their peers, they chose Donald Trump. Four students volunteered, and they created an image based on the problems everyone had listed. The image was of three students holding hands but not wanting to hold hands with the fourth person. I asked the rest of the class, "What is this image about?" Those viewing the activity responded: "They are the wall"; "Maybe Trump put them in jail, and they were holding hands to give each other hope"; "Maybe they are Mexicans building a wall to keep Donald Trump out"; "Maybe they are representing how they are not accepting others because those two people were not holding hands."

This image was powerful to see, but even more so was listening to these sixth-grade students' interpretations. The first response invoked the wall—this time with the idea of using it to keep themselves (and Mexicans as specifically mentioned) safe from Trump. The other understandings of the image call attention to the isolation children and families may have been feeling at this time. Likewise, the children mentioned the issue of incarceration, imagining that people were put in jail (detained); yet imprisoned people could give each other the hope needed to keep going. At that point, though I had not yet communicated to the students that I was interested in issues of immigration, I knew the topic would be important for them too. These various themes of fear of Trump, deportation, and especially the wall would continue to resonate with students and would be exemplified through interviews, theater skits, stories, and jokes.

Similarly, during an image-theater exercise, we decided to "activate" the still images by adding voice and movement to them. The image the students wanted to act out was the one of Trump building the wall. As two students began performing their improvised skit, one of the lines that stood out to me was: "I am going to build a wall and I am going to make Mexico pay for it!" In response, Paola, 11 years old and playing the role of then-presidential candidate Hillary Clinton, responded, "I am going to build [a wall] around your house! And if you become president then I will build a wall around that house too!"

Paola's exclamations are powerful. They demonstrate the importance of staying away from Trump, but also how she critically and creatively thinks of ways to problem-solve and prepare for the possibility of a wall dividing Mexico and the US. The ingenuity of simultaneously allowing the wall to be built *but* with the purpose of isolating Trump is laughable and at the same time serious in communicating the strong feelings students had against him. There is also something striking about stating that if he became president, then the wall would be built around the White House, which is so representative of US power and democracy.

Aside from building a wall around the White House, children wanted to dig a tunnel for immigrants to go through. Like the rest of the nation, the children were also captivated by news stories of Guzmán's escape and recapture.[24] For the Trump administration, El Chapo's capture was a tweet-worthy accomplishment that ostensibly justified the inappropriate claims about Mexicans. In a lighthearted and joking tone, children in the class often idolized El Chapo, branding him a hero of sorts like Robin Hood or Pancho Villa. During one of the theater exercises, one of the students asked, "What are we gonna do if Trump builds a wall?" Jorge (age 12) responded, "We're going to dig [under] the walls. I'm going to be like El Chapo. Like in the song when it says you're going to build the wall."

Jorge was referring to the popular rap song by YG titled "FDT" ("Fuck Donald Trump"), featuring Nipsey Hussle from the album *Still Brazy*. In the song, artists say, "All the 'n——s in the hood wanna fight you / Surprised El Chapo ain't tried to snipe you / . . . If you build walls, we gon' prolly dig holes." This song served as an anti-Trump anthem in Black and Brown communities like South Central Los Angeles. It specifically calls for unity among all people in resisting Trump; for example, it evokes the Watts Uprising when communities protested police brutality, and calls for unity between Bloods and Crips for the sake of helping better the community and protect children: "God bless the kids, this n—— wicked and wigged / When me and Nip link, that's Bloods and Crips / Where your L.A. rally? We gon' crash your shit." Children in the class associate with the song and its message, which generates ideas about how to resist and outsmart the numerous institutional barriers that affect the safety of children and many of their family members.

Children also imagined being present the day the wall was "confirmed." In one of our improvisational theater exercises, one student started to act as if he were Trump finalizing the construction of the wall. In the middle of the exercise, he said "wait," ran to his backpack, pulled out a piece of paper and a pencil, and took a moment to write some lines. When he revealed the paper to us, it seemed like a formal declaration of policy, and the student read it in a powerful voice. He began with the title, "Donald Trump's Wall Confirmation," and followed with, "I want to build a wall between Mexico and America, and if someone digs under, it's going to have to die by my soldiers. So, until I sign this paper, I will not build this wall." This 11-year-old put himself in Trump's shoes, attempting to embody his political power and authority. In his declaration or confirmation, he already anticipated that some people would object to the wall; he created a consequence for those who would not comply by saying that someone who dug under it would have to die at the hands of soldiers. For children this is not hard to believe as they are constantly confronted with images of Border Patrol agents, police, military, and other figures of enforcement. When the student playing Trump made this border-wall "confirmation," other students automatically responded:

> MULTIPLE STUDENTS: Boo!
> RODRIGUEZ VEGA: Hold on.
> STUDENT: Throw tomatoes!
> RODRIGUEZ VEGA: Do people think that that is accurate?
> MULTIPLE STUDENTS: Yeah, yes.

In their impulsive response, students chose the cartoonish option of booing someone off stage and throwing tomatoes at them to indicate disagreement. The creativity of the student playing Trump in this scene did not go without objection from his peers. When I asked this student how he was so good at playing Trump, he stated, "I just watch how he says what he says in the news." The mannerisms and the relentless firmness in his voice were impressive. As children continue to experience the fallout from immigration policies, it is important for adults to know that children are paying attention. They are thinking critically and, more importantly, creatively about the ways to challenge this difficult moment full of fear for immigrant communities.

The topic of the wall feels much closer to children than it actually is. Patty, who is 11 years old, made a statement in one of our classes that offers some insight into how children in border states understand the wall. After the "Wall Confirmation" skit had occurred, a student walked in late to class, and I then asked students to share with the newcomer what had happened. Patty raised her hand and said, "Es una obra de Donald Trump que va a firmar el papel para que, para que construya . . . la pared, que, este . . . que divide a Los Ángeles y México" (It is a play about how Donald Trump is going to sign the papers so that he builds the . . . the wall, that, umm . . . that divides Los Angeles and Mexico). Everything

Plate 1.1. Gabriel (High School).

Plate 1.2. Carla (Elementary School).

Plate 2.1. Cynthia (Elementary School).

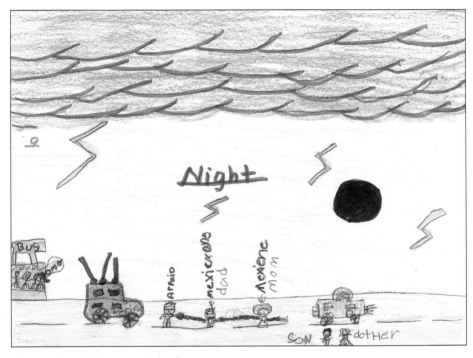

Plate 2.2. Luisa (Elementary School).

Plate 2.3. Isela (Elementary School).

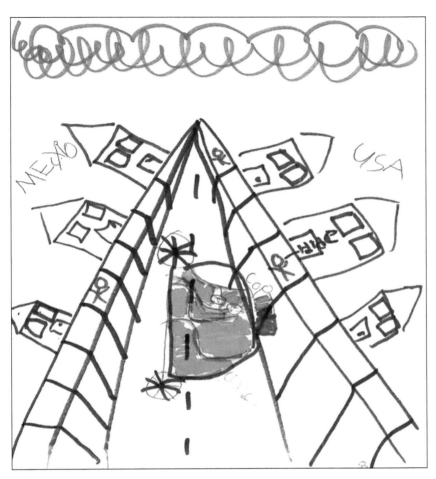

Plate 2.4. Fernando (Elementary School).

Plate 2.5. Angel (Elementary School).

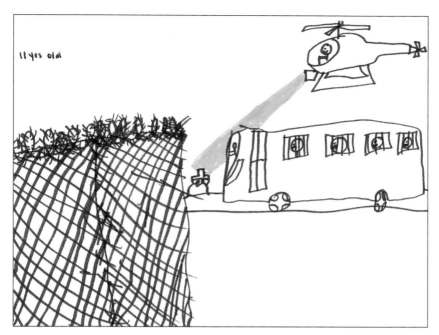

Plate 2.6. Mario (Middle School).

Plate 2.7. Julian (Elementary School).

Plate 2.8. Pedro (Middle School).

Plate 2.9. Luis's Drawing (Middle School).

Plate 2.10. Image Theater (Middle School).

Plate 2.11. Ernesto's Drawing (Middle School).

Plate 2.12. Julio's Drawing (Middle School).

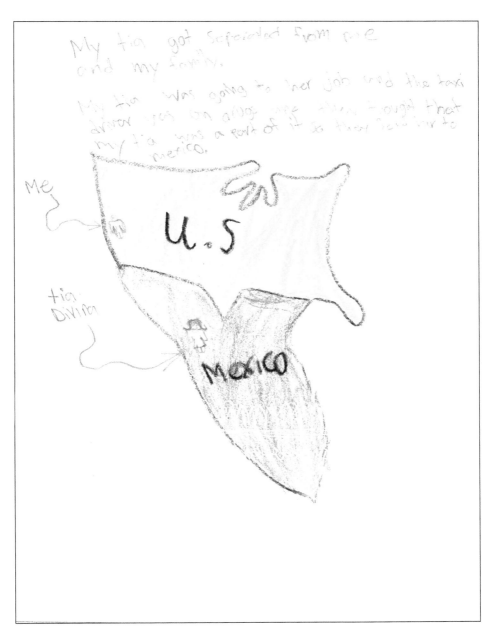

Plate 2.13. Max's Drawing (Middle School).

Plate 2.14. Brandon's First Drawing (Middle School).

Plate 2.15. Brandon's Second Drawing (Middle School).

Plate 2.16. Elisa's Drawing (Middle School).

Patty said was accurate except that the wall will divide more than just Los Angeles from Mexico; it will divide the entire US from Mexico. Yet her statement exemplifies how, for Patty, her whole world is Los Angeles, where she lives and where her immediate family lives.

This statement reflects how intimately these issues are affecting the students' lives. It is as if Patty had said that the border wall was going to divide her neighborhood from Mexico, illustrating that children sometimes internalize events and what is shown in the news in ways that are not physically or legally feasible. In turn, we must be attentive as researchers, educators, and community members who are involved with young children of immigrants. Amid so much chaos and "fake news," it is increasingly important to dispel myths and distinguish fact from fiction, particularly because anti-immigrant sentiments are embedded in many forms of communication and in society.

Fears of Detention, Deportation, and Absences

During my two years working with sixth-grade students in Los Angeles, it was clear that political turmoil, anti-immigrant policies, and uncertainty about the future induced distress and concerns about the possibility or reality of familial separation. These separations occurred in various forms: some involved family members from whom the students had already been distanced; there were also cases of reconnection with family after being separated for some time; and some separations were from family members who lost their lives on the border. The following examples highlight the various manifestations of fear related to separation exhibited by the children in California.

Nosotros, cuando venimos, teníamos papeles como mi mamá, siempre ha tenido visa. Y como ahora nos quedamos a vivir aquí, perdió, mi mamá, su visa. Y mi abuelita estaba muy viejita, y mi mamá sufrió mucho porque se murió.

[When we came, we always had papers like my mom. She had a visa. But since we stayed to live here (overstayed the visa) my mom lost her visa. Then when my grandmother was very sick and dying my mom suffered so much, because my grandmother died.]

Julia was only 11 years old. Yet even at a young age she was very aware of her and her mother's legal status. She described how she and her mother overstayed their visas when they arrived from Guatemala and became undocumented. For many immigrants who are undocumented, returning to their country of origin is impossible because they may never be able to return to the US without putting their lives in danger and spending thousands of dollars to hire a coyote.[25] Thus, many families like Julia's often endure painful separations for extended periods, particularly when a family member is very ill or dying or when a joyous occasion takes place, such as weddings or birthdays. Families on either side of the border cannot come together at times when it would be culturally, socially, or religiously expected.

Julia was not the only one in her family who expressed difficulty and sadness in not being able to reunite with extended-family members; she also witnessed the pain this caused her parents in the US, particularly her mother. Multiple children shared experiences about the death of grandparents and the family having to mourn the loss from across the border. After Julia shared, almost all the children raised their hand wanting to share a story about a time they could not visit a family member in their country of origin because of issues with documentation status.

Max was usually a quiet boy. His parents migrated from Mexico when he was little. When it was time to assign characters, Max volunteered to play Trump. The class got a kick out of seeing his dark-brown complexion paired with the bright yellow wig. When a student began a conversation about the border and family members, Max reflected:

> My aunt got deported to Mexico. She used to live here in the USA, and one day she was going to work in a taxi, and the taxi driver was, like, on drugs and then the police stopped him, and since my aunt was in the taxi, they arrested her. She didn't really know that the taxi driver was on drugs, they didn't do a drug test on her so they just took her to the jail and deported her.

This is another case of a young person struggling with the separation of a family member. In contrast to the situation with Julia's family, Max's aunt lived with his family in one house. On her way to work, Max's aunt got into a taxi that was pulled over while speeding and moving erratically. Although she did not know it at that moment, the taxi driver was under the influence and was arrested on-site. As the police questioned Max's aunt, they realized that she was undocumented when she could not show proper identification; this prompted police officers to call ICE to intervene. Hence, even though she was the passenger, she came into contact with law enforcement and was questioned about her legal status. Eventually, this traffic stop resulted in her deportation. This is another example of criminal and immigration law coalescing and of how many undocumented immigrants become intertwined with criminal law because of their legal status by way of programs like 287(g) and others like it.[26]

In Max's drawing (plate 2.13) we see the representation of the US where he is, and of Mexico where his "Tía Divina" is now living after her deportation. Although his entire immediate family is no longer with the aunt, in the drawing he singles himself out. He shows where he is located on the map, Los Angeles, and shows his aunt in the northeastern part of Mexico. The longing for his aunt is evident in the puzzle-like drawings of him and his aunt, emphasizing the distance and the border between the two. Max's drawing and story resemble those of many of the children who shared about a family member who had been deported.

For a similar case, we turn to Brandon who was one of six children. He loved dogs and playing video games with his siblings. He was born in Los Angeles and predominantly spoke English, although he said his dad spoke a lot of Spanish. He was not certain if his dad was documented or not, but he did know that his mom was born in the US. His mixed-status family had encountered the law at various moments in Brandon's life. For example, one day during class, students were sharing what they had done that weekend. Instead of sharing about that, Brandon wanted to tell me why he had been absent from the last theater class; he said it was because he had to go see his dad.

Later, when I looked at his drawing (plate 2.14), I realized that what he meant was that his dad had been detained in jail. So, rather than going to school, Brandon and all his siblings went to court for his dad's hearing. His drawing details how the entire family traveled by bus to the jail's or court's parking lot. His image has very little color, mainly drawn in gray pencil. Only a few colorful items stand out, like the sun, the road with a blue P for parking, and the large brown door.

Inside he draws small rooms with one person in them, representing jail cells. Each stick figure representing detained individuals in those cells is frowning. The only figure that is smiling is the one in the corner sitting on a chair, representing the guard. This figure of the guard is reminiscent of Foucault's panopticon of surveillance, where one person can see everyone around.[27] The anticipation of being watched at all times creates what Foucault calls docile bodies.[28] Brandon added text to his drawing that says, "My dad went to jail. He had his turn to call, when we [k]new, we went to pick him up. I was sad." It was important for Brandon to have the time to draw this and process what he and his family had gone through. He was able to express his sadness more profoundly in the drawing than when he told me he simply could not come to class because he "had to see his dad." Later I asked Brandon to draw a picture about what he wanted to happen. The next image was about Brandon's dad getting out of jail in two more months, which he described as four weeks in the drawing.

Later, as we checked in during class with our Rose and Thorn activity (used to describe one negative and one positive of each student's day, weekend, or experience), Brandon shared with everyone that his dad was detained in jail. Other children responded by sharing their own stories about detention, jail, or imprisonment. As their energy led them to talk all at once, I had to gather the group and have one person speak at a time. When the other children were asked if they knew someone who had gone to jail, some raised their hands and others just shouted, "My uncle . . . ," "My brother, he is getting out soon . . . ," "My sister went to juvie." Then I asked, "How do you feel after they can come out?" They replied, "Relieved," "Happy," "Hallelujah!" Then Brandon shared, "You get worried that your mom or dad might do something bad again." The separation between him and his father was painful, and it was clear that Brandon was sad about the possibility of not being able to see his dad for a long time if he got "in trouble again." This way of thinking illuminates how children make sense of the carceral system and learn to internalize ideas of respectability—who is a good or bad person, what makes a good or bad immigrant.[29] As the above examples demonstrate, immigrants can be detained and deported through police-ICE collaborations for matters like being victims of crimes, simply jaywalking, or having a broken taillight. Thus, it is not one's deservingness, worth, or value that determines whether one can stay in the US but, rather, how much one can avoid any contact with law enforcement.

One of the many exercises in class was to make a drawing of future goals. Brandon used this opportunity to draw about his upcoming birthday and what he wanted to happen. In the drawing, the main theme was his reunion with his dad. Brandon had wished that this would happen in time for his 13th birthday, which was in four weeks. This image (plate 2.15) is the opposite of his last drawing, where he specified that in court, he was feeling sad. Here, in his birthday drawing, there are colorful balloons, ribbons with lights, a four-layer cake, and gifts. The smiling stick figure with a squiggly mustache is labeled "my dad" and the small figure is labeled "me." This image centers a moment of reunification, rather than a location as his previous image had highlighted.

Following is another example of the sadness that migrant children feel when they leave family behind. During one of our check-in activities, students were sharing their drawings of what they had done during the weekend, on which Mother's Day happened to fall. Students shared about going out to dinner and having celebrations for their mothers. I noticed that Elisa was not as animated as she usually was when it was her turn to share. She showed the circle of students a cartoon of a woman, and under it was a sentence in Spanish that read, "I missed my mom, I have not seen her in two years." Elisa was 12, but she was 10 when she migrated to Los Angeles from El Salvador. Once she arrived, she met with her aunt and cousins who were born in the US. Although Elisa was happy to be in Los Angeles with her extended family and to be attending school where she was learning English, she became very depressed because of how badly she wished to be with her mother, especially on a special day like Mother's Day.

Elisa was one of the many child migrants who had risked their lives to reunite with someone in the US, where they hoped to have a better life. Many children making the trip do not reach their destination; some lose their lives along the journey, others are detained at the border, and, based on their age, some children are sent to special detention facilities where they live for an extended period and are then reunited with their family members in the country of destination. Although Elisa's mother wanted to reunite with her daughter and come to live with her sister in Los Angeles, the journey north had proven too dangerous; just the previous year their 20-year-old nephew Alex had died while attempting to cross.

One day, with tears in her eyes, Elisa explained the term "immigrant" during one of our theater classes. Her cousin Erick, who was also 12 years old and participated in the theater class, told us what had happened to them that was making Elisa emotional. He said, "We did not know anything about my cousin until we saw on the news that his body was found on the border." At that moment Erick also began to cry. Students approached and hugged both Erick and Elisa. Neither of them could verbally tell me more as they were overwhelmed with emotion. I told them we could take a break, or a moment to organize our thoughts by putting them down on paper or drawing something. Other students shared their own stories to comfort Erick and Elisa by explaining that they also knew people who had died trying to cross or even talking about movies or news stories they had seen that resembled something like Alex's experience. Since sharing stories was not seeming to help, I decided to have everyone sit quietly and reflect on this story or draw something that they wanted to share. Furthermore, I took this time to check in on both Erick and Elisa to make sure they were okay; I told them they could take a break or join the activity. They decided to join the drawing activity, and Elisa then created her drawing.

This image (plate 2.16)is an altar, an homage to the life of their cousin Alex, whose name is written on the small cross. The drawing is a way of processing his death and remembering him. The moon and the bright yellow sun frame the drawing with two cacti that represent the desert. Located between the two saguaro cacti, the most important part of the drawing is a television set that bears the name of the nationally syndicated Spanish-language news show *Primer Impacto* (First Impact) where they found out about Alex's death.

Later, when I saw Elisa's drawing, I learned that her aunt had not wanted her son to come to the US, but he had wanted to help her make more money for the family, and so had convinced his two uncles to help him pay for a coyote to get him here. Although they waited for him in Los Angeles, he never arrived. The family in El Salvador said that he had not returned there either. As time passed by, one day Elisa, her cousin, and her aunt were watching the Spanish-language news program on TV where they saw that their cousin's dead body had been found on the border. His body was sent back to El Salvador, where the family buried him without telling anyone. Elisa shared that the thought of her cousin's death continued to cause the family immense sorrow and pain.

This information was something that Elisa and Erick had a very hard time articulating verbally. Yet their drawings and what they did manage to share were so moving that the class "coincidentally" ended up creating their final performance about a similar story. Here a child migrant, also named Alex, makes it across the border with the help of two other child migrants and with guidance from a magical creature who is half human and half coyote. The opportunity to re-create this tragic story was moving for the cousins, their family, the class, and the audience that witnessed it.

These accounts of immigrant children's fear of separation in Arizona and California provide context to their everyday lives as they encounter state-sanctioned legal violence. This violence comes in the form of immigration policies as well as rhetoric they are often exposed to through the media. Immigration policies are affecting children by increasing their stress and fear of family separation. To some degree the possibility of being separated from their parents is realistic and fills them with worry, but telling their stories, drawing, make-believing, and performing give these children a method of relieving some of that tension. These policies in Arizona and California carry destructive consequences for children of immigrants. Art and art making allow us to visualize the possible impact of this fear on their lives. The next chapter describes the response of children in Arizona to the fear induced by policies that threaten their lives.

3

Response

Children in Arizona

Over the last decade, as deportations have increased, children have become hyperaware of authority figures in their neighborhoods and society. In Arizona, children were overly aware of anti-immigrant legislators, lawmakers, and enforcement officials, in particular Sheriff Joe Arpaio. As we have seen, an overarching theme of fear pervades immigrant children's artwork, mainly exhibited through narratives of separation relating to detention, deportation, and borders. Yet children are not passive in the face of this fear. The children with whom I worked responded to and processed the fears spurred by the legal violence they and their communities faced through their artwork. Immigration raids were commonplace in Arizona at this time, and even if children did not know of someone who had been detained or deported, they still lived in fear of it happening to them. The local and national media outlets were especially quick to cover the latest immigration-raid sites in the Maricopa County area, making such raids a constant headline news story. Much like Donald Trump, Sheriff Joe Arpaio was a fan of seeing himself on TV. Giving at least one press conference or interview per week, Arpaio was a household name and an ever-present entity in children's lives. His performance as "America's Toughest Sheriff" utilized old tropes of the Southwest. These cowboy tropes were reinforced through his use of horses, tanks, the Tent City jail, and the emasculating and criminalizing of Latinx immigrants with pink underwear.[1] These same tropes were represented in the children's drawings.

This chapter aims to make sense of how children in Arizona responded to the fears of family separation. It also highlights the pervasiveness of key characters and icons representing immigration policy and danger in children's drawings from 2008 to 2012 in Maricopa County in Phoenix. The characters reflected in their art included sheriff's deputies, police officers/"cops," Immigration and Customs Enforcement (ICE) agents, Highway Patrol and Border Patrol (*migra*) officers, SWAT-team personnel, and security guards. In terms of the frequency[2] of characters in all the drawings, Sheriff Joe Arpaio was mentioned more times than any other person in the category of actors, which included people like parents and other family members, peers, or others. We will see how through their art, the children responded to the presence of Arpaio and the impact of racism on their lives.

Plate 3.1, drawn by 12-year-old Daniel, gives us a candid account by a child of immigrants. Both of Daniel's parents migrated to Arizona from Mexico City; he was born in the US and struggled to understand why he did not have the same right to keep his family together as other children. In his drawing, Daniel makes sense of why his family is in danger and offers one of the most poignant examples of how Arpaio affected children. The drawing, which includes a large image that looks like a campaign poster for Arpaio, could be interpreted in the vein of political and campaign-imagery traditions. It seems to reference the well-known and iconic American patriotic posters from World War I, like the James Montgomery Flagg's "Uncle Sam Wants YOU for U.S. Army" poster from 100 years ago.[3] Flagg's poster was a widespread campaign advertisement that appealed to the public's rising feelings of patriotism as the country entered a world war. Daniel is similarly motivated to play off patriotic iconography and elevate it by strategically turning it on its head, using elements of sophisticated political-cartoon style by incorporating symbols like the Mexican flag, the colors of the US flag, and political slogans.

In the drawing, a large sheriff is placed in the center of the page with the words "FREEDOM IS AMERICA'"" and "YEAH RIGHT!" below as the backdrop to the entire image. Here, the sheriff holds two protest signs in each hand—one reads "100% RACIST" and the other "Mexicans are not Humans." In this image, the sign that is held high with pride is the "100% RACIST" one. However, the sign that is partially hidden but still visible is the one that dehumanizes a sizable portion of Arizona's population—Mexicans. The lack of humanity and outright racism represented in Arpaio's signs is what Daniel considers the motivating force of policies that tear at the human and social fabric of the community. Similarly, to illuminate the racist undertones of Arpaio's identity, Daniel draws him wearing a tie with the word "Mexicans" crossed out. The design and colors of the tie evoke those of a familiar representation, the Confederate flag. Under Arpaio's foot is a stomped Mexican flag. Daniel's image is rich with symbolism and messages about what it means to belong in this society and how it feels to be excluded from it. The image unmistakably critiques Arpaio's racism and xenophobic ideals about the "American Dream" and sheds light on the perception of him in Arizona's Mexican-immigrant community.

Daniel's drawing reflects the kinds of messages he receives from society about his identity as a Mexican American youth in a place where racial profiling is commonplace. The image of the Mexican flag or the word Mexican are represented four times in this drawing, all in hateful tones. This is worrisome as we know that negative societal messages make it difficult for children to develop an adaptive and positive sense of self.[4] This image also demonstrates the kind of indignation that children in Arizona use to resist racism. "FREEDOM IS AMERICA" is drawn and carefully designed in a patriotic red, white, and blue color scheme that illustrates an important critique of popular notions like American exceptionalism, the American Dream, and the frontier spirit.[5] Daniel adds a sarcastic undertone to these ideas that children are taught every day at school. Under "FREEDOM IS AMERICA" he draws the words "YEAH RIGHT!" in gray, highlighting his skepticism about this popularly advertised and globally known tagline claimed by the US. At an early age Daniel already has the creativity and talent of a political cartoonist, utilizing tropes, color schemes, and savvy political commentary to understand his position in American society. When I showed this drawing to Daniel's parents, they told me they had both recently sat him down to make a family plan of what he must do if they were to be detained or deported. They had notarized a document that would allow Daniel to live with a close family friend. Ultimately, this image brings to the forefront questions about school practices such as the daily recitation of the Pledge of Allegiance when children of immigrants must return to a home under threat of familial disintegration at the hands of the state they pledge allegiance to. Children feel, see, and experience legal violence through immigration policy and anti-immigrant rhetoric. This image demonstrates what happens when the authorities that are meant to protect and represent concepts like security, freedom, and peace are the very entities that threaten children's safety and well-being.

Figure 3.1 is by Mayra, a middle-school student who decided to do a write-up for the prompt meant to help generate ideas for a community mural: (1) What is the problem? (2) How do you feel about it? (3) What can be done to change it? Mayra decided to answer with a series of bullet points. She quickly narrowed down "the problem" to Arpaio, as labeled on the left. Then she described why he was the problem by stating that he treats people like animals, "doesn't care about separating families, is raises [racist], and has a *pansa de burro* [donkey's belly]." In this write-up Mayra quickly mirrors the dehumanization she feels when she is treated like an "animal" by expressing how she thinks that Arpaio looks like a donkey with a big belly. In that moment Mayra decides to cope with feelings of humiliation and fear through humor by pointing out something comical and, in her mind, embarrassing about Arpaio. This practice of coping through comedy was common among children in Arizona. They often talked about Arpaio treating immigrants like animals and about wanting him to see them as people.

Mayra then addresses the third question of the prompt: What can be done about this problem? She again centers on Arpaio and calls for people to "fire him, send him to jail, send him to Mexico, and put him in the electric chair." The suggestions get more serious to the point that she asks for the death penalty to be used against the sheriff. Perhaps she believed that the crimes of taking parents away from their children deserved to be punished with death. However, from that daunting suggestion she tones it down to a more "civil" option that elevates her voice as a citizen: "write to the president." This suggestion indicates her positive perception of President Obama during that time. Mayra and many other children from this community thought Obama would apply a sense of justice and stop Arpaio if they simply asked him. Mayra then adds her own category to the prompt where she presents the "effects" of this problem and again reminds us that Arpaio treats people, Mexicans specifically, like animals. Here she is reiterating the dehumanization that she and her immigrant community feel in Arizona. Her personal addition of thinking about the effects of such a problem points to the self-reflexive nature of Mayra's answers and to the trust that is built between the young person and the individual administering the prompt.

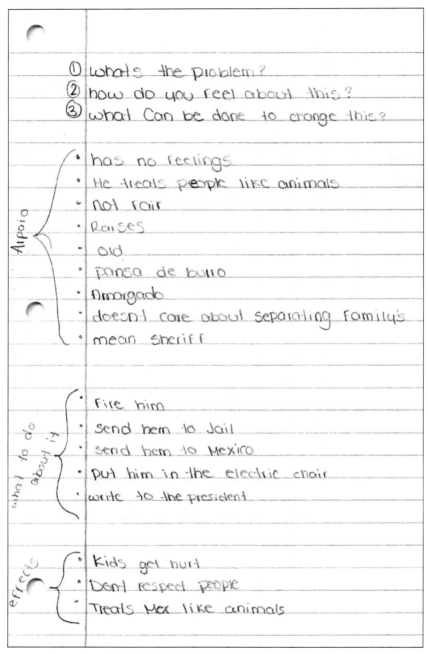

① whats the problem?
② how do you feel about this?
③ what Can be done to change this?

Alpaio {
- has no feelings
- He treats people like animals
- not fair
- Raises
- old
- pansa de burro
- Amargado
- doesn't care about separating family's
- mean sheriff
}

what to do about it {
- Fire him
- send hem to Jail
- send hem to Mexico
- put him in the electric chair
- write to the president
}

effects {
- Kids get hurt
- Dont respect people
- Treats Mex like animals
}

Figure 3.1. Mayra (Middle School).

Children were thoughtful in responding to the prompt "What is the problem? How do you feel about it? What can be done to change it?" Sergio, a middle-school student, wrote a short essay (figure 3.2) on his ideas about the most challenging problems he saw in society. He stated that immigration is the major problem in Arizona—not the immigration itself but the impact of anti-immigrant policies enforced in ways that create unlivable conditions for immigrants. Unlike with mere images, here Sergio provides context for the reasons why people migrate. Then he pinpoints the problem: "In Arizona the Sheriff, Joe Arpaio, arrests any person that looks like Mexican no matter if they are US citizens or not. He sends them to jail where they get beat up and treated like animals. . . . That leaves there kids alone in the USA away from there [sic] parents and [to] get adopted by a family if lucky."

Sergio's testimony relating to those who are in danger of deportation points to the perpetual and systematic fears that immigration laws foster. He states that in Arizona, just *looking* Mexican is enough reason to be arrested and detained or deported via racial profiling. Even if you are a US citizen and have a right to be in the country, you are not safe. This is the result of communities being tormented by policies like 287(g) and SB1070,[6] where police-ICE collaboration makes everyone who has any contact with state authority a target to be questioned. Even long before these policies were officially introduced, legislated, and enforced, immigrant children and their families already felt unsafe to be in public because the way they looked, the music they listened to, the language they spoke, or the car they drove were sufficient reasons to be profiled and asked for documentation. When these policies were introduced, however, those fears only became more palpable as they were officially sanctioned by the state.

In this community, Brown people have experiences with hostile laws even when they are not the direct targets. The overlooked consequences are that bystanders, community members, or as demonstrated here, children of immigrants are affected by these laws. Particularly for children of immigrants, though they may have been born in the US, as many are, having an undocumented parent invokes what scholars have called a "master status" where the undocumented status of one's parent dictates the way a mixed-status family can live their lives.[7] Even though children may have citizenship, they still feel endangered. Here, Sergio presents a

> One major problem in Arizona is immigration. People all over the world is immigrating to U.S.A to have a better life and education for themselves and family. But most of immigrants come from Mexico to close states like Arizona. In Arizona the sheriff, Joe Arpaio, arrest any person that looks like mexican, no matter if they are U.S. citizens or not. He then send them to jail were they get beat up and treated like animals. In desperation they sign there own deportation and get send back to Mexico. That leaves there kids alone in U.S.A away from there parents and get adopted by a family if lucky.
>
> This make mexicans and other people scare, sad, unfair and worried. IF you ask me I would say I feel like a slave living soppusly in a free country. Now theres almost nothing to do about this but if we get anough people to be against immigration and sheriff Joe Arpaio now the people that come for a better life won't continue to be slaves.

Figure 3.2. Sergio (Middle School).

powerful perspective that concurs with Mayra who stated that Mexicans were being treated like animals, reiterating a sense of dehumanization and othering. This perception also highlights the double standards of American patriotism. Sergio ends his essay by saying, "I feel like a slave living soppusly [sic] in a free country." Illuminating the ties between enslavement and racism, something that resonates for children like him, he is able to think critically about the label of America or the US as a "free country." Although most of that statement is daunting, he ends, like Mayra, on an empowering note. Asserting that if people get organized against Arpaio they may be able to gain liberation, he points to and finds inspiration in abolitionist traditions that have previously liberated African Americans from enslavement and granted them civil rights.

Plate 3.2 and figure 3.3 provide additional examples of how children in Arizona view authority. The first image was made by Jaqui in elementary school and the second by Sarai in middle school. Jacqui's drawing depicts a city scene with a car with sirens behind three people (a young girl, a woman, and a man); in front of the people is another vehicle. Above that is a statement in Spanish that reads: "el arpayo [sic] es malo con los mexicanos y los trata mal. No es justo me ase sentir mal, quiero que lo corran para que lla no fastidie!" (Arpaio is mean with the Mexicans and treats them badly. It's not fair, he makes me feel bad, I want them to fire him, so he won't bother us!)

The image's setting is an intersection, indicated by the cars, road, and streetlight on the right. It is important to note that even as an elementary-school student at a young age like 6, Jaqui shares the common knowledge that driving is a dangerous and unavoidable risk that undocumented immigrants must contend with on a daily basis especially when driving to and from work. Even on holidays and special occasions, immigrant families often stay home because alcohol checkpoints can put their status in danger even when they have not been drinking. This is particularly true in Arizona because it was one of the first states that implemented the 287(g) agreements which forged the national (ICE) and local (police) partnerships. Hence if one is pulled over even for a routine check, the risk of detention and deportation is exacerbated if one does not have a driver's license. Precisely because undocumented immigrants are denied driver's licenses, this is one of the most common ways in which immigrant communities' interaction with law enforcement puts their families at risk. Driving is a principal way that immigrants become vulnerable to detention, and children are highly aware of this danger. The scene appears to be of a mother being taken by the police. Jaqui draws a small girl on the left of the central figure, who could be herself. After years of news coverage that centered

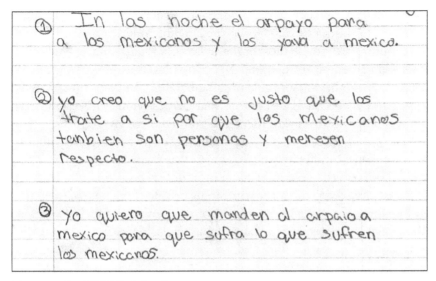

① In las noche el arpayo para
a los mexicanos y los yava a mexico.

② yo creo que no es justo que los
trate a si por que los mexicanos
tanbien son personas y meresen
respecto.

③ yo quiero que manden al arpaio a
mexico para que sufra lo que sufren
los mexicanos.

Figure 3.3. Sarai (Middle School).

on the children left alone after a car of undocumented immigrants is pulled over and the passengers are detained, it is not surprising that this is what she portrays.

Sarai also focuses on Arpaio and his treatment of Mexicans in her response to the prompt. In English her answers are:

(1) In the night Arpaio stops the Mexicans and takes them to Mexico.
(2) I think that it's not fair that he treats them like that because Mexicans are also people and deserve respect.
(3) I want them to send Arpaio to Mexico so he can suffer what Mexicans suffer.

She proposes that Arpaio should literally endure the same suffering her community deals with, thus mirroring that pain onto the sheriff. For Sarai justice means deporting Arpaio and eliminating the threat of his presence from the streets of Maricopa County. Rather than perceiving them as signs of protection and safety, like other children Sarai reiterates the threat that police and enforcement officers represent for communities of color, in this case, Mexicans.

Overall, there was an overrepresentation of authority figures in the drawings children created compared to other characters like parents, family members, and peers. Most often they incorporated a depiction or statement about Arpaio, and their drawings focused on how they viewed his effect on the Mexican immigrant community in Phoenix. In their drawings, children regularly confused the various kinds of authority figures they encountered. As we have seen, they would include a sheriff's deputy and a police car in the same image, indicating that the type of state enforcement agency did not matter; all were similarly threatening. Another kind of confusion involved the difference between the word "*immigration*" and the notion of *anti-immigrant sentiments*. Children would not make statements about immigration being bad or the hot-button issue, but only talk about anti-immigrant policies, ideas, people, and agencies as constituting the main dilemma. Finally, children also conflated the terms "Mexican," "immigrant," and "undocumented," using them interchangeably despite widely different meanings and connotations. In turn, these mistakes call attention to the complex reality that mixed-status families always encounter.

Responding to Racism

Some of the drawings we have already examined have portrayed narratives of violence, racism, disrespect, and rights. The images below most clearly exemplify these themes. The first drawing (see plate 3.3) is by Eduardo, an elementary-school student, who depicts a nighttime arrest by sheriff deputies in a police car. We know it is nighttime by the positioning of a half-moon on the top left corner. Children were keen on drawing big bright suns, and when the quintessential drawing of the sun was missing it was almost always intentional. The scene is of a Brown man, wearing a shirt that reads "I'm Mexican," on his knees with both hands in the air and his face looking down. He wears a baseball cap, something that construction workers do to protect themselves from the extreme heat and sun in Arizona. Pointing guns at him are two orange-colored, smiling authority figures labeled "Sheriff." Although the officers are identified as sheriff's deputies, the car they are driving is a police vehicle, again reflecting the conflation of various enforcement officers.

This image demonstrates the outright physical violence and racism that the Mexican community encounters in Arizona. At age 7, Eduardo knows that during the night sheriff's deputies will use their weapons against unarmed Mexicans. Having a brown body is enough reason to be shot. This narrative is also one that gets overly portrayed in the media and is talked about at grassroots level. At the community center where the children came after school, they would tell each other these stories about people getting pulled over, deported, or killed as if they were sharing scary stories around a campfire. It is unfortunate that at the age of 7, children are already aware of the racial hierarchies and dangers, particularly at the hands of law-enforcement officials like the sheriffs in Eduardo's image.

Sandra's drawing (see figure 3.4) represents one of the ways the border was characterized by children and youth in Arizona. Her image is set on the US-Mexico border. This depiction provides insight into her perceptions of how race, ethnicity, phenotype, and racism affect immigrants in the US. On the Mexico side are three splayed bodies with frowns drawn on their faces. On the US side is a large stick figure wearing a big hat like the one Uncle Sam typically wears. This figure is signaling toward the border and to another person on the US side. The other character is much smaller and has a perplexed expression, indicated by the mouth drawn open in a circle rather than the common line, smile, or frown. A short dialogue between the two figures is illustrated with two word bubbles. As the Uncle Sam figure points to the border, the smaller figure says, "But I'm a *citizen*"; Uncle Sam replies, "you *look* Mexican." Sandra uses an added emphasis, underlining the words "citizen" and "look" in red. Linking these words communicates the difference between being a citizen and looking like one. Children like Sandra critique the fact that in society, whether a person phenotypically "looks" undocumented matters more than whether that person is indeed a US citizen, highlighting how whiteness is the signifier of membership and inclusion against which everything is measured. This image also reveals how even though US citizens are not supposed to be deported, historically there have been violations of that right, particularly when the person has not been White.

As many activists and advocates for Black Lives Matter and immigrant rights have indicated, citizenship will not protect a person from

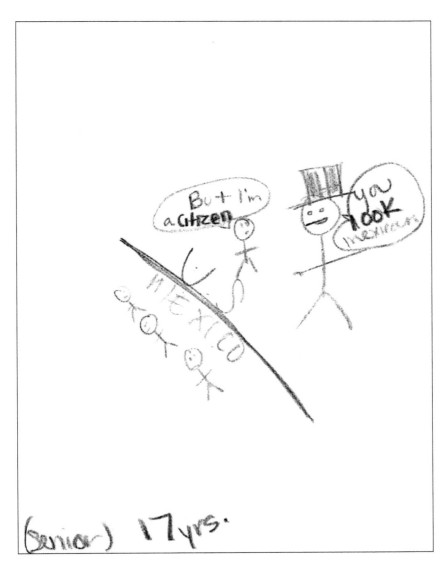

Figure 3.4. Sandra (High School).

racism or danger. Positing that citizenship is not enough, Sandra calls viewers to be more focused on what is needed: respect. This image also evokes a not-too-distant history of the Mexican Repatriation program. During the Great Depression in the 1930s, hundreds of Mexicans and Mexican American US citizens were put in trains and deported south of the border against their will, often to places they had never been.[8] In 2006, (now ex-) Arizona Senator Russell Pearce suggested that Arizona should revive a similarly racist policy called Operation Wetback. In this operation, which took place in 1954, US citizens were similarly "deported back to Mexico" in violation of their birthright citizenship, which enabled them to remain in the US.[9] A year later Pearce, the author of Senate Bill 1070, circulated an email to neo-Nazi and White-supremacist online groups including the Ku Klux Klan to request their support for his efforts to pass this infamous bill.[10] Along similar lines, under President Trump's administration Pearce established a "denaturalization" task force that aimed to make permanent residents and citizens vulnerable to deportation and included the mission of revoking citizenship from children born in the US to undocumented parents.[11] As we have seen, children report what they see in their community through their drawings and testimonies, exposing the racism, violation of rights, and legal violence they experience as the result of policies put in place by people like Russell Pearce.

Figure 3.5 also demonstrates the sentiments children harbor about racism and their desire to be respected. In it Julio, an elementary-school student, wrote: "The Sheriff Joe Arpaio will realize that we want him to respect us and our family just like we respect him. I want Joe Arpaio to stop hating us for our skin color." To Julio the sheriff is not a symbol of safety or order but a representation of disrespect and racism. Ironically, while the virtues of respect, kindness, and compassion are what children are taught to practice in school from an early age, because of their race or immigration status society may not always live up to its standards of respecting each individual.

The final image (figure 3.6) in this chapter, created by Ruthie, a high school student, concerns the carceral system's practices. Although it is difficult to see, the image is informative about the human rights violations that many imprisoned people in Arizona experience. It is unclear if it refers to prison or detention centers, though it could be a critique

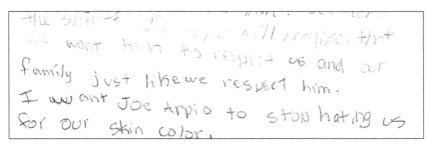

Figure 3.5. Julio (Elementary School).

of both. The drawing depicts a man in a cage on the left side of the paper, and on the bottom right is a home with three people inside saying, "where is dad?" Above the person in the cage there is pink text in bullet points:

No rights to have clean clothes.
No rights to have shower.
No rights to call home.
No rights to food or be with his kids.

Young people like Ruthie are aware of the violence, racism, disrespect, and violations of human rights that undocumented people experience. bell hooks emphasized the importance of maintaining strong family bonds between parents and children, but in Ruthie's drawing they have been deeply severed. In her book *All About Love*, hooks states, "Severe separations in early life leave emotional scars on the brain because they assault the essential human connection—the parent-child bond which teaches us that we are lovable. The parent-child bond which teaches us *how* to love. We cannot be whole human beings—indeed, we may find it hard to be human—without the sustenance of this first attachment."[12] For a country with an extreme dependence on this population, it is worrisome that children are fearful of losing the parent-child bond at such an early age. Gender-studies scholar Juana Maria Rodriguez reminds us that cultural theorist Lee Edelman articulated concerns about children being imagined as future subjects of the nation through repressive disciplinary power in the name of future promise.[13] Indeed, the US prison-industrial com-

Figure 3.6. Ruthie (High School).

plex predicts future incarceration rates based on children's fourth-grade reading levels, indicating that an inability to read is a predictor of criminality.[14] Over the years the effects of such inability have fostered a disproportionate number of incarcerations for Native American, Black, and Latinx youth.[15]

The children in Arizona are not the only ones who show a preoccupation with incarceration, race, and the ways immigrants are treated in the US. The next chapter explores the stories of children in Los Angeles, particularly those from Central American families who also experience racism, violence, and dehumanization. Although there are similarities in the ways immigrant-origin children generally respond to racism, there are differences between the experiences and reactions of children in Arizona from 2008 and children in California during 2016. As we will see, children's response to anti-immigrant sentiments, rhetoric, and policies became more direct, intense, and dire. This may in part have been caused by President Trump's more direct and public attacks on immigrants compared to President Obama. Particularly during Trump's administration, national immigration policy came to mirror the constant reality of children in Arizona. Unfortunately, children all over the country are now exposed to anti-immigrant sentiments. Although Arizona children's drawings, stories, and responses were not as violent, they foreshadowed a worsening situation that was on the horizon for the rest of the US.

4

Resistance

Children in California

In the California of 2016, children mirrored in their artwork the societal dehumanization, violence, and harm they experienced. As a result, responded with righteous indignation to the policy plans of President Trump. Overall, in both Arizona and California, children demonstrated their association of legal violence with authority, particularly with figures like Arpaio and Trump. Interestingly, children in both states saw President Obama as a sympathetic ally despite his having set the foundation for an enforcement-focused immigration system. Perhaps the 2012 executive order to pass Deferred Action for Childhood Arrivals (DACA) created the perception that Obama was a proimmigrant president despite his restrictive asylum policies and failure to provide a real path toward citizenship for the millions of undocumented people already in the US.

Framing a Response of Violence, Death, and Social Mirroring

How children understand and internalize violence, racism, and death can help determine their overall well-being.[1] Children tend to mimic what they see adults doing, thereby internalizing the structure of their society, culture, and family. Similarly, as babies' brains develop, healthy attachment to a parent is vital in achieving chemical balance and optimal brain development.[2] Later in life, the amygdala region—the part of the brain that controls affect and self-soothing in times of stress—helps develop the ability for proper decision-making. All of this, in turn, affects children academically and behaviorally. Problems are likely to arise when attachment is broken. Indeed, the earlier the attachment is broken, the more damage this can wreak on the life of child.[3] These findings from the fields of psychology and child development suggest that when young children are separated from their parents through structural factors—like detention/deportation, imprisonment, or parenting from across borders—the effects on young children's brains and life outcomes are detrimental for them and for society.

Often after internalizing, children turn to mirroring. Coupled with the risk factors of living in poverty, inadequate education, and perpetual violence in their community, as children in immigrant families come of age, they receive a series of societal messages about their cultural, ethnic, and racial group. Through societal treatment, media representations, and political sentiments, this social mirroring can influence children's identities in detrimental or positive ways.[4] When mirroring reflects negative images, "adolescents may find it difficult to develop a flexible and adaptive sense of self."[5] Children of immigrants seem to disproportionately receive negative messages from society when compared to White nonimmigrant children. They then mirror some of the ideas they are exposed to, particularly the anti-immigrant and anti-Latinx rhetoric that has become commonplace. Children have a keen awareness of the perceived epitome of power, whether it is in the form of a political figure or an administrative entity. Anthropologists have long documented the mirroring behavior between, for example, gangs and military groups, in which one group replicates the behavior, dress, and ideas of another to gain some of the power it holds.[6] Similarly, children imitate power.

In California, some of the children I worked with both internalized their precarious social positions through coming to understand perceptions of enforcement authorities as symbols of safety and justice, and, in symbolic ways, mimicked the structural and systemic violence in their communities. As a way of ameliorating their desperation for familial cohesion, their art represented themes of death. Although they do not literally kill Donald Trump, for example, children attempt to kill what Trump represents in their lives. As an act of desperation in the form of mirroring, children may adopt the ridiculing or the dehumanizing behavior of someone like Trump and employ it as a way of rebelling, resisting, and having a chance to survive and assert their humanity.

In the work in Los Angeles, in contrast to the solely visual and writing-based work in Arizona, children mimicked and imitated those with authority, including parents, teachers, celebrities, politicians, gang members, or soldiers. There may have been richer opportunities to engage in these mirroring representations because their class focused on theater, not just writing and visual art. Even if at times these forms of imitation are innocent, they can foster situations of danger and detriment. To navigate racism, children may mirror back the hate and violence they experience in their lives. For them, imitating and replicating power is an attempt to grasp the little power they can create. Often violence becomes cyclical, and children are powerful messengers of the ill-intentioned narratives we see in popular media. Yet often children mirror this negativity with a strong sense of righteous indignation.

Caged Children: California's Response of Righteous Indignation

In *Code of the Street*, sociologist Elijah Anderson argues that life circumstances in poor communities—such as lack of jobs that pay living wages, limited basic public services (police response in emergencies, building maintenance, trash pickup, lighting, and other services that middle-class neighborhoods take for granted), the stigma of race, the fallout from rampant drug use and drug trafficking—result in alienation and absence of hope for the future. Living in this sort of environment places young people at special risk of falling victim to aggressive behavior. However, there are some elements that can mitigate this impact. Some protective factors, like a stable home life, can help children have a healthy sense of self and feel protected. However, not all children experience or develop these protective factors, especially under a system of detention and deportation. Thus, children and young people are confronted with learning a set of "street codes" comprised of informal rules governing interpersonal public behavior. Anderson posits that at the heart of these street codes is the quest for respect. In what he calls street culture, respect is viewed as an external entity, one that is hard-won but easily lost and so must constantly be guarded. Overall, the code of the street is a cultural adaptation to a profound lack of faith in the police and judicial system, and a loss of faith in others who could represent safety. Youth in Anderson's study viewed police as part of the dominant White society and as not caring about protecting inner-city residents, as demonstrated by the lack of response when called and by their harassment of youth on the streets.[7]

Critical scholars have also demonstrated some of the dangers of color-blind thinking when it comes to interactions between communities of color and police officers.[8] In some communities, enforcement officers represent a threat rather than a source of safety.[9] In sum, today's authorities no longer offer hope to this generation of young people.[10] The recent reports on gun violence concur that placing cops in schools have not made schools safe. Rather, there has been a transformation from disciplinary problems into criminal violations that result in negative outcomes for young people. Instead of making schools and children feel safe, police presence has cemented what scholars call the school-to-prison pipeline as children get entangled with the law for otherwise acceptable childlike behavior. Ultimately, not all schools are places of joy and critical thinking that can support students. Instead, they often function as "institutions of containment and control that produce pedagogies of conformity and oppression that kill the imagination by teaching to tests."[11]

The association of police and violence also extends to notions of death and fear of dying. It is important to note that children's capacity to comprehend death varies heavily depending on their cognitive ability and developmental phase.[12] As noted, stress and lack of parental attachment can hinder children's cognitive capacity.[13] In studying children's comprehension of death, Speece and Brent found that not all children understand its irreversibility. They did assert that the usual age children start thinking about death is between 5 and 7, meaning that from an early age the phenomenon of death becomes important.[14]

Children of immigrants in Los Angeles are aware of the current difficult political moment. In their schools, they are often unafraid to speak back and resist. Building on the concept of social mirroring propounded by Carola Suárez-Orozco,[15] it is useful to explore how children mirror societal dehumanization and violence, particularly when they grow up in urban neighborhoods like South Central Los Angeles or experience the trauma related to possible family separation. Children may use drawings, performances, and interviews as tools for navigating racism, but it is important to remember that their attitudes are not always positive. To gain control and safety in their own lives, children often mirror violence with dehumanization and dark humor toward certain authority figures.

During the pre- and postelection periods in 2016 and 2017 when I worked with children in South Central Los Angeles, students were creative in thinking of solutions for the dilemmas that anti-immigration rhetoric and policies present. Most students' recommendations and ideas were humorous in nature, at times calling for the impossible to be done or turning the world upside down and offering new perspectives. In all the play, humor, and satire that children expressed, however, one theme came up often enough to merit special attention. Although it was playful and humorous, it is important to focus closely on this frustration that children were feeling as it provides unique information about their experiences. Death was a significant factor in the coded transcripts and analyzed images. Children were preoccupied not only with the death of migrants on the border but with the forces that endanger the lives of children and their families. When I quantified all their statements, death was one of the topics most often mentioned. Sometimes the death of Trump was presented figuratively, comically, purposefully, and symbolically. The following examples are rich with descriptive information about how children demonstrate righteous indignation and attempt to find solutions through the elimination of hate speech, anti-immigrant rhetoric, and racist remarks. Most of these quotes come from in-class discussions during the theater exercises, but I also draw on interviews with parents and children to offer context.

Dehumanization and the Media

I turn now to three images that demonstrate children's emphasis on the media in representing death and violence related to immigration, recalling Elisa's drawing (plate 2.16) about the moment her family in Los Angeles found out that her cousin who was migrating from El Salvador had died on the border. Plate 4.1 tells the story of how a young boy met his father who had crossed the border to reunite with his family. While the dad says, "I crossed the border," a television set centered in the image shows a close-up of a face with blond hair labeled "Donald Trump." As families worried about their fate in the US given their immigration status, television sets monitored the news and reported on topics like the border wall, separations, and the latest set of statements from the president's Twitter account.[16]

Similarly, the photograph from the final performance in 2017, the program's second year, centers on the news reporter as one of the main characters in the play (see plate 4.2). The prop he is holding is a television frame with the words "Samsung Smart" to resemble the television many people have at home. This reporter or journalist is the conduit for the important information that immigrant or mixed-status families need to know to stay safe on a daily basis.

Reflecting the importance of the media, the first example indicates the severity of anti-immigrant rhetoric. During one of the class sessions, I asked students to watch the news and report back on what most concerned them. To maintain some level of focus, I asked them to take a piece of paper and coloring materials and create a drawing about what they found to be most interesting or worrisome. Almost all the children drew something about Trump, and having them share their drawings led us directly into a conversation about the president, his policies, and even his family.

Here children made sense of what they were seeing in the world:

RODRIGUEZ VEGA: If you could tell Trump something what would you say? Who knows what they would say? ¿Quién sabe lo que le diría?

BETTY: Yo! . . . ¿Por qué es racista si tu mamá es de Canadá y su esposa es de Rusia? [Me! . . . Why is he so racist if his mother is from Canada and his wife is from Russia?]

RODRIGUEZ VEGA: Okay, good point. Danny, what would you say?

DANNY: That why is [he] racist? We didn't do nothing; we didn't kill anybody from his family or nothing, why is he being like that to us? Is like . . .

JESÚS: Is like we could've taken his life—

DANNY: He's wife didn't have papers then why he didn't report [deport] her?

RODRIGUEZ VEGA: Okay.

DANIEL: They do have papers—

DANNY: I said his wife didn't—she wasn't American.

JESÚS: I would say he's lucky that he made it to president because he's super sexist . . . like people don't want Hillary to be president because she's a girl.

RODRIGUEZ VEGA: Okay, wait raise your hand everybody . . . Josue what would you say?

JOSUE: Why deporting those . . . if you were from Mexico would you deport yourself?

RODRIGUEZ VEGA: Okay, last one.

DANNY: I would've said—why do you want to be like Hitler?

ASSISTANT TEACHER: Hitler?

DANNY: Yes I said Hitler—like Betty said, like his mom—¿De dónde era su mamá? [Where did you say his mom was from?]

[Laughter]

BETTY: De Canadá. [From Canada.]

RODRIGUEZ VEGA: Okay, de Canadá—

DANNY: I agree with Berta, Hitler his parent were Jewish and watch it didn't work out for them.

The children struggled to understand how someone who came from an immigrant family or who was married to an immigrant could himself be so anti-immigrant. The line that stands out is from Jesús: "Is like we could've taken his life," implying that there could be a possibility of killing Trump. But since that had not happened, Danny cannot understand why Trump would hate them so much and spew such racist notions about Mexicans, Central Americans, and immigrants in general.

After questioning Melania Trump's nationality or documentation status and why Trump was not trying to deport his own wife, Danny told everyone that he would ask Trump why he wanted to be like Hitler. This took the conversation in another direction. To the teaching assistant, the comparison to Hitler came as an extreme measure. When Danny's statement is questioned, he echoes Betty's claim that Trump's mother is not from the US or that he also comes from immigrants. And that, like Hitler, Trump is anti-immigrant even if he hates something that he also embodies or that is part of him. Despite Danny's belief, Hitler's parents were not in fact Jewish even if that idea animated Danny's thinking.

More than thinking about death and killing Trump, this example illuminates the ways in which children in South Central Los Angeles think critically about history and present-day implications. The comparison to Hitler often connotes intense emotions as most people have a strong reaction to anything that compares to the magnitude of the persecution of Jewish people during the Holocaust. Danny's comparison to Hitler as a disparaged individual in history seems to attempt to bring Trump down so that he, too, can disappear. Comparing him to the "worst person in history" almost dehumanizes him and makes him a sort of cruel monster. To children like Jesús and Danny, stating that they could have taken Trump's' life and comparing him to Hitler comes easy, particularly during Trump's first year in office when tensions were especially high.

This comparison reflects the severity of the then-prevailing situation, as children portrayed Trump as the modern-day Hitler. In fact, education scholars such as Giroux have documented the ways in which media and political parties on both sides of the political aisle have compared Trump to Hitler and Mussolini, overtly calling him out as a tyrant, fascist, or neofascist.[17] Children are astute in picking up on these sentiments. Ultimately, in drawing a comparison between Hitler and Trump, 12-year-old Danny embodies a "radical optimism" with regard to stopping Trump. Such hope, as Giroux explains, entails living without illusions and being fully aware of the practical difficulties and risks involved in meaningful struggles for real change, without losing optimism.

Mirroring Dehumanization: Government's Duty to Take Out Donald Trump

The children in South Central Los Angeles are constantly surrounded by death. They encounter the notions of afterlife, killings, and assassinations from what they see on television, but they are also confronted with death in the lived realities of their neighborhood, and at this school, the increasing deaths of parents with cancer. Given the constant presence of death, it is not surprising that it would manifest in their school activities and art creations.

In the following exchange, the children can be seen embracing a belief that the government is an almighty entity that has the responsibility to make things right in society. This discussion took place during one of the brainstorming theater games; Lilia (the most newly arrived immigrant student from Guatemala) was giving her group directions on where to take the scene. She began her role as director of the scene:

LILIA: Van a asesinar a Donald Trump. El gobierno lo tiene que hacer.
[They are going to assassinate Donald Trump. The government has to
  do it.]
¿Okay? Ahora tienen que hacer lo que dicen, ya?
[So now you have to do what they're saying. Ready?]
WHOLE GROUP YELLS: Three! Two! One! . . . Action!
JUAN: Hazte como si tienes una pistola y la vas a apuntar a ellos.
[Act like if you have a gun and you are pointing it at them.]
JUAN: I wanted to be one of the soldiers. La bazooka!

This scenario demonstrates Lilia's initial directions. She orders that those students playing the role of the government must assassinate Trump. Then another student, Juan, adds that those playing the government should act like they have a gun and point it at "them," though it is not clear if "them" refers to Trump or the government. Clearly, the students are not reticent in taking this radical approach. In the middle of the scene, a student starts to complain that he wanted to have a role in the skit of playing a soldier. Then Juan yells for him to include a bazooka rather than a gun.

The inclusion of a military weapon like a bazooka is important to note. The children I observed are enthralled with weapons and militarization. Particularly for boys in this class, if there was an opportunity to include something related to the army, police, or fighting, they took full advantage—often, as in this example, to the point of extreme measures. Bazookas, rifles, machine guns, bombs, and grenades were often part of their play even during recess and after school. Significantly, however, the children positioned these weapons of destruction in relation to eliminating Trump as a way of gaining relief from their worries about war, deportation, racism, and family separation. The children were calling on government officials and entities to use their power to change society by removing Trump. In this case and in the examples below, I argue, Trump is a proxy for the harsh conditions their families face.

The following exchange exemplifies how students in this class continued to bring up Trump's campaign promise of building "the wall." Particularly during the campaign period, children talked and laughed about it a lot. This is one of the ways the daily Trump news would make its way into our class, our theater exercises, and into children's improvisational lines. In this scene, Diego was excited about getting to direct a skit. As everyone sat around the small and cozy carpeted bleachers of the library room, we prepared to look down at the improvisational skit that a small group of students had planned. The actors scattered to find their places. One student took a deep breath, crossed his arms in front of his chest, and stood as tall as his four-foot frame allowed. Diego, our momentary director, yelled "All freeze!," and as the actors looked like statues about to come to life, he commanded, "Action!"

DIEGO: All freeze! . . . Action!

JOSE AS TRUMP: I want to build a wall between Mexico and America, and if someone digs under the wall, [they will] die from my soldiers. So, until I sign this paper, I—I will now build a wall with this . . . contract.

DIEGO: ¡Matalo! [Kill him!]

JOSE: I have a call.

DIEGO: A real call?

(Ringing of a student's cell phone)

RODRIGUEZ VEGA: Okay, you step in. [points to another student] You're Donald Trump right now.

JOSE AS TRUMP: Wait, I can just call my mom back—[puts his phone back in his pocket]

DIEGO: Porque el gobierno—el gobierno los tiene que matar. Okay, denle.
Ahí está Donald Trump. [Because the government, the government has to kill them! Okay, go. Donald Trump is right there.]

Although this scene is in bad theatrical shape, the actor embodying a politician gave us important messages about the children's thoughts and motives for choosing these characters and these specific events. Jose felt the pressure of wanting to keep the role of Trump, as it is highly coveted by students. Diego, annoyed by the interrupting phone call, also pressured Jose to finish the scene because the whole story had not been told; there was still the part about where the government kills Trump. Although, when Diego says, "Because the government has to kill them!

Okay go, Donald Trump is right there," the audience thinks that it is Trump who will be killed by the government, that is not so clear. The government killing "them" can also imply killing immigrants, as Trump has ordered that soldiers must kill anyone who attempts to dig under the wall when trying to migrate to the US.

Even with the passion of the students and the attentive audience, we ran out of time as Jose's mom called once again; we had to end class then and there. We never got to see if Trump was going to be killed by the government or if Diego was going to have students act as immigrants who get killed by Trump's soldiers. However, what is evident is that for these students, death is not an outlandish option to bring up, and whether it is Trump who gets killed or immigrants, death is unfortunately all too natural an occurrence and thought. As children pick up messages from society about who they are, they are also extremely aware of the many deaths occurring on the border as people attempt to migrate.[18] All this is compounded by the legal violence their families and community experience in their daily lives through both the effects of immigration policy and the rhetoric of the media. Although our society takes legal, social, and familial measures to protect children, it is telling that children of immigrants in South Central Los Angeles do not receive equal protection compared to White children in more affluent communities.

Police presence is commonplace in this Watts neighborhood and, through media, children and families encounter military commercials, movies, and video games. Scholars have long noted the purposeful targeting of military recruitment in Brown neighborhoods.[19] A disproportionate number of Chicanos and Mexican nationals have died in conflicts ranging from World War II to Vietnam and Afghanistan.[20] To these young middle-school boys, the military is one of the only ways to achieve upward mobility.[21] This data also concurs with findings and lived experiences of how children see themselves as police officers, soldiers, or even gang members in attempting to claim some power that they currently do not hold.[22]

The planning for the play took a dramatic turn of events. As we were cleaning up and preparing to leave the library where we had conducted our theater class and rehearsed our skits, one of the shier kids, Leo, approached me and asked:

LEO: Can we continue to do this?

RODRIGUEZ VEGA: What?

LEO: The thing that we're doing with Donald Trump.

RODRIGUEZ VEGA: Next time?

LEO: Yeah! . . . What if [alluding to killing the government] be better?

RODRIGUEZ VEGA: I don't know! Why would it be better? Why would you want the government to be killed?

LEO: For their actions.

RODRIGUEZ VEGA: You think it'd be better?

LEO: Yeah, like for more action.

RODRIGUEZ VEGA: What—how would that change what's happening now?

LEO: Because if he does that—the soldiers . . . obviously, it would give it more action.

RODRIGUEZ VEGA: But why?

Although Leo's reply, "For their actions," implies that the government has been "bad" and that removing it makes sense, Leo is also interested in giving the skit more action. He thinks that killing the government is a good idea not only because they are complicit in anti-immigrant/Latinx laws, violence, and deaths but also because "we get better theater." Though I continued to probe why he thought we should take this approach, he did not elaborate further than to say it was for action's sake.

Even if Leo is not able to fully articulate his thoughts, it is clear they are not only about giving the audience some excitement. Leo began to think critically about the actions of "the government" (it is not clear how he defines that entity), and he called their actions out. There is an underlying sense of wrongdoing that he is expressing. Perhaps he believed that the government should do more to protect people, but instead, Leo thought the government was too corrupt to help them.

Use Military Arms to Take Out Donald Trump

The children I worked with were not only concerned with issues of immigration but also aware of broader, complex issues related to geopolitics. One of the topics that came up during our reflection activities was that bombings and war in other countries worried them. In their perspective, Trump was responsible for the bombing that was creating war and hurting other people. The two images below demonstrate this theme of Trump's misuse of military arms.

The first drawing is about the bombings that were taking place in Syria during 2016. The bombings were ordered in the spring of 2016 before Trump was elected. It is interesting that the students saw Trump as responsible even though he was not elected until November. However, ingrained in students' minds were news stories that showed devastating images of destroyed buildings and injured families. In figure 4.1, Adrian, age 12, wrote, "When the USA send a Boom [Bomb] it [to] Syria!" In the drawing Adrian depicts a large rocket-like bomb that is shooting up toward the sky from a tube-like object. Next to that there are two figures, one in a suit with high blond, almost neon hair—a feature used often to portray Trump. Then there is a smaller figure with a hat on and a green uniform, meant to represent a soldier holding a remote-control device that is used to fire this missile. The setting of the image is a US military base as characterized by the US flag and the barricade-like compound

Figure 4.1. Adrian's Drawing.

Figure 4.2. Joaquin's Drawing.

on the right. In this image not everything is colored; in fact, most is in gray pencil tones. The only things Adrian colored and thus emphasized in his drawing were the words in the image, the missile with fire, the soldier's uniform, and Trump's hair.

Another example of children's worries about national safety is Joaquin's drawing (figure 4.2), which is representative of foreign relations in the Middle East. Like many of the young boys in the class, Joaquin was obsessed with military films, video games, and facts about the army. They knew about the various weaponry and the military branches that one could join. This knowledge may have resulted from heavy and disproportionate military recruitment in poor Black and Brown communities like the one where Joaquin and Adrian lived.[23] Joaquin also wrote a short statement to explain his image: "Trump put bombs on a different city, and I want to stop war." Unlike Adrian's image above, here Joaquin drew an incoming bomb. The setting is in a city with a tall building and many smaller ones with people inside. Most of them are on fire and in each of the doors there are small circles that look like people's heads. Most of the image is shaded in dark colors and has somber tones of black, gray, red, and yellow.

Figure 4.3. Mateo's Drawing

What may be most striking about the image is on the left side. Joaquin drew a small figure with a smiling face and red hair, and above the figure is a bomb coming into the town. The bomb is labeled with the word "Trump" in the center. It is traveling fast, as indicated by the brown dust or air that is left behind as it flies and the yellow-greenish wick on top. It is significant that Joaquin named the bomb after Trump; he suggested that Trump was the bomb that was going to destroy cities and cause death and pain. Children did not care only about immigration policy and the way their families were affected by Trump's plans; they were also aware of the Trump presidency's effect on the rest of the world and on other children. Here Trump is literally the symbol of destruction, and thus, in the children's logic, if you want to stop this destruction you must first stop Trump.

In figure 4.3, Mateo wrote, "Donald Trump [is] trying to report us and built [sic] a wall and trying to start World War 3 with North Korea." All are actions that would greatly alter a young person's life. Mateo also drew a high wall with barbed-wire fencing on top. On the left is a portrait of Trump, who appears to be standing at a podium with his name on it. In front of him is a microphone used to say what is in his thought bubble: "I will build a wall!!" Then on the lower right side is the image of a young child with a sad expression who wears a shirt bearing an image with a similar expression, with a sad and exhausted face and the tongue out. The kid also has a thought/speech bubble that shows the symbols of questions and exclamations, indicating confusion and danger. A second bubble just has the word "No!!" These thoughts seem to indicate what Mateo is feeling in response to the many actions that Trump is proposing to take, including his approach to international relations and the exercise of US military power. The next section demonstrates how the children mirror this idea of Trump's destructiveness by trying to destroy him first before he destroys the world—or more specifically, their world.

Mirroring Use of Military Arms

As we have seen, children in Watts—the boys in particular—were very preoccupied with military topics. This was perhaps because of the long legacy of military recruitment of Brown bodies in rough neighborhoods or possibly because of society's glorification and commodification of wars, violence, and arms. Given these factors, when thinking about death having to do with government, elected officials, or powerful entities, children often invoked military lingo and perspectives in our stories, theater, drawings, and interviews. In the first example, students discussed the plotline for the final performance of the second year of the class, which coincided with Trump's first year in office. During a brainstorming session about what should happen, Joel started the dialogue:

JOEL: Like, can maybe Trump get mad because they don't want him to lose votes, or maybe they would get him in jail.

RODRIGUEZ VEGA: Okay, so we have various stories, like Trump turns nice, Trump goes to jail, what else?

OSCAR: He's shot.

JOEL: We go to the White House!

RODRIGUEZ VEGA: And what do you do at the White House?

DANIEL: You scream—

JOEL: You shoot and dodge.

OSCAR: Can we? Like a sniper—

By bringing in the sniper idea, Oscar affirmed his classmates' notions about killing Trump. Here Oscar takes a different direction from Joel, who suggests that Trump goes to jail. Prior to this idea, another student suggested that Trump actually "turns nice" like a "good guy." These non-violent suggestions did not get support; other students suggested that when students arrive at the White House they encounter Trump, who has been shot by one of the snipers. Their scenarios connoted secret missions with the late inclusion of the sniper character. It is important to consider why the children felt motivated to resort to violent means in seeking to change what is happening.

In the previous section on governmental responsibility to kill Trump, the students had suggested adding a sniper as a main character. The young boys in the class were eager to play the role of a sniper in the final performance. More than five students at a time raised their hands asking to take that role, although I did not cast it and in the end we did not include that part of the story at all. Instead, through more dialogue about what we *did* want to see, we found alternative endings. These also resonated with the class, involving ideas like an impeachment of Trump or the return of President Obama. The ideas about killing Trump never seemed noteworthy at the moment. It is only in retrospect and through careful analysis that it became clear that the idea of eliminating him was a common response to the children's dehumanization.

The next example highlights the directly spoken lines from one of the practice skits of a forum-theater exercise. In this type of skit other students can jump in and take a role or verbally suggest alternative actions, lines, or a different ending. In this example students invoked the often-overused trope of "good guys vs. bad guys" that the media popularizes and is ingrained in the status quo. Other versions of this binary include "cowboys vs. Indians" and "cops vs. robbers." This skit depicts a confrontation during one of the presidential debates between Donald Trump (Mario) and Hillary Clinton (Patty):

> MARIO AS TRUMP: I would not let people get in this country.
> PATTY AS CLINTON: People will be coming from other countries, and nobody would be taken.
> MARIO AS TRUMP: Yes, but I will [take them].
> PATTY AS CLINTON: There'll be more people, and there'll be more country.
> MARIO AS TRUMP: I will not let the—[*here Mario playing Trump falls to the ground holding his chest*]
> DARIO AS THE REPORTER: He got shot!
> AUDIENCE: [Laughter]
> DARIO AS THE REPORTER: Got shot, yeah you did it! You did it! They're not going to build the wall!
>
> [*Trump jumps up and speaks in a mysterious and sinister tone*]
>
> MARIO AS TRUMP: Aha! You tried to kill me, but I have a ballistic vest.

Better than any telenovela these children watch with their parents on the Spanish-language channels, this skit had students sitting at the edge of their seats. Because of its improvisational nature, no one knew what would unfold, not even the actors themselves. Mario and Patty—or Trump and Clinton—engaged in a lively verbal altercation as they debated immigration policies and shared their thoughts on who should gain membership in the nation-state. Dario, the reporter, had a minimal role but his actions were emphatic. He held a pantomimed camera on his left shoulder and a fake microphone by holding a cell phone in his hand. He dramatically panned left, then right, quickly and precisely as each candidate began their first word.

Here, the role of the reporter represents the link between the general public and these political figures. Dario narrated the events and loudly exclaimed "He got shot!," which surprisingly became a comical moment for the class. All children watching responded as if something hilarious had happened; the action then intensified when Trump revived from his wound, shouting aloud an "Aha!" in an evil-villain tone similar to that of the "bad" guys in a movie or cartoon. He kept the tension high by engaging his invisible killer, saying that despite the attempt to kill him he was still alive thanks to a "ballistic vest." At the time, I did not know what exactly a ballistic vest was; I had to look it up to learn that it was a warfare or policing object. In popular culture, the vest is used as a military accessory in movies, and in superhero or villain tales. In the skit, this ballistic vest is a fictional weapon that affords powers to a "bad guy" or "evil villain."

Children's imaginary use of these combat tools to kill Trump represent the often-used tropes in children's films and stories of taking out the bad guy or a battle between good and evil.[24] Although it is initially alarming to learn about children who want to kill the president, it is not all that surprising given the way the entertainment industry uses common problematic tropes of good guys vs. bad guys when creating material for children to consume. In the movies, when a bad guy is killed, the killer generally does not die, does not go to jail, does not feel remorse, and does not get deported. Rather, that person becomes the hero of the story and is the one who saves the day!

In expressing a desire to kill Trump, the children thus demonstrate that they want to be their own heroes in saving the world. To be the hero, one must kill the bad guy. It is noteworthy that in their skit there is no role assigned to a student to be a killer or sniper. The invisible killers in their plays could really be anyone. It almost does not matter who it is, but rather that the killing is done. In almost all the examples in which the children incorporated death in their plays, they relied on a well-known vocabulary of militarized language and knowledge of weapons and how they function, as well as the various roles available in military missions most often portrayed in film, television, and video games.

Symbolic Death

Plate 4.3, drawn by Mary, depicts a cartoon version of Trump that resembles the characters in the show *South Park*. In this image the character of Trump is giving a speech as US president and in his thought bubble there is an image of a little girl crying next to what looks like a red cage. During the time this image was created in 2017, Trump had not publicly admitted to implementing his zero-tolerance policy that put more children and families in cage-like detention centers. However, the zero-tolerance policy was tested during that time and children were aware that it was part of Trump's immigration-enforcement strategy. Certainly, images of children in cages or "chain-link-fenced rooms" had already circulated through social media even during Obama's second presidential term. To the children, images of other children in cages without their parents was a daunting symbol of death since children need the care of a parent to survive.

Often, children were appalled by the statements Trump would make every week along his presidential campaign trail. At the same time, there was an excitement about the possibility of the first woman president of the US. Other students were saddened that Obama was no longer going to be president. The next image represents one student's thoughts about the 2016 election. I asked everyone to draw what they wanted to happen in the election, including whom they wanted to win. Lalo, an 11-year-old, made an image (plate 4.4) and wrote a statement that reads, "Trump lost the election and hillary won. Trump lost because no one likes him only a few people like his wife and his son [sic]." In the image, both characters are standing with hands on their hips in what looks like an assertive pose. Yet Trump has a deep, dark frown with what look like bloodshot eyes and dark circles around them. It also appears that he is hurt and bleeding from the side of his face. He is positioned slightly behind his opponent but at an angle, which indicates instability. Conversely, Hillary looks pleasant and is smiling. Behind them waves a great big American flag.

Symbolism is another tool that children harness in their varied arsenal of calls for Trump's elimination. These examples are powerful and important to understand as they provide insight into how children may internalize, mirror, or replicate violence and power as they see or experience these in society. Together, the next quotes represent symbolic ways of killing Trump that venture into the metaphoric realm.

Mirroring Symbolic Death

Usually, theater class started right on time as children ran from their classroom to either the library or the multipurpose room that functioned as the school's auditorium and cafeteria. In the library, children would sit around in a small semicircle that looked like a ministage with bleacher seating. This space was lined with a carpet and typically served as a place to read with small groups of children. In this intimate space I got to know the students and build the rapport needed to candidly speak about their fears, dreams for the future, and family circumstances. Not every skit was daunting and about pain; some had joy and laughter too. During one of our brainstorming activities, the imagination of one of the students made everyone laugh so hard that Jorge, one of the silliest kids in the class, farted. After this embarrassing moment for Jorge, we had to pause the session and gather our composure.

In these sessions Juan, 11 and one of the smallest students in the class, was quiet but funny and often had the best one-liners. His big glasses weighed on his nose a bit and he was always holding a video-game gadget. The rest of the class thought he was cool because he was good at drawing and sometimes let others play with his Gameboy. In one scene Juan had volunteered to play the role of Trump and asked me if he should have a mask of Trump's face, like the presidential masks that robbers wear when they are sticking up a bank in a movie. To his request to buy a Trump mask, I replied:

RODRIGUEZ VEGA: You're not gonna put on a mask of Donald
Trump—
LEO: He's gonna be like with rabies and—
JUAN: Like I got rabies—[starts barking, acting sickly and funny]
LEO: He'll be like "Come on, give me attention" [roaring]

Juan and Leo comically described the way a Trump mask could be used in the play. They took it to another level by making Trump seem animalistic like a dog with rabies. Juan then added the body movements of a zombielike choking dog falling to the ground. This immediately made everyone laugh. Leo added some sound effects to Juan's portrayal of a rabies-infected Trump zombie with some loud roaring like a dinosaur. Although Juan and Leo's playful ideas and acting were hilarious to the class, they are important to note. These means of dehumanizing Trump and making him seem comical helped to release some of the fear students harbored when discussing disturbing political topics. Through laughter the children gained some power back, an approach that correlates with research on children using laughter to cope with sickness and pain.[25]

Even if the lines and stories created by the children are comical, they have a lot to teach us about their ideas of society and who holds power. The next scenario offers a quick but charged statement about the proposed wall Trump had claimed would "Make America Great Again." In one of the skits, in which children are migrating across Mexico to make it to the US, three children portray the journey of many Central American people. In one scene, as the cool desert night falls on the three characters, they bid each other good night in the following way:

LUIS: Everybody, good night!
JOY: They're building a wall now—
JUAN: Rest in peace—

In this example Trump is not dying. Rather, in response to the building of the border wall, Juan adds an unrehearsed and spontaneous RIP. He tells his partners "Rest in peace" in a nonchalant way similar to how Luis bids everyone "good night." This normalization of death is evidenced by the lack of any dramatic ending. Instead there is a sudden admission of what the US-Mexico wall would mean for migrants on the journey north. For them and possibly their families, the building of a wall could mean the end of life for people they may know or the expectation of imminent death for many others. Although some argue that children tend to normalize notions of death because of their exposure to it through video games, movies, and make-believe, it is also evident that to Juan and other children in South Central Los Angeles, the wall symbolized death.

The next example represents Trump's loss of power through the elimination of his physical appeal. There was a lively discussion about how to personify Trump in the end-of-the-year play. This performance took place during his activity on the campaign trail, where he proposed many of his anti-immigrant ideas. Although, at the time, Trump winning the election did not seem a realistic possibility, the children wasted no opportunity to make fun of him, thereby attempting to end his power by destroying his image.

LAURA: Ahí con todos los pelos. Me pongo la peluca. [There with all the hairs. I can put on a wig.]

MIGUEL: I am the president and I'll put a turkey on my head.

JORGE: No, don't vote for president. Vote grandma [Hillary Clinton] and grandpa [Bernie Sanders].

CARLA: That would be funny. His hair.

LAURA: We could put hair in his *sobaco* [armpit].

RODRIGUEZ VEGA: Okay everybody, let's see. How many people want the Trump thing in there?

MARIA: If his hair falls off!

RODRIGUEZ VEGA: Yes, you can make it whatever you want. Some people don't want it. Explain what you mean.

JORGE: Well . . . because he could be like a bald-headed Trump!

RUTHIE: No, no, it's important—

DIANA: Yo si quiero que sea. [I do want that to happen.]

This excerpt sheds light on the metaphors for nullifying the power Trump has in society, particularly through the symbolism of his hair. Rather than killing Trump, like Juan and Leo in the previous example, here Miguel seeks to ridicule and dehumanize him by suggesting that putting a turkey on his head is the way to go. This created a mental image that inspired people to laugh and see Trump as a clown. Then, Jorge told people not to vote for Trump but rather to vote for "grandma" or "grandpa"—Hillary Clinton and Bernie Sanders, who, because of their age, were like many of the children's grandparents. Then quickly the conversation returned to the hair when Laura suggested putting blond hair on the armpits of the student who was going to play Trump. Again, Laura attempted to make a joke out of Trump's hair. Other students suggested that Trump be left bald under his wig.

Many students wanted this to happen; the excitement was palpable. Indeed, after seeing the power of this scene in the final performance, it was clear that this was the part of the play that changed everything. At that moment, with the drop of Trump's wig, not only did the audience members laugh, stomp, and clap but the outcome changed as the main characters were able to make it to the US when Trump ran away crying because he had lost his hair. Here this removal of his hair represents his loss of power. His hair had become a stand-in for his identity and the most critiqued part of his aesthetic presentation.

Mirroring Death

Of all the issues that children brought up during the election and Trump's first year in office, the building of the US-Mexico wall received the most attention. Aside from fear of being separated from their family members as the top concern, children did not want a wall to be built. To some of them, its construction meant that they would never see family members who lived in Mexico or other parts of Central America. Others were worried that if a wall were to exist, more people would die on the border when trying to cross.

Ultimately, the wall represented death and irreversible separation from those the children loved. The children's reaction to this impending feeling of doom was righteous indignation. Children believed that "disappearing" Trump was the solution to the fears they faced in their lives. In the next four examples, the children described what their best-case ultimate scenario would be. The events of the election coalesced with other timely high-profile news stories. During a theater exercise, students were creating a skit about the election and the various speeches candidates were making. When the Trump character was killed in one of the versions of the play, students began to laugh out loud to the point of disrupting the activity. I paused the class, attempting to help them to regain their composure, and this dialogue came after:

> RODRIGUEZ VEGA: I have a question, everyone—why do you want to keep talking about Donald Trump?
> JULIO: Because we hate him!
> SARA: And we want him to get assassinated, that's why.
> STUDENT IN BACKGROUND: [He's gay!]
> CARLOS: There's nothing wrong with being gay.
> LUIS: But racism, that is very wrong.
> JULIO: I'm gonna send El Chapo on him!
> SARA: El Chapo está en New York. [El Chapo is in New York.]

In this excerpt, the students quickly responded that "we hate him!" as another student emphasized that "we want him to get assassinated." Multiple students spoke over each other to respond to my question. Within one of those responses, one student called Trump "gay" as if attempting to demean and insult him. Quickly another student responded with "There's nothing wrong with being gay," and another followed up with a term they often used to describe Trump, racist. In the background (not caught by the audio recording) a student yelled, "I'm gonna send El Chapo on him!" to which someone else replied, "El Chapo is in New York." In this discussion the children positioned their strong sentiments about Trump with the highly sensationalized capture of El Chapo, but just before the mention of El Chapo someone voiced a homophobic slur. This slur was quickly challenged and the children immediately resumed their planning, calling on El Chapo to help them. Ultimately, the children felt so desperate in wanting Trump to go away that the idea of him being assassinated seemed to be the only solution.

It was clever and even comical for the children to bring up the highly sensationalized character of El Chapo, but it also suggested the ways in which they were seeking an alternative source of justice, particularly when the state represented a danger to them. Children in Los Angeles encountered police presence regularly and at times told stories about the police being scary and shooting people. At the same time, many students romanticized the notion of becoming police officers or military enforcers. It was clear that the children saw Trump as being on the side of authorities like the police. But they also knew that the police had power, so they also wanted to imitate the police in the theater performances. This juxtaposition was present throughout the school year. Some saw the police as the helpers and others as the threat. It is noteworthy that in the case of asking for help to do away with Trump the children did not think of the police; rather, they looked to a figure like El Chapo. In some of the places where the children's families come from, like Mexico and in particular Sinaloa, drug lords like El Chapo embody the trope of a Robin Hood who takes from the rich to give to the poor. Perhaps they saw El Chapo as a superhero who could step in, defeat Trump, and save the day as they had commonly seen done in cartoons and movies.

During class children shared many ideas they wanted to enact. Usually, toward the end of the school year, children tended to have favorite icebreaker games and theater exercises that they wanted to repeat every time we met. In such activities we tried to act out a scenario with various students attempting to play the same character in different ways until a resolution was found. The great theater practitioner Augusto Boal called this method "forum theater." I suggested doing a skit about a phone call in which two people would talk on the phone and create a conversation without having planned anything. The goal of this activity was to teach students to play off each other on stage, to improvise something that made sense. To my suggestion students responded:

> RODRIGUEZ VEGA: The skit, the phone skit—
> JO: The car crash—
> SONIA: The car crash—
> JESS: And Donald Trump.
> RODRIGUEZ VEGA: Okay.
> DANNY: And then he dies!

When I suggested we do the telephone-conversation skit, the children ignored my suggestion and asked that we do one about a car accident instead. While Jo offered this idea initially, Sonia repeated it to emphasize her preference. Then Jess stated that we should add Trump to the scene. When I said okay, as if to try to understand, Danny added "And then he dies!," implying that in the skit Trump should die in the car accident. It is unclear if the children were consciously choosing Trump's death as endings to their skits and stories or if this happened organically.

Either way, these repetitive outcomes are significant. The children felt overwhelmed and helpless to stop their parents' detention or deportations in real life, and thus in a space of make-believe they were not shy about eliminating Trump and imitating power. Through my interviews with parents and children, it was clear that the children were aware of their parents' (and in some cases their own) undocumented status. Parents had plans in place for extended family or neighbors to be legal guardians of their children just in case they were detained and did not come home.

Often during the skits where students killed Trump, other students would lose their focus by laughing so hard that I had to take time to help them catch their breath and collect themselves again. These moments highlight the importance of imagination and creativity for children, and also the ways that, unfortunately, violence is an all-too-common force in their lives. Opportunities like these also offer young people an emotional release and a method to process those emotions. One event happened at the beginning of the year, before the children had killed the Trump character in their theater skits. As this was one of the first times the idea of killing Trump was raised, it evoked a particularly strong response from the class audience and the actors themselves:

RODRIGUEZ VEGA: All right, all right, all right.
ALL: [Laughter]
RODRIGUEZ VEGA: Why is this so funny to you?
CELIA: Because they killed Donald Trump [laughs].
ALL: [Laughter]
FLOR: Why are you laughing so hard?
ALL: [Laughter]
FLOR: Take a break, take a break, both—
RODRIGUEZ VEGA: Yeah, get it together. Everybody, take a deep breath.

In this example as I tried to keep the students' attention, it felt almost impossible to quiet the class down and focus on the task. Most students saw theater as a time to play, to be outlandish and loud. For example, in one of the skits "Donald Trump" as played by Mario fell to the ground in what looked like a 12-year-old body acting very old and having a heart attack. Mario's body made a loud thud as he fell carelessly without fear of getting hurt. He became motivated by the reaction this could engender from his classmates. Unsurprisingly, Mario had the class in tears and bellyaches from their cackles. I attempted to ask the students why this scenario was so funny to them, and only one person had enough composure to respond. Celia, who was usually a very serious student and too shy to volunteer for any roles, shouted in a loud explanatory voice, "Because they killed Donald Trump" and let out a light laugh and a sigh.

In a room with loud laughter and bodies gasping for air as children held their stomachs, Flor stood out. She was the director-narrator for this scene, and she was giggling but had stopped laughing. Flor helped people to add suggestions to the play. In forum theater Flor's role was that of the joker—the intermediary between the audience and the actors, and the bridge that made sense of the scenario. A bit frustrated that the scene was paused, Flor asked everyone, "Why are you laughing so hard?" People did not reply but just kept laughing. Then she implored them to take a break. I echoed Flor's statement, asking the children to try to catch their breath and deepen their exhalations. In a political context in which Trump was promising to make immigrants' lives so difficult that they would be forced to return to their countries of origin, his sudden death symbolized a turn of events that children were used to seeing in action storybooks and comics. Even children who were usually shy tended to laugh and agree with the elimination of Trump. The power of laughter was palpable and striking. Especially because fear can often be paralyzing, and this was a time that children described as "scary," making light of a fearful situation reaped a great response of relief and fun. When the children either ridiculed or eliminated Trump, they felt empowered and less afraid. Perhaps the great and uncontrollable laughter stemmed from the fact that this situation was very hard to imagine actually occurring. The delicate balancing of comedy and tragedy in life and theater was something the children were unafraid to explore.

Philosopher Jorge Portilla discusses the popular Mexican practice of *relajo* (satirical fun), where laughter caused by "satire, the grotesque, parody, jokes" is used to undo the seriousness of the situation and creates a liberatory sense of noncompliance.[26] This *relajo* is a sort of invitation to join a "disordered movement," a form of challenging authority that El Teatro Campesino[27] often employed through their *actos*,[28] *carpas*,[29] and collective memory.[30] In this political time, where the collective memory surrounding the border is full of stories of pain, separation, death, and trauma, laughter becomes a mighty antidote to the paralyzing power of fear. Indeed, in such situations "only the magic of laughter could radically and credibly suspend the seriousness of the entire social system of oppression."[31]

In our brainstorming activity students were thinking of options to include in their rendition of the most important news on television, which, as usual, involved Donald Trump. In their frustration and fear of being separated from their family, they opted to just eliminate Trump. In the exchange below, as the children were debating, a disagreement arose. I tried to serve as a mediator among them all, but the children in this class had gotten so comfortable with each other that they no longer needed me to step in to help generate conversation. Instead they were ready to persuade each other, like Dulce, who thought that it was better "to change Trump's mind than to kill him."

> DULCE: Tiene que cambiar su opinión. [He has to change his mind.]
> CELIA: We have to assassinate Trump.
> BETTY: No, tiene que cambiar su opinión también. Tiene que pelear para que Donald Trump no construya la pared. [No, he has to change his mind, so we fight so Trump won't build the wall.]
> JUAN: Can I speak?
> RODRIGUEZ VEGA: Si, explícales lo que quieres hacer. [Yes, explain what you want to do.]
> CELIA: Van a matar a Donald Trump. [They are going to kill Trump.]

Such a debate involving different ideas and actions was not unusual. Some students tended to appeal to Trump's morality or the immigrant status of his wife. Others cared little about convincing him to change his mind; instead they often took extreme measures of putting an end to Trump altogether in the scenarios they created. Dulce and Betty were two of the students who wanted to convince Trump to stop deporting people and work it out through theater. Others, like Celia, were adamant that the only option was to "assassinate" him. Celia even cut off Juan, who was trying to speak, to say, "they are going to kill Donald Trump." It is unclear if the children took this option because they had no hope of appealing to his benevolence and rationality. They may not have seen Trump changing his mind as a real possibility; or it may have seemed something too hard to achieve so that, in their frustration, they opted to just eliminate him, possibly mirroring the goal of anti-immigrant legislation (*as in Operation Endgame*) and legal violence that seems aimed at eliminating immigrants and their children.

The children dehumanized Trump in multiple ways. Most of them compared him to animals. For example, during the first class session I had with the students I asked them, "What issues are most important to you?" Students responded with many concerns such as "the drought in California . . . the border wall, deportations, Donald Trump (yeah, DT!). Donald Trompas!" I was interested in the many ways they described

Trump. One of them, "Trompas," was especially intriguing. When I looked up *trompas*, it was defined as "Horn, snout, mouth, lips, or blubber lips." Trump as Trompas is a play on words that calls attention to the lip movements and gestures that Trump employs when he speaks. It satirized his statements as coming from an animal, as a snout is a body part of a pig.

This type of dehumanization tactic was not unique to the children in my class. The comparison of disliked individuals or groups of people to animals, and specifically to pigs, is common. El Teatro Campesino, for instance, used pig masks to portray the *patroncito* or boss during their *actos*. Their goal was to empower farmworkers, and using *relajo* was instrumental in making fun of the boss and making him seem less scary.[32] The pig mask along with an imaginary limousine were kitsch props that El Teatro Campesino used to represent symbols of power, thereby using humor to mitigate fear of the ranchers.[33] Similarly, other communities under the threat of police brutality have referred to police officers as pigs.[34] As stated in setting forth the ideology of the Black Panther Party, "we need power, desperately, to counter the power of the pigs that now bears so heavily upon us."[35] Scholars have also discussed what is known as the "fascist pigs theory," which maintains that only people with certain dispositions, such as authoritarian personalities, are attracted to police work given its violent nature.[36] In this context, it is understandable that calling Trump a pig would be part of the children's vocabulary as they attempted to gain some control over their lives and safety.

As we have seen, the children in Arizona were keenly aware of the presence of law-enforcement personnel as authority figures in their lives, as was most notably seen in how often they referred to then-Sheriff Joe Arpaio. Through his deportation raids, Arizona felt the heavy-handed immigration enforcement implemented by the Obama administration's 287(g) programs.[37] Similarly, the children in California were very focused on Trump and his role in the harsh policies affecting their lives. They did not shy away from imaginatively taking their power back from Trump. Their skits and brainstorming offer insight into the thoughts of children living at the nexus of an "immigrant-addicted economy" and draconian anti-immigration policy enforcement, along with a failing approach to foreign policy in countries south of the border.[38] Through children's cultural productions and art we can better understand how their lives frequently intersect with the law because of their families' legal status. Their visual narratives illuminate the material effects of legal violence in their lives through the merging of immigration and criminal law. The children demonstrated acute awareness of the violence, racism, and dehumanization that put their families' cohesion and lives at risk. They responded with righteous indignation that mirrored back the threats they experienced.

During the two years in which I worked with children in South Central Los Angeles, the children presented creative, out-of-the-box, and quirky solutions to the dilemmas that anti-immigrant ideas and policies present. Most of their recommendations and ideas were humorous in nature. Yet it is striking that in all their plays, humor, and satire there was a constant theme of violence, dehumanization, and death. As we have seen, the tools for navigating racism are not always positive. The children mirrored societal violence, dehumanization, and death as means to navigate a racist, xenophobic society and gain control and safety over their lives through righteous indignation. These dynamics warrant serious consideration, as they illuminate the detrimental impact that anti-immigrant politicians and policies have on children of immigrants. Rather than literally killing someone, the children attempted, in their "assassination" of Joe Arpaio or Donald Trump, to kill what they embody—racism, danger, and hate. In enacting righteous indignation and desperation, they mirror and mimic the negativity they see around them. Children see the elimination, ridiculing, or dehumanizing of these political figures as a way of rebelling, resisting, and possibly having a chance to survive. Children thereby assert the dignity and humanity of themselves and their families. However, the power of art and healing did not end here. As we will see, the art-making process allowed the children to create more cathartic strategies to address their problems and fears.

5

Resilience

Art-Healing Praxis and Possibilities for Restoration

Children in Arizona and California exposed the destructive consequences of legal violence through their drawings and stories. They also reimagined life-shattering fears into moments of joy, creativity, agency, and resilience. Praxis, as theorized by the eminent educator Paulo Freire, allows for theory to become action.[1] The act of creating through the process of art making allowed children the time, space, and opportunity to lean into their imagination. In doing so, they learned coping mechanisms for stressful times. The repetitive and calming moment of practicing art lowers children's stress hormones, such as cortisol and adrenaline.[2] Once their nervous system calms, their body is no longer in fight-or-flight mode and levels of toxic stress decline, allowing for their body and mind to enter a parasympathetic state.[3] Here, a person is better able to rest, digest, and signal to the body that physical healing can begin.[4] An art-healing praxis is thus helpful for children to calm their fears and explore solutions in a trauma-responsive[5] and healing-centered way.

This methodology of praxis through art and healing helped the children to create scenarios that would be difficult for adults to imagine. The children moved back and forth through destructive and dehumanizing ideas to embodying peace and possibility. The process was not always linear, but the critical thinking motivated the children to ponder what was possible. They constantly reflected on what world they wanted. The healing was also collective. There was lots of laughter as the children brainstormed performance ideas and shared stories about their drawings. Comedy and satire were essential in extending that comedic relief to their family members, teachers, peers, and school community. Knowing that positive emotions, optimism, and humor provide resilience to stress,[6] it is essential to understand how this work can aid in reversing the damage of legal violence and trauma in children of immigrants. This chapter illuminates the ways children in Arizona reimagined possibilities through a praxis of art and healing and how the children in California embodied more positive alternate realities.

Arizona: Reimagining Solutions That Cultivate Agency, Hope, and Resilience

The drawings we have seen thus far have painted a gloomy picture of children's lives in Phoenix. Yet, even under draconian anti-immigrant policies and threatening living conditions, these children demonstrated agency, hope, and resilience. For instance, in Victor's drawing (figure 5.1) he takes us back to an image we saw earlier, in which Daniel drew a cartoonish Sheriff Joe Arpaio holding a protest sign. Here Victor, age 16, has drawn a sheriff's deputy in full riot gear—something commonly seen in Arizona protests and gatherings sparked by the highly contested legislative policies. This type of uniform was also typical of what children might see as they watched the news with their parents. However, instead of holding a sign with hateful or racist language about Mexicans as in Daniel's drawing, Victor created a contradictory image of peace. This sheriff's deputy's sign reads "I (love) Mexicans" while he is dressed in full SWAT-like gear. This image is a reaction to the overemphasis on anti-immigrant messaging, which was specifically also anti-Mexican, during this time in Phoenix. As the population is predominantly Mexican, children also reflected on cultural symbols and identity.

This image was created in response to the question "What do you wish would happen?" from the original prompt in Arizona's community center. Students' artwork addressed questions that included: (1) What is the problem? (2) How do you feel about it? and (3) What do you wish would happen? This drawing shows the dialectical process of children's thoughts and demonstrates that they want to be loved and accepted in their communities, by everyone, even those they fear. Moreover, they aspire to transform that fear. If sheriffs *actually* loved Mexicans and Mexican Americans, then Mexican immigrant youth like Victor and Daniel would feel safe and more included. This image demonstrates that possibility.

Lupe, who was 11 years old, drew the next image, an imaginative representation of "WORLD Peace!!" (see plate 5.1). On the left stands Sheriff

Joe Arpaio, gazing directly at "Pancho," a Mexican on the right. There is a short dialogue between them where the sheriff says, "Hi, How are you!" and the Mexican responds with "Hola." Above them is a large blue cloud and a bright sun at the corner. The colors and positioning of the characters invoke a pleasant emotion and a nice day between two equals who are meeting on friendly terms.

Similarly, Chris also calls for world peace. As a high school student, he was one of the first people in the group to draw "Pancho" as the quintessential Mexican who would shake Joe Arpaio's hand (see figure 5.2). This handshake would become the catalyst for the peace that the children in Arizona described. Chris talked about Pancho being a *jornalero* (day laborer) who would shake Arpaio's hand. At this time day laborers in Arizona were especially vulnerable because of the highly visible way they had to look for work, outside of home improvement and department stores and in plain

Figure 5.1. Victor, "I Love Mexicans."

sight of local authority. It is important to note that to Chris and other youth, this handshake is not only a symbol of amicable resolution but of "WORLD PEACE!!," as written as a subtext to multiple drawings. Although most of the anti-immigrant policies in Arizona were especially severe in Maricopa County, for the children in this community, Arizona was their entire world. In their minds, if Sheriff Joe Arpaio and a Mexican were to shake hands all would be well in the world.

Jason, a 9-year-old elementary-school student, made figure 5.3. The drawing is divided into two sections. The one on the left shows two individuals fighting each other with fists up in the air and a large cloud

Figure 5.2. Chris, "Pancho and World Peace!!"

overhead. In contrast, the image on the right has a clear sky with a half sun and a large rainbow, as if to say that this image takes place after the storm. The two stick figures on the right have their hands extended to one another, and on the outside of their hands is a large heart representing love between these two figures. The drawing is a direct comparison between two realities, one of which could drastically alter the children's lives. As such, the importance of these drawings is that they show the only way the children can dream of world peace happening.

Figure 5.4 is another representation of what the children believed was possible. This image, drawn by 7-year-old Carly, creates the vivid world that many of the children attempted to communicate in their drawings. Carly drew the very real racial differences between "Arpaio and the Mexican," but without any suggestion of power distinctions or evidence of racism. They are equals, as indicated by their identical height and by their hands touching. They stand on what look like hilltops, conjuring similarities to Dr. Martin Luther King's famous "I Have a Dream" speech in Washington, DC, in which he declared that his dream was to see Black and White children on the hilltops of Georgia in a future where people "would not be judged by the color of their skin but by the content of their character."[7] Dr. King created a verbal image with his speech in which people who are usually at odds are united by holding hands. This drawing also invokes his last speech, "I've Been to the Mountaintop," in which he described in detail his vision of future equality.[8] Because children at this age often learn about the civil rights movement only in the context of Dr. King's work, they apply this language to their own struggles for freedom.

At the bottom of the mountain, Carly drew small groups of people exclaiming "Yay" and "World peace." There is also an image of a road

Figure 5.3. Jason, "Heart Split."

Figure 5.4. Carly, "Arpaio and the Mexican."

with a car driving from one side to the other. However, unlike in many of the images we have seen, driving does not entail a risk of being pulled over, detained, and deported. Here it is simply a usual activity in a world where one's skin color is not a reason to be racially profiled, detained, violated, or killed. The world that Carly creates is a place with singing birds where the sun is huge and shines down with a large smile and everyone has joy.

The final image we will consider is by Javier, a middle-school student who created this drawing when debates about Senate Bill 1070 became daily topics on the news and in private and social settings. The drawing's focus is the iconic Virgen de Guadalupe, located in the center of the image with a Mexican flag placed above, below, and as the wings of the cherub holding the Virgen up (see plate 5.2). This symbolic figure is reminiscent of the imagery used during the Mexican Revolution, by the United Farm Workers movement, in the Chicano student walkouts, and in the post-2006 immigrant marches that were held all over the US.[9] The Virgen continues to be an important symbol of hope and faith in the people's movement for equality and dignity. Surrounding her are masses of people with signs that read "No More Sheriff," "3 words that represent Guadalupe: (1) peace, (2) love, (3) hope;" and "Stop Arpaio and his Rage." The banner placed at the top of the drawing says, "Stop the SB 1070." The protest signs in this image were commonplace for people in the immigrant community during protests and rallies that were held all over Phoenix and in other parts of the country. For the children, these signs asserted the cultural symbols that had given their families strength and hope for the future, particularly during oppressive and uncertain times. The Mexican flags placed multiple times around the image indicate that for this young person, being Mexican is something to feel pride in, not something to hide or feel shame about. Here Javier is not hiding his or his community's ethnicity or nationality. On the periphery of the Virgen are other iconic symbols that also represent peace, like hearts, white doves, and peace signs. In addition to those symbols, Javier juxtaposed a symbol that looks like a "Do Not Smoke" sign, but with the word "ARPAIO" in capital letters crossed out; Javier thus suggested that if Arpaio were not present peace would exist.

The children and young people in Phoenix not only emphasized the hardships caused by family separation but also provided avenues for possible solutions. They assumed agency in exploring what peace in the community would look like and demonstrated the many lessons children learn from society at a young age but often forget to practice in adulthood. These lessons—kindness, respect, friendship, and love—are not childish or only for children; they are powerful and necessary for everyone. Young people are more than capable of being critical thinkers, and through art they can potentialize their transformative suggestions and bring their powerful imaginations to fruition. This was also clear as the children shared with each other the drawings that they created, opening space for dialogue. At the end of each session the children held minigalleries where they got to "show and tell," and eventually, at the end of the summer, they put on a show for the community and were able to feel greater ownership and agency about their drawings and messages of hope.

The children with whom I worked in Los Angeles grappled with a different political period. Although distinct in geography and temporality, these places do have important aspects in common. In 2008–10,

Arizona was the center of anti-immigrant legal experimentation. Almost ten years later, the ideas implemented there were now in effect across the country. In Los Angeles migrant children and children of immigrants now feared the same sort of family separation due to detention or deportation that the children in Arizona had feared before them. However, the children in both places also demonstrated resilience and possibility using art-healing praxis.

California: Embodying Solutions and Healing Trauma

One morning during a drawing activity, I asked students to draw a picture about what they saw on the news or what concerned them. Manny, a 9-year-old, shared his drawing and added that he was mainly concerned about Trump. The image included Trump, North Korea, and "the wall". He shared that what he saw made him afraid of the future—the uncertainty of what might happen made him think the worst. Manny echoed what many of his classmates felt: a fear of being separated from their families. Through the activity of creating art, though, Manny and his peers were able to deeply explore their thoughts and fears. Some were able to vocalize their concerns by talking, others embodied possibilities through theater, and some visualized a future through drawings. Most notably, as we will see, they were able to find solace in new possibilities for the future.

Self-Portraits

I now discuss four cases that offer examples of work by students who participated in the self-portrait class at the school taught by Judith F. Baca. Through a curriculum that centers students' dreams and future aspirations and with the help of teaching assistants they got to design and create a digital self-portrait that was permanently installed on the elementary school's wall, collectively forming a mural of portraits and aspirations. The first is Manny's self-portrait (plate 5.3). At 9 years old, Manny was aware and critical of racism. The image he created contained little information about his future aspirations or favorite hobbies, even though those were supposed to be the central theme of his portrait. His focus was on his ethnicity and pride in his Mexican American identity. Similar to other examples, his dislike of racism is indicated by the way that word is crossed out. It is significant to note that a screaming Trump is placed on the top left corner. Often in Western cultures, the most important part of an image is situated on the top left area as this is the direction in which we read written work, top left to right. Here Manny includes the side of Trump's face, but also crosses it out. For Manny, racism is represented by including the face of Trump, who believes that Mexicans are drug dealers and rapists, a perception that drove his goal of building a wall on the US-Mexico border. It is evident that Trump's statements during the election affected both documented and undocumented Mexican American families, with a specific impact on the lives of young children.

However, demonstrating resilience, Manny's facial expression reveals a slight smile and direct eye contact with the viewer. The confidence is evident because, although he is looking up, he does not shy away by casting his gaze down or off to the side. His body posture is open, and closest to him is a small circle that looks like a sign with the Mexican and US flags. In between them he proclaims, "Yes, I am both of them." This statement is powerful, especially from a 9-year-old. It reveals Manny's sense of self and the way he has embraced his multifaceted identity, shattering the stereotype that he must be one or the other. He unifies the two cultures by breaking this binary and in doing so asserts his agency in the world.

In the second portrait (plate 5.4), Diego, a 13-year-old, indicated that he wanted to be a professional soccer player. He said that if being a soccer player did not work out, then he would be a basketball player or maybe even a football player, although soccer was his first love. Throughout the drawing we can see the importance of sports in Diego's identity and life. However, the drawing strongly juxtaposed these interests with the face of President Donald Trump hovering above. As in the previous portrait, Trump's face had a harsh red cross near the eye, which took up most of the face. This political symbolism informs the viewer of Diego's strong dislike of Trump and what he represents. The following quote is from the artist statement he displayed next to his work for the showcase at the end of the year, thereby explaining what he drew and how he saw himself:

My name is Diego and I want to be a soccer player and stop DONALD TRUMP from sending immigrants and stop being racist. I'm 13 and when I'm a soccer player, a pro one, I wanna donate my money to hospitals and donate my hair to kids that have cancer. I wanna help others, homeless that lost their jobs and their house, people that can't leave weed, drugs. I'ma help them get a new life and a family [sic]. I'ma teach my kids to not mistreat other people and to not think they are more than others [sic]. To respect others even tho they don't have a job and smell nasty. Homeless are still people and they are like us and need to respect them or let them be.

Diego had many intentions to help others and was committed to a variety of causes; yet his primary concern was to stop Trump, which he felt both responsible for and capable of doing. Diego specifically pointed out two issues with the then president: the racism he believed he embodied, and the possibility of sending immigrants back. All of this could pose a problem for Diego and others like him. Diego came to the US from El Salvador with a coyote when he was 10 years old. His mom shared that they were separated for a period of two years. She worked very hard to save money to bring him, but she could only save $1,000 because she was being exploited where she had first started working as a live-in nanny. To bring Diego she had to ask all the people she knew to lend her money; she ended up collecting $10,500 to pay the coyote.

When Diego made it across, she was very happy to be reunited but had to work long hours for an entire year to pay back all the money she owed. Diego, for the most part, was happy to be reunited with his mother in Los Angeles but had a hard time learning English and would spend too much time alone while his mother worked. Although Diego and his mother had been together in the US for three years, she was constantly worried that police might pull her over for a traffic violation or any other minor infraction that could result in her being detained and eventually deported. Diego shared the same fear. However, during class, it was not evident that he was afraid; his excitement, participation, and talkative nature made him seem carefree and outgoing.

In fact, most children projected a calm and positive demeanor during the art class. Yet, under that calmness, fear and anxiety were commonplace. One of the children's favorite activities was to impersonate other

Plate 3.1. Daniel (Middle School).

el ar Tipayo es malo con los mexicanos y los trata mal. no es Justo me ase sentir mal. quiero que lo corran para que El no Festidie.

★
100%

6

Plate 3.2. Jaqui (Elementary School).

Plate 3.3. Eduardo (Elementary School).

Plate 4.1. "I cross the border." (Middle School)

Plate 4.2. Samsung TV Character (Middle School).

Plate 4.3. Mary's Drawing (Middle School).

Plate 4.4. Lalo's Drawing (Middle School).

Plate 5.1. Lupe's Drawing (Elementary School).

Plate 5.2. Javier, "Stop the SB 1070." (Middle School)

Plate 5.3. Manny, Self-Portrait. (Elementary School).

Plate 5.4. Diego, Self-Portrait (Middle School).

Plate 5.5. Marla, Self-Portrait (Middle School).

Plate 5.6. Jeanette, "President." (Middle School)

Plate 5.7. Julio, "Trump." (Middle School)

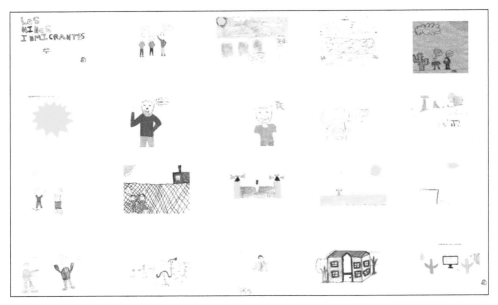

Plate 5.8. "Storyboard, Part 2." (Middle School)

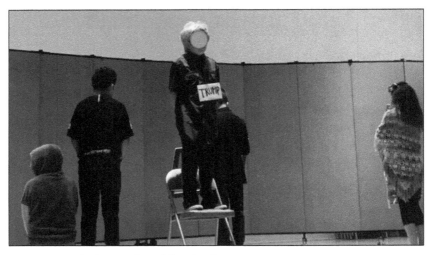

Plate 5.9. Camilo, "Trump." (Middle School)

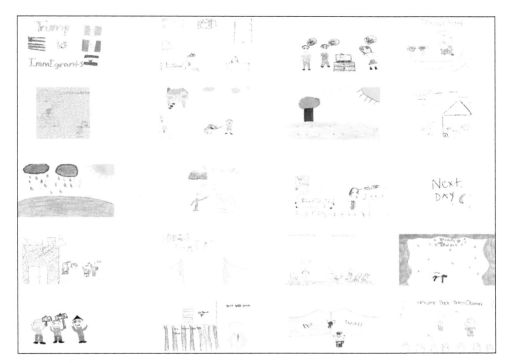

Plate 5.10. "Storyboard, Part 1." (Middle School)

Plate 5.11. Sara, "Confronting Trump." (Middle School)

Plate 5.12. Juan, "Confronting Trump." (Middle School)

Plate 5.13. Carolina, "Confronting Trump." (Middle School)

people. They would put on fake mustaches and act like adults. For example, they pretended to be truck drivers, or upset mothers demanding kids to clean their rooms. Children also took on roles of power, such as portraying the president, military personnel, bosses, police officers, and even "mean" teachers. One of the many students who resonated with this sort of play was 11-year-old Marla. Marla was one of the girls who truly developed her voice in the course of the theater class. She started off being very shy, but it did not keep her from volunteering for theater games and icebreakers. This motivated other girls to participate and be more outspoken. One day during a theater activity, the students started talking about violence in the community. Marla volunteered to play the role of a cop—a role only boys had previously wanted to play. Later I learned that Marla actually wanted to be a police officer when she grew up. But not just any police officer; Marla asserted that she hoped to be what she called a "nice" officer. Although she was insistent on becoming part of the system in this way, it is important to note her way of vocalizing this critique of police. Surely a child growing up in South Central Los Angeles is affected by a reality of police violence that has been all too common for many generations.[10]

When it came time to make self-portraits, Marla again personified the role of a police officer, holding sunglasses to her face as well as a police hat (plate 5.5). Although the portrait showed her wearing a Los Angeles Dodgers T-shirt and jeans, she brought in additional police enforcement symbolism by standing in front of a Los Angeles Police Department (LAPD) car; children in South Central Los Angeles were highly aware of these because of the pervasive policing of their community.[11] Yet, contrasting with the police car and the accessories was a large thumbs-up-giving Donald Trump with a red "denied" sign on his face. The large letters next to him exclaim, "We can STOP Donald Trump" with the STOP in red. The image of Trump and the statement about stopping him take up as much space on the portrait as Marla does. This image powerfully suggests that, for Marla, stopping Trump was as much a part of her identity as was the importance of becoming a police officer. In a sense, for Marla, stopping Trump was almost her first duty. Trump literally took up space and importance in her personal life, so much so that she needed to include him in her own self-portrait that was to become part of a permanent mural installation at the school.

Next to Marla's picture, her artist statement reads:

My name is Marla, and I am 11-years-old. My portrait is about me being a nice police officer. What I mean by that is me stopping DONALD
TRUMP FROM SEPARATING FAMILY! [sic] Another reason why I
want to be a police officer is because it has always been my dream job. I
also am doing my dream job because I want to help the community.

Again, we see that the only time Marla capitalized anything was when
she was making a statement about Trump. One of her statements was
about stopping Trump and the other was about stopping him from separating families. The latter assertion was ambiguous as to whether she
meant the separation of other people's families or was referring to her
own family. Despite this ambiguity, the importance of keeping families
together was evident and Marla transmitted this message with great
urgency.

It is also necessary to look deeper at the career Marla had chosen.
Again, it is important to note that she added the word "nice" before "police officer." When communicating to attendees at the art showcase what
her portrait was about, she said, "This is me stopping Donald Trump, I
am a police officer, but I am not with him, I am one of the good ones."
This statement is powerful because, although it is similar to tropes used in
American mainstream movies, as we saw regarding notions about "good
guys vs. bad guys," "cowboys vs. Indians," "cops vs. robbers," Marla complicated the role of police. To her, not all police were bad or good; however, with this statement she acknowledged that there was a relationship
between the president's ideas and enforcement officers. This may imply
that Marla previously had negative experiences with the police or had
witnessed police behaving in "mean" or "bad" ways. Although she did not
talk about police violence, police brutality, or the role of police officers
in her community, her use of the word "nice" posited a critical question
about the community's perception of police presence and surveillance.

Jeanette, who was 12 years old, was a first-generation immigrant who
came with her family from Central America. Although she did not mention Trump, she made a powerful statement with her portrait (plate 5.6).
Her dream and future aspiration was to become the president of the US.
In the portrait she looks strong and confident, holding up her hand to say

hello to her fellow constituents. Although there has never been a president who looked like her and immigrants cannot legally become the US president, her embodiment of that position of power was radically imaginative and defiant. This is particularly significant when contrasted with news of Central American children and families detained at the border and vulnerable to so many dangers on their journey toward the US.

Theater: Trump I in 2017

Twelve-year-old Julio donned a yellow wig as he became Donald Trump for our play *Los Niños Inmigrantes* or *The Immigrant Children* (plate 5.7). In this play, as Trump, Julio paraded along the San Diego–Tijuana border to check out the place where he wanted to construct the wall. There, he confronted three Central American children who were crossing to reunite with their parents in Los Angeles. As they were crossing, the magical half-human half-coyote stopped them when he saw Trump at a distance. The children and the coyote observed Trump talking to Obama about the wall. The most important part of the play—aside from the children arriving in the US safely—happens when Julio's (Trump's) allergies get irritated by the dust at the border. He lets out a very powerful sneeze, making the blond wig fly off his head in the most dramatic and unexpected way. In response, the audience roars with laughter and disbelief. Julio enjoyed this moment in the play. Through the satire created in the performance, power was taken away from Trump. As the laughter subsided, Trump no longer seemed as scary as before; instead he was defeated by being exposed as a vulnerable mortal human being predisposed to baldness. This is the power of children tapping into the transformative potential of art.

All the self-portraits demonstrate the vision children harbor for themselves and society. They seek to find resolutions to the problems that spark fear in their lives. And in so doing, they assert their humanity, seeing themselves as future presidents, leaders, and adults with agency, and as living a future with joy and laughter while they help others. They are thus able to embrace their whole selves as complicated and nuanced people. The children's agency did not come easily, requiring countless practice sessions and rehearsals, but it nonetheless flourished during theater exercises and in the final performance.

The Many Hopes

As vocal as the students were about their concerns, most students still had hope that things could get better. The following interaction is indicative of the hope or resilience children commonly demonstrated. Although this was not an attitude shared by every one of them, overall the children agreed about wanting to make things better. During one of the check-ins, we talked about the various news stories on television and what we thought of them:

> EDUARDO: I hope he doesn't build the wall!
> MARTA: I hope he doesn't send immigrants where they lived.
> CARLOS: I hope he doesn't deport people from the United States.
> ROSA: Or that he doesn't start World War III.
> MARTA: I agree with Eduardo.
> RODRIGUEZ VEGA: You agree with Eduardo? What specifically do you agree with?
> MARTA: On that, he doesn't build the wall.

As hopeful as these students were, they also demonstrate concern for what is happening in society. The students begin talking about the wall and suddenly there is a *hopeful* escalation of concern about sending people back or deporting them from the US, and, finally, about starting World War III. The last student brings the interaction back to where the first student began, hoping that Trump does not build the wall. Although there were many aspects of Trump that concerned these children of immigrants, building of the wall resonated as one of the top priorities. Nevertheless, they did not despair, showing that they were both well aware and positive.

Final Theater Performance from Year 1: Los Niños Inmigrantes

Each year we used storyboards to digitally project the drawings children made on a large screen above the state. This helped visually describe each scene of our performance. That way, if there was a parent or community member who did not understand the language the children were acting in or was lost, they could follow along on the screen that projected the images above the stage. The storyboard could be read from top left to right; this version comes from year 1 of my time in the school in California, which coincided with the 2016–17 election (see plate 5.8). This performance was deeply affected by the earlier-discussed story of Alex, where children in the class were distraught by the death of their classmate's cousin who had been trying to cross the border from El Salvador to the US. In this story Alex was the main character, but this time, in the play, his fate was not death; rather, he received help from other children and from a magical desert-crossing creature. Although Alex and his friends run into Trump on the border while he is checking on his wall, they defeat Trump through wit and humor. This victory was not just for Alex, or the children in the play, but for the audience members and their families.

The children surmounted the alarming possibility of death in the hot desert, overcame the threat of animals like snakes, stayed safe from being captured by the Border Patrol, and, most importantly, their parents demonstrated agency in helping to ensure that their children made it across the border. In the performance, when Trump's wig falls to the floor because of his mighty sneeze, the children laugh as Trump runs away from a debate with Obama. Here that opportunity of humor is what allowed for safety; at this moment humor was the antidote to fear.

Final Performance from Year 2: Trump vs. Immigrants

During the second year of the class, students were more encouraged than ever to put on a play in which they discussed the most important topics they saw on the news. As in year 1, Trump was a major character and part of many conversations. In a scene for the final performance, 12-year-old Camilo enters the stage playing the role of Trump, one of the main characters of the play, while the entire family is watching the news on television. As President Trump, Camilo stands on a chair to make his announcement as the family turns around in the background. Next, we see Camilo stand tall with his hands behind his back to portray authority and power (see plate 5.9). In that scene he declares that the plan for building the wall is underway and the wall will be finished in a month, which makes the audience laugh. When he is done talking, he jumps off the chair as if diving into a pool, and the family comes back to life by turning around as the news anchor finishes the segment. "That's all folks, please watch this again during the evening news!"

In this play, *Trump vs. Immigrants*, the media plays a key role. In the scenes with the family, the television is always on, and when the news comes on regarding immigration and Trump, the entire family gathers attentively around the screen. In plate 5.9, for example, we see Camilo as Trump giving one of his epic speeches. Incredibly, while Camilo plays the role of Trump, he looks confident and unbothered by the booing that comes from the audience every time he steps on stage. When I asked him how he prepared to do this part, he replied, "I just watched the news with my family, like the family in the play." Children easily commented in class about the news stories they watched on TV or about radio shows that dealt with immigration. In general, Spanish-language media played a major role in the lives of immigrant families, particularly during this politically charged time.[12]

At this moment of the play, the family is worried that the dad has been deported, and even the dog refuses to play at the park because he is depressed. But Diego, the other main character playing the part of the family's young child, is motivated to act. He decides that he will go to school the next day and organize his classmates to march to the border wall to confront Trump. Students at his school are compelled to take action, thanks in part to what they see on the news and their racist teacher, who wears a "Make America Great Again" hat in class. As they make their way to the border with their signs and banners, they confront Trump giving a speech. The play ends with two "Men in Black/CIA agents" coming to announce that the ballots were wrong and Trump is actually not the president, and yet neither is Hillary Clinton. To everyone's surprise, the CIA decides to bring Obama back for a third term while government agents carry Trump away kicking and screaming. This makes the audience laugh and clap because they see that the person who threatens the family in the play, and possibly their family in real life, has been removed in a comical way. Although, in real life, a president is unable to hold office for a third term, the children's imagination had no limit. They created an outcome where a person they trusted—despite the actual ways his policies enforced anti-immigrant systems—had the opportunity to return as president. In the children's minds, Obama was the president they wished was still in office.

Plate 5.10 is the storyboard the children created for the second year's performance. This final drawing is of President Obama coming back to claim his seat in the Oval Office. In this storyboard, the other things that Diego (the main character) accomplished were to defy his racist and Trump-supporting teacher who wears a MAGA hat and likes to bully the Mexican students. Diego and his classmates go to the border and take matters into their own hands, demonstrating agency as we saw with the self-portraits in the previous section.

Solutions and Agency

There were additional ways the children created solutions in their drawings. For example, the proposition of Obama coming back to office was one that also came through in their drawings, where they interrogated a problem they saw in society. Diego, the student who wanted to become an athlete, created an image that identified the problem as Trump building what he calls a "great great wall" that is similar to the Great Wall of China, which the children were learning about in school (see figure 5.5). For Diego the real problem was that Trump was what he called a racist who wanted to send people back to their countries and that he "sucks" as president. His most logical solution was to give Obama another chance.

Additionally, Sara proposed to confront Trump. When I asked her what she would say to him in her image, she drew a girl asking him "Why are you so mean?" and Trump replying "Whatever!!" (see plate 5.11). Then the person on the right says, "You would not like it if they report [sic] your parents!" Children in this context often confused the word "*deport*" for "*report*." The way that language could be used interchangeably between schooling and the prison-industrial complex was uncanny. Children described getting reported to the principal's office or having school detention in the same way that people are described as being held in immigration detention and getting deported. They also made sure to point out that the word "detention" was bad in both circumstances. Although some scholars have discussed the "school-to-prison pipeline" and how schooling can replicate systems of oppression, particularly in schools where children of color attend, here the children are also aware of the ways language around schooling resembles the

Figure 5.5. Diego, "Trump as the Problem."

prison system and immigration detention, ultimately normalizing locking people in cages or sending them away.[13]

Plate 5.12 is another example of how children propose to make their voices heard. The drawing shows Trump in his typical blue suit on the right, and next to him is a wall that resembles the part of the border that has already been constructed with bars. This wall looks especially like the one on the San Diego–Tijuana border, which is the entry point for most children who cross to and from Mexico. However, unlike in other drawings, here we cannot see children or adults responding to Trump's claims. There is a set of word bubbles or clouds with messages of unidentified people in reference to his goals. They communicate messages of noncompliance like "Don't take people," "Let them go," and "We want people free." In this image the symbol of resilience that represents the solution is the brown wooden ladder that is drawn against the border wall, peeking over the top. This ladder represents the notion that even *if* the wall is indeed built, people will find a way to migrate by jumping over it.

In the final image, Carolina, age 10, created a picture of a beautiful bright day in a green field. There are two people depicted, one with dark skin and brown hair and another person so white that one can barely distinguish the face from the white background of the paper (see plate 5.13). The person with blond hair is also labeled as "racist" and a small blurb below reads, "I want to change Donald Trump's opinion and make him now [know] that every raise [race] are [sic] the same." Carolina's intent was to acknowledge that she felt unsettled by Trump, but like her classmates, she thought of options to confront him and let him know what she believed. In this case she indicated that talking with him would help change his mind.

In this way, through the praxis of art making, the children harnessed coping mechanisms that could allow healing to begin. It was helpful for them, like the youth in Arizona, to imagine other possibilities. Seeing themselves in a different way was also powerful, as the children in California were able to gain perspective and understanding in re-creating story lines they originally feared. It was especially helpful for children to use theater as a practice of embodiment that allowed them to step into someone else's shoes, be it a parent, a police officer, or even a politician. Through this art practice, solutions, joy, agency, and resilience were able to emerge.

A Schoolteacher's Perspective

Theater, make-believe, drawing, re-creating, and using their creativity were transformative for the children I worked with in Arizona and California. The following excerpt is from an interview I conducted with the full-time teacher of the sixth graders in Los Angeles that captures the essence of what I believe is at stake when children are given the opportunity to use art. Ms. Solis explained:

> I haven't seen the full effects, but to take a kid like Carlos, to take a kid like Jay, and Daniel, who were very troubled, with so many behavioral issues. All the teachers were like, "How do you do it?" I'm like, "I don't know." Because they were notorious at that school from kinder until sixth

grade to be terrors. Everyone was fed up with them. The fact that they were excited about something and did participate, and did a good job, it's amazing. I really think it was healing them and it's a shame, I wish they could just have started doing it earlier. . . . I mean, for sure it helped them emotionally because it brought them a sense of a place where they felt maybe they were not being judged by their academics. It was just, "I'm going to take this character, and I'm just gonna roll with it, and it's fine, I'm not being graded." It took that pressure off performing academically in a sense. Even academically, some of them really took it up a notch with their reading scores so maybe there was some sort of influence. I know it helped empower them with self-esteem and self-confidence. It got them excited to do something different where they were able to express themselves and be someone else. I think it was fun for them. For some of them it was a relief or escape from who they are.

As Ms. Solis noted, the momentary escape from their real lives and pressures opened a place where the children could explore their emotions and possibilities. A praxis of art and healing would be useful for other teachers, scholars, researchers, and caretakers aiming to achieve similar outcomes. Indeed, the process of imagining and embodying alternative realities that differed from oppressive social structures was useful in stimulating resilience and healing in these children exposed to trauma and toxic stress.[14] If we want society to become a place of real care and liberation—especially for the most marginalized—then these transformative ways of creating and imagining alternative worlds are vital for young people. As Bettina Love[15] reminds us, it is not enough to hope to not be separated from one's family. Why not harness the potential in children to thrive and not only survive?

The In-Betweenness of Imagination

Children of immigrants are especially savvy at navigating one set of norms and language at home, and then, as soon as they step out of their homes, beginning to navigate various contexts of code switching and adaptation. Even within the family unit, children of immigrants serve important roles as family translators, interpreters, and spokespeople.[16] Although these roles are important, children must still navigate hierarchies within the family, precisely because they are children. This skillful navigation is what literacy scholars like de los Rios and Garcia have called "translanguaging," which centers on the practices of bilingual students.[17] Subcomandante Marcos of the Ejército Zapatista de Liberación Nacional (Zapatista Army of National Liberation or EZLN) stated, "Queremos un mundo donde quepan muchos mundos" (We want a world where many worlds fit),[18] and that is exactly what children teach us. As children of immigrants live in constant transitions of worlds between home and school, their perspective encompasses many worlds in one, creating extraordinary capacity for mental ambidexterity replete with creative possibilities.

Similarly, children of immigrants create new value systems of images and symbols that connect them to their families and schools in ways that are safe, loving, and bravely offer us hope. This form of differential consciousness allows for coalitions of creativity and establishes sites of opposition or resistance to dominant norms.[19] Anzaldúa's *Nepantla* or third space is similar to what Homi Bhabha called a third-space consciousness, an "alien-territory", and a "split-space" where those who are in-between carry the burden of rearing a vanguard.[20] Children of immigrants are thus the vanguards of the third space or in-between space and use imagination to re-create situations, structures, and systems that harm their lives and endanger their family cohesion. As theorist Terry Eagleton discusses, this creative space is a fruitful one: "Children make the best theorists, since they have not yet been educated into accepting our routine social practices as 'natural,' and so insist on posing to those practices the most embarrassingly general and fundamental questions, regarding them with a wondering estrangement which we adults have long forgotten. Since they do not yet grasp our social practices as inevitable, they do not see why we might not do things differently."[21]

This ability to think differently underscores the immense importance of children's imagination. Not only is imagination important for their own lives but also for the communities and families where the children come from. Theater and other forms of creative expression are essential for thinking about the future and allowing children the time and space to dream up all the possibilities in life. As Adrienne Maree Brown reminds us, in life as in theater, there is an elemental need to embody in order to learn, but it all starts with imagining. We are in what Brown calls "an imagination battle," as she powerfully reflects about the future and how to get there from this specific current moment, adding:

> Trayvon Martin and Mike Brown and Renisha McBride and so many others are dead because, in some white imagination, they were dangerous. And that imagination is so respected that those who kill, based on an imagined, radicalized fear of Black people, are rarely held accountable. Imagination has people thinking they can go from being poor to a millionaire as part of a shared American dream. Imagination turns Brown bombers into terrorists and White bombers into mentally ill victims. Imagination gives us borders, gives us superiority, gives us race as an indicator of ability. . . . I often feel I am trapped inside someone else's imagination, and I must engage my own imagination in order to break free.

Inspired by the work of Octavia Butler, who worked her whole life at imagining the future, Brown positions us as carriers of that responsibility, where a visionary exploration of humanity must start with imagination.[22]

Like Brown, Appadurai reminds us that imagination is important for those migrants who are on the way to the US as well as for those who are already here.[23] He adds that we need to shape the force of imagination into something constructive, because if we do not, we will continue to spin off in directions of fear, anxiety, and anger.[24] I agree that imagination is not just for the elite; rather, it is a right for everyone. "The imagination is no longer a matter of individual genius, escapism from ordinary life, or just a dimension of aesthetics. It is a faculty that informs the daily lives of ordinary people in myriad ways. It allows people to consider migration, resist state violence, seek social redress, and design new forms of civic association and collaboration, often across national boundaries."[25] Art does precisely this for children—it allows them the time, space, and method for imagining. This is especially helpful for those who experience difficulties at such early points of their lives. Certainly, there can be no love without justice, therefore, we must live in a culture that "not only respects, but also upholds basic civil [and human] rights for children."[26]

Conclusion

Art as an Offering

People of color are denied access to art
for the fear that if they get their hands on it,
they'll write their own stories
and understand the value of their lives.
—bell hooks and Amalia Mesa-Bains, *Homegrown*[1]

The vulnerability of undocumented families has been made more visible than ever before. The deadly COVID-19 pandemic took the lives of nearly one million people in the US alone and decimated places of employment for the immigrant labor force. At-home social distancing in heavily populated communities has been nearly impossible, further highlighting health disparities and disproportionate impacts of the pandemic on people of color and immigrant communities. These events made daily life feel surreal and threatening. The early 2020s also marked a vital election year, and Black Lives Matter uprisings around the country brought to the forefront the ways violence systematically coalesces with racism. Asylum-seeking families continued to wait in camps at the border for an opportunity to enter the US while hundreds of children separated from their families in 2018 were left in limbo as their parents had not been found after being deported. Although much of the country sighed a breath of relief when Joe Biden won the presidency, those aware of the detrimental impact of Obama-era immigration policies found themselves anxious to see if the Biden-Harris administration would differ in its approach to immigrants.

Perhaps most relevant to the ideas presented in this book, in 2021 hundreds of bodies of Indigenous children were found in church grounds in Canada and in the US. These children had been separated by force from their families, communities, and tribes at the turn of the

20th century and forced into so-called Indian boarding schools to be Americanized. Almost 100 years later, their bodies were returned to their ancestral homelands from which they were violently taken. The eerie dynamic of migrant children also being separated from their families as the bodies of Indigenous children were found evokes the legacies of family separation that have existed on this continent since the colonization of the Americas.

Based on over 10 years of work with immigrant-origin children in two different border states, Arizona and California, this book has offered a glimpse into the lives of immigrant children and their families. Through an analysis of 300 children's drawings, theater performances, and family interviews, we have engaged with accounts of children's challenges with deportation and family separation during two different political moments.

Children of immigrants are the fastest-growing segment of the US child population.[2] By 2040 one in three children will be growing up in an immigrant household.[3] Despite the increasing numbers of immigrant children and the dependency the country will have on this generation in the future, anti-immigrant policies targeted at undocumented adults at the national and local levels continue to affect these children in detrimental ways.[4] This book has aimed to provide insight into the lives of children who live at the nexus of an "immigrant-addicted economy" and draconian anti-immigration policy enforcement.[5] Combined with a failing approach to foreign policy in countries south of the border, these circumstances are disastrous for immigrant communities and their children. Through the lens of legal violence, we have seen how children's lives regularly intersect with the law, often creating chronic and toxic stress in the lives of children and their families.[6]

The visual narratives of the children's drawings and performances are the material effects of legal violence on their lives through the merging of immigration and criminal law. However, this book has shown that children are resilient and can use art to cope with and resist these laws. As we have seen, children of immigrants and migrant children respond to legal violence through harnessing agency. Often, literature on immigrant children deems them passive, enforcing narratives of victimization, but we have seen them here as agents of their own stories, through theater, drawing, and *relajo* (satire), they speak back and reimagine destructive situations in ways that adults sometimes cannot, offering us alternatives and hope.

Such agency is not unique to my participants; children have had to become spokespeople because of the extreme dehumanization of adults in communities of color, such as 5-year-old Sophie Cruz, who ran up to the pope to deliver a drawing and letter in which she asked him for help for her undocumented parents, or 9-year-old Katherine Figueroa, who was the first person to ask President Obama for administrative relief for her parents who were detained for three months. Or 9-year-old Zianna, who spoke on CNN in 2016, asking for an end to police brutality and the killing of Black people. Moreover, students from all over the nation have spoken up and organized to end gun violence. To understand what is occurring, we must address the concerns of all these young people, who courageously confront the challenges of our time. Thus, we need to create spaces that foster dialogue through art both in and out of schools.

School Implications

The American system of schooling, meant to assimilate students into a labor hierarchy of social class, is not working. We must change the schooling system dramatically and build it anew. In the meantime, we need massive structural changes that establish art programs to complement traditional school subjects. Mehta and Fine's *In Search of Deeper Learning*[7] reminds us that urgency must be met with hope; this book makes clear why art, civic education, social-justice-oriented learning, and culturally relevant curriculum are needed in schools. Art provides an avenue to foster deeper learning with cognitive, social, emotional, and academic benefits. In the face of dangerous defunding of art programs in intercity communities, it is important to equip teachers with the trauma-sensitive and culturally sustaining tools of creativity needed to work with immigrant youth. For that reason, I propose that universities and teacher-education programs preservice teachers to utilize nontraditional methods of teaching that complement children's strengths, like creativity, curiosity, and imagination. They also must understand the complex legal webs that envelop children of immigrants and immigrant communities as a whole. In terms of educational policy, it is important to work with future educators and school leaders so that they will understand the specific learning environments needed to help children heal and cope with traumas of deportation. Currently, schools unfortunately find themselves unprepared to talk about this subject and underresourced to deal with the psychological and emotional consequences. It is imperative that schools are at the forefront of immigration-justice demands. Schools need plans in place that prepare them when responding to familial deportations, neighborhood violence, and other forms of trauma. Consequently, educators and researchers should employ artistic and expressive methods when working with children and aim to develop new methodologies that include performative and visual approaches. These outlets can provide candid and descriptive information produced by children, while at the same time affording meditative, reflective, and innately healing effects through the art-making process. These methods are particularly powerful when working with children who are shy, learning a new language, or have experienced trauma in their lives. Funding must be generously prioritized for more and longer afterschool art programs that provide a safe place for children to stay while their parents are working.

For children of immigrants, and children in general, creativity is a way to process the experiences of loss, violence, and fear. However, I concur that our wholeness does not just emerge from looking closely at pain but also from creating a community that is open to humor, love, laughter, and playfulness in the present moment.[8] Ultimately, the goal of this book has been to expose the fact that criminalizing migration is state-sponsored legal violence and human torture that fosters generational cycles of pain and trauma. Yet, nevertheless, through theater, drawings, and *relajo* (satire) children can transform and heal.

Policy Implications

This book has described only a portion of a larger set of immigration policy changes implemented or attempted by the Obama and Trump administrations to restrict immigration to the US.[9] Based on the most recent studies that have been conducted since 2017,[10] these policies appear overall to have harmed youth development. These studies show negative consequences for mental health and well-being for youth who experience both specific policy-driven experiences like detention, but also among the larger group of immigrant-origin children who experience the general cumulative effects of policies implemented both at the border and within the US in areas of enforcement, asylum, documentation status, and integration.

Much remains to be investigated concerning the impacts of these policies on the well-being, learning, and development of youth, as well as the mechanisms through which these effects occur. For that effort, a variety of qualitative and quantitative methods could be used to complement the "Cops Off Campus" organizing efforts happening round the US. Above and beyond the usual recommendations to conduct more participatory and creative research, I suggest the following: First, cross-national collaborations may be useful to delineate the experiences of children and families during their migration or attempts to migrate to the US. As one example, a qualitative study by Medina and Menjívar of members of mixed-status families described the experiences of family members in Mexico after deportation.[11] Large-scale transnational projects like the Mexican Migration Project that transformed our understanding of migration from Mexico to the US[12] could be replicated with more of a focus on children's experiences.

Second, although experiences in policy-relevant settings like detention centers may be almost impossible to investigate directly during detention, there may be other potential methods to obtain information about these experiences. To my knowledge there have only been a handful of studies of youth in detention since 2017.[13] However, accounts from individuals released from these centers may illuminate the experiences of youth and their family members who have been detained. Retrospective accounts such as these may be powerful in the absence of real-time data from within difficult-to-access settings.

Third, the community-level impacts of policies on youth development have been underexplored. When many immigration policies are restrictive, their cumulative impact may occur through a variety of community-level processes that have been discussed as potential mechanisms but have been rarely studied. For example, Bellows's study[14] of the impact of heightened enforcement and deportation activities on lowering county-level academic achievement during the Obama administration should be replicated with the addition of time-by-location data on deportation raids that have occurred more recently. That study used the

Stanford Education Data Archive; the addition of a national data set tracking student achievement in all districts and counties by year would offer high potential for understanding effects of immigration not only on the traditional mental health and well-being indicators that dominate in this literature, but also on policy-relevant outcomes such as academic achievement and educational progress.

Finally, further efforts should document how mitigating factors and resistance may result in positive outcomes among immigrant-origin children in the face of adverse policy contexts in the US. The data in this book show that immigrant-youth contributions in domains like art, protest, and resistance are widespread instantiations of civic engagement, leadership, and resilience processes. Understanding further the circumstances and contexts in which children and youth may engage in such acts of resistance will help guide future policy as well as interventions in schools, communities, and other contexts. Overall, the research literature on impacts of specific immigration policies on youth development is still nascent.[15] However, the dramatic accounts of recent policies' harmful effects create an urgency to document the consequences more completely for youth and to leverage those data to improve national policy and inform local action.

Lastly, I must reiterate the need for an immediate overhaul of immigration policy and a well-resourced family-reunification program that prioritizes parents of documented *and* undocumented children. Rather than adding more children to an already overburdened foster-care system, it would be best for families to never separate in the first place. Additionally, there is a need to better fund programs that aid in the physical and mental well-being of children and mixed-status families. Realistically, these recommendations are temporary "Band-Aid" solutions to a complex issue of problematic foreign policy all over the globe and, as described in this book, with significant implications south of the US border. US interventions in Central America along with NAFTA/CAFTA and other polices that propel people out of their communities and into the US for survival must be understood as the catalyst for migration. Finally, we must #AbolishICE, as it has served as the structural tool to deport and separate millions of families since its establishment in 2003. Finally, under any circumstances, may we never cage children again.

This book is an offering to future generations, a refusal to forget. The drawings of kid stick figures with tears streaming down their faces, parents in shackles torn away from their children, police cars detaining fathers, and feelings of metaphoric and literal caging of families have been ingrained in my heart and mind for the last 13 years. I have sought to make visible the fears and pain of children I met in Phoenix and in Los Angeles. Along the path of exposing the pain, I also learned about the will to find joy in everyday life even while living in fear and in hiding. The resilience and imagination that art allowed children to demonstrate are what I cling to in moments when I lose faith in society. With this work, I implore those who have seen the visual testimonies of children and learned about their stories to not allow history to repeat itself.

ACKNOWLEDGMENTS

Divino cielo te ruego
Permiso para cantar
Me persigno luego y luego
Y empiezo por saludar
Agua, tierra, viento, y fuego
—El Siquisiri (Laguana Prieta)

To all my relations:

I wish this book did not need to exist and that I did not need to write it. The responsibility of sharing these stories and drawings has never been something I have taken lightly, and the images shared with me have weighed on my heart since 2008. The sheer fact that you are reading these words today means that there was an enormous web of support that sustained me as I uncovered these narratives. Starting with an acknowledgment to the land, thank you to the caretakers of the unceded territories where I lived and worked on this book—the Tohono O'odham, Akimel O'odham, Diné, Hohokam, and Gabrielino-Tongva, also known as Phoenix, Arizona, and Los Angeles, California.

To begin, I want to thank the young people. Together we created, discussed, laughed (a lot), cried, played, performed, snacked, and imagined. Thank you to the parents and caretakers who welcomed me into their homes and trusted me. Thank you to the teachers, administrators, and community-center workers who allowed me to build new ways of teaching. I also acknowledge the steadfast support of Jennifer Hammer at New York University Press—my dream press! I am also grateful to the reviewers who provided thoughtful and supportive feedback through their careful readings.

I also want to thank the César E. Chávez Department of Chicana/o and Central American Studies at UCLA. It was an honor to be part of the first doctoral cohort. In particular, I want to thank Leisy Abrego and

Judy Baca, my fiercest theory and praxis partners who also doubled as my advisers. I hope this book reflects your splendor in creating powerful and much-needed work. You both forged road maps where there were no trails. I was also extremely fortunate to count on the unending support of Carola Suárez-Orozco, Gaye Theresa Johnson, and Charlene Villaseñor Black, who were instrumental in the formation of this project and forever forces of inspiration and models for femmetorship.

This research was made possible through generous funding from UCLA's Eugene V. Cota-Robles Fellowship, the Graduate Research Mentorship Program, the UC-MEXUS Dissertation Research Grant, the Institute of American Cultures in the Chicano Studies Research Center, and the Ford Foundation Dissertation Fellowship. A very special thanks to the Social and Public Art Resource Center (SPARC) in Venice, California, for their training and collaborative partnership with the Los Angeles Unified School District (LAUSD). Thank you to the New York University Provost's Office for providing me the time to think through my project and create the initial drafts of this book, especially to my unwavering postdoc mentor and one of the greatest champions of my work, Hirokazu Yoshikawa. Hiro, you are not only a scholar of immeasurable caliber but also a truly kind person. A special thank you to those I met while at NYU—Stella Flores, Charlton McIlwain, Farooq Niazi, Ifrah Mahamud Magan, Sarah Rendon Garcia, my writing group of Leila Adu-Gilmor, Luis Rodriguez, Kayla DesPortes, Joe Salvatore, and Mercy Agyepong, and finally my postdoc sister, Ariana Valle. I am appreciative of Arlene Dávila, who set this book plan in motion by putting me in touch with the editors at NYU Press. My book blossomed during my time as a University of California Chancellor's Postdoctoral Fellow at UC, Santa Barbara, under the mentorship of Dolores Inés Casillas in the Department of Chicana/o Studies. I am incredibly fortunate to have her support and that of Mark Lawson, Kimberly Adkinson, and Ernestine Harrison at the UC President's Postdoctoral Fellowship Program office. Finally, thank you to the American Association of University Women for a book grant that supported part of the book subventions that allowed for most of the children's drawings to be printed in color.

I would be remiss to not acknowledge the people who made this ambitious project move—my undergraduate art-teaching assistants in each year of data collection in California. Thank you, Erendirani Aparicio Chavez and Jatziry Callejas. Your genuine excitement to teach theater with me was apparent in the joy of the children. A special thank you to the detail-oriented brilliance of Eva Amarillas Wong Diaz, who was an incredible research assistant. Jordan Beltran Gonzales, your careful attention to detail and dedication to helping make sense of these sentences will forever be appreciated. Thank you as well, Cathy Hannabach and the folks at Ideas on Fire for fueling my thoughts with your editorial support.

I did not make it this far by myself. Growing up as an undocumented young person in the projects of South Phoenix required me to stand on the shoulders of many intergenerational giants. The many mentors and femmetors I've had span across time and space; they have been guideposts along a trying journey. Thank you, Gustavo McGrew, Christina Marin, Diana Miller, Judy Butzine, Steve Seidel, Daniel Solorzano, Abel Valenzuela, Marivel Danielson, Carlos Vélez-Ibañez, Edward Escobar, Carla Melo, Rosalee Gonzalez, Laura Esquivel, Martha Ramirez Oropeza, Leo Chavez, Vilma Ortiz, Irene Vega, Cati de los Rios, Martha Gonzalez, Michelle Téllez, Maria Malagon, Emir Estrada, Lilian Chavez.

This book is evidence of what community organizers have been saying for decades. I am indebted to these spaces of possibility and acknowledge my time at Puente Human Rights Movement of Arizona as formative to the development of this book. I also want to give a shout-out to Mijente, Tonatierra, the National Day Labor Organizing Network (NDLON), People for People, and all community spaces that continue to fight the good fight.

Thank you to my community of friends and comrades of Arizona—Bryant Partida, Alexis Aguirre, Carlos Garcia, Gabriela Reza, Ruben Lucio, Miguel Zarate, Gregorio Montes de Oca, Candelaria Montes de Oca, Maria del Carmen Parra Cano, Renato Ramos, DJ Portugal, Perla Farias, Nuvia Nevarez, Sandra Castro, Ernesto Lopez, Diana Perez Ramirez, Opal Tometi, Virginia Cano, Manuel Saldaña, Valeria Fernandez, Victor Hugo Rodriguez, SentRock, Victoria Villalba, Chela Meraz, Luis Avila y a el grupo de El Break, Violeta Ramos, Elvia Zamora, Alfonso Parra, Vania Guevara, and Daniel Rodriguez. Thank you to the many people who let me live with them—Jazelle Rodriguez and Mama Oli, Arlin Guadian, Julian Arredondo and Mima, la familia Garcia-Jara, and Ruthie and Sarai Santos. To all members of Teatro Movimiento Ollin (TeMO) and all the Nopalerxs from Teatro Nopalero. I want to acknowledge my extreme fortune to count on the love, magic, and sisterhood of my *comadres*, Dulce Juarez, Angelica Medina, and Courtney Peña.

A major shout-out of appreciation for my extended community and chosen family from Arizona, to California, to Boston and back! Starting with my queens and king, Leigh-Anna Hidalgo, Jack (and the entire) Caraves family, Anisha Gandhi, Rose Simons, Angelica Becerra, and Christine Vega. Our group chat and unending support for one another through joy, love, and care is revolutionary. Thank you to Rocio Garcia, Kristina Lovato, my Harvard *hermanas* Vanessa Monterosa and Dianne Sanchez Shumway. Thank you to Jeanette Acosta, Aarti Shahani, Sushma Sheth, Emiliano Bourgois-Chacon, Michael Moses, Sharim Hannegan-Martinez, Christina Zavala, lil'Zoa Lopez, and the El Teatro Campesino crew—Seth Millwood and Alejandro Nuño, Shirley Alvarado del Aguila, Marco Loera, Ernesto Yerena, Andrea Gomez Cervantes, Mickey Ferrara, Uriel Rivera, Omar Gonzalez, Carlos Rogel, Davida Persaud, Kaelyn Rodriguez, Brenda Nicolas, Lucy Leon, Rafael Solorzano, Melanie Cervantes, Juliana Urtubey Otálora, Olmeca, Diana Cervera, Lauren Guerra, Juan and Jessica Redin, Ariana (Diosa) Rodriguez, Yuri Velasco, Lizardo Uribe, German Cadenas, Laura Minero, Gomez, Johnathan Perez, Yessica Rodriguez, Avilia Guardiola, Gary Trujillo, Michael Trejo, the East Side Café Son Jarocho Community, El Centro Cultural de Mexico en Santa Ana, Las Hormigas del El Hormiguero, and Los primos Morales from Civil Coffee in Highland Park who kept me caffeinated and excited with their requests for updates about the book. My team of wellness that kept me alive and on the path of healing through acupuncture and herbs—Andrea Peganos, Lisa Hyun Kim, and Dr. Elena. This book was fueled during late night sessions of writing, thinking, crying, and dancing to the genius of Billie Holiday, Nina Simone, Juan Luis Guerra, Silvio Rodriguez, Selena, Jenni Rivera, Celia Cruz, Lauryn Hill, Mos Def, and Lin-Manuel Miranda.

Gracias a toda la familia en Mexico, los Vega Beck y los Rodriguez Menchaca, especialmente a Marcela Vega y a Giselle Portillo.

At the center of my heart is my family. I inherited my dad's love for books and learning. He never got to see this book realized, but I know he would be proud from the ancestors' realm. To my mom, *gracias por tu creatividad y cariño. Tus palabras de apoyo no fueron en vano.* I thank my brother and sister—Victor Manuel and Alejandra—for their love and support. I offer this book to my niece and nephews—Jaylene, Jayden, and Julian. Love you all, and remember, the sky is the limit!

To my love, Arleen. Thank you for pouring so much love and life into my days. Our dancing, silliness, and romance fill me with joy. I love you and our pup, Lupi, so much.

APPENDIX

Overview of Methodology

The tools of inquiry included qualitative interviews, observations, surveys, and an analysis of children's drawings, journals, and theater performances. Since my work in California included both interviews and artwork, I used separate analytical strategies for each data set. First, I professionally translated and transcribed interviews and coded them through Dedoose—an online software. Then, with the visual data from Arizona and California, I used previous methods of visual coding.[1] I employed a protocol of visual-content analysis by creating codes—such as Content, Actors, Emotions, Nations, and Aesthetics—that were quantified to capture the narratives in children's art. Together, this creative data captured the verbal *and* visual testimonies of migrant children.

To do this work carefully I equipped myself with knowledge, resources, and tools. I worked with the Institutional Review Board (IRB) representatives at UCLA to ensure that I had IRB approval to engage children in this work, and I also went through the necessary procedures with LAUSD to be able to be present at the school having cleared all the background checks and medical prerequisites. As an additional precaution, I collaborated with a school psychologist, a drama therapist, and several community organizations that provided training in conducting research with vulnerable youth. I have purposefully and painstakingly developed these collaborations to ensure an ethically responsible project. The parents of all children agreed to allow their children to participate in this work and I kept no personal or identifiable information. Each child and parent had bilingual information about the class and study; I also made myself available over the phone and for home visits to talk with any family members. Furthermore, since this is a vulnerable population, I made sure to anonymize all sites and gave pseudonyms to all participants.

BUILDING RAPPORT

Check-ins helped center students who had a hard time following instructions, staying on task, and listening. After check-ins, we shifted focus to our plan for the day. Check-ins also allowed me to establish a space and time to get to know my students and build rapport with them, which was essential to my pedagogical practice in creating a horizontal or democratic learning environment, where students are seen as active agents able to coconstruct knowledge and learning with their teacher and peers.[2] As aforementioned, this form of education is based on Paulo Freire's *Pedagogy of the Oppressed*, which seeks to position problem-posing pedagogy as a form of teaching that centers students' needs and concerns. Problem-solving pedagogy stands in sharp contrast to what Freire called the "Banking Method of Education," where the teacher operates as a banker who deposits knowledge into students' empty brains. This deems students to be passive beings, void of their own knowledge or life experiences. Thus, I sought the opposite in my class where the learning was meant to be horizontal rather than vertical/top-down. To do this, we used a variety of methods that I will elaborate on below, including Rose and Thorn activity, meditation, Theater of the Oppressed/Boal-style theater games,[3] and the storyboarding.

CHECK-INS: ROSE AND THORN ACTIVITY

One of the most important activities that students enjoyed was called the Rose and Thorn check-in.[4] This activity involved spending some time reflecting on the day or week. Students then pick one memory, event, or aspect of their day that was a rose—a positive or beautiful thing—and then a thorn—a negative aspect or something that hurt. This worked particularly well in smaller groups of no more than 10 students. Sometimes half of the class time would be used for this activity as students had lots to share, prompting me to ask them to draw their rose and then their thorn on occasion. This activity fostered rich dialogue and deep reflection among students who learned about their classmates and offered support.

MEDITATIONS FOR FOCUS

When students were particularly rambunctious, the use of meditation truly helped. My teaching assistant and I would take turns leading the activity while the other watched students who played, stood up, talked, opened their eyes, or were not taking the activity seriously. One of our favorite meditation activities was to ask all students to lie down on the auditorium floor where we worked. We asked them to take deep breaths and trust that they were safe as they closed their eyes if they wanted, or focused their gaze on a particular point on the ceiling. Once they were calm, we took collective breaths to bring our attention back to the present moment and space. We took time focusing on breath, making the exhalations longer than the inhalations and then giving them time to create a goal/intention for the workshop and for what they wanted to get out of it. Then, we asked students to commit and fully participate. Once the deep breathing was over, we asked students to slightly move their bodies, and finished with stretches to warm up the body for either a theater game or an activity.

Another meditation activity that involved movement was the tree meditation. We asked students to stand in a big, spacious circle facing out. With their eyes closed, we guided their breathing to deepen and relax. Then, we asked them to imagine a tree and talked them through becoming that tree. Through this imagination exercise, we asked them questions to keep their mind on the task, such as: How tall is your tree? How wide is the trunk? How many leaves are there? What colors do you see on your tree? Is it swinging? Then, we would ask students to move as their tree moved; some would sway side to side gently, others looked like they were in the middle of a storm with harsh and fast movements. Other students stretched their arms out to the sky as tall branches trying to reach the sun; others would touch the ground and focus on their roots. As we asked students to relax and open their eyes, we were able to calmly transition to a voice exercise, discussion, or activity.

One of the most important reasons for including meditation in the curriculum concerned the multiple benefits of meditation and mindfulness for children who have experienced trauma. Benefits include increased attention, better grades, and the ability to deal with stressors.[5] The brains of children who undergo intense trauma cannot process emotions or make logical decisions as they are unable to distinguish between right and wrong; yet meditation has the power to balance their brain, repairing the damage caused by stress.[6] As such, it is essential to include meditative and mindfulness components in the teaching of immigrant children, whose lives are often unpredictable and heightened with stress by the possibility of deportation and family separation.

THEATER OF THE OPPRESSED AS PEDAGOGY

Once students were ready to use their bodies, we transitioned the class to a Theater of the Oppressed icebreaker, theater game, or exercise. As mentioned previously, Theater of the Oppressed has various components including Image Theater, Newspaper Theater, Forum Theater, Invisible Theater, Rainbow of Desire, and Legislative Theater. During this class I mainly used the first three forms: Image Theater, Newspaper Theater, and Forum Theater. Image Theater uses the body to create frozen images that can represent issues facing the participants or viewers. Through the molding of images, participants can gain depth and visual understanding of those issues. Images can also be made to represent solutions to problems people might be trying to solve. There is also a way to activate images by adding voice or sounds to each of the frozen participants. Those on the outside looking at the image can treat it like a gallery of sorts, where one can pay attention to the ways people create body positions, dynamics, facial expressions, and relationships between other images or frozen statues. In the end, the image looks like a photograph capturing an important message. This style of theater proved very useful in inspiring children's imaginations and brainstorming. Image Theater is especially powerful because it is so easy to do, but mainly for its "extraordinary capacity for making thought *visible*."[7] For children of immigrants and for children in generally, this can be extremely helpful in finding nonverbal ways to express themselves.

Newspaper Theater was an important tool for getting children to engage with what is happening in the media. Before class, I reminded students to watch the news with their family, listen to the radio, or read a newspaper and pick the most important story. This generated a great deal of conversation about current events. Most often the topic discussed had to do with politics. Once we had collectively created a story, we made a skit from the students' contributions where students got to play the various characters involved in the story, and then we discussed what we saw or did not see represented. The discussion of what we saw was essential as it afforded opportunities for critical thinking and dialogue.

The final form of Theater of the Oppressed we used was Forum Theater. In Forum Theater, it is important to designate a joker; in Brazilian Portuguese the joker is also known as the *kuringa*. The joker (*kuringa*) is the link between the "audience" and the "actors" and facilitates dialogue between the two. However, the roles are blurred as the audience can inform the actors and even join them to play out their suggestions. Once a topic or problem is collectively chosen, people quickly assign roles and attempt to play out the scenario. In between the acting, the joker can freeze what is happening on stage and ask the audience for direction. The audience can then advise characters on what to do, or members of it can come up to the stage and play that character themselves if they maintain their own positionality. Collectively, all participants come up with the solution to the originally posed problem. In acting out the solution, participants are empowered in their real lives. Children were very involved in this form of theater and always favored playing the role of the joker. Once we had clearly chosen the topics, we often transitioned to methods used by the famous Chicano theater group El Teatro Campesino; specifically, we followed their use of *actos*.

EL TEATRO CAMPESINO'S *ACTOS* AS PEDAGOGY

Popularized in the 1970s, El Teatro Campesino used theater to organize, inform, and empower farmworkers alongside Cesar Chavez, Dolores Huerta, and the United Farm Workers.[8] An *acto* can be defined as a "short, improvised scene dealing with the experience of its participants."[9] Although popularized in the United States by El Teatro Campesino, *actos* are not unique to Chicanos. According to Valdez, the founder of El Teatro Campesino, the most important part of an *acto* is not the ideas of the artist or individual but rather the social vision of the community.[10] Moreover, the five goals of *actos* are to: (1) inspire the audience to social action; (2) illuminate specific points about social problems; (3) satirize the opposition; (4) show or hint at a solution; and (5) express what people are feeling.[11] A key aspect of an *acto* is to empower the participants and the audience to lose their fear and diminish the person in power through satire and comedy. This was one of the children's most important strategies when talking about political issues regarding Trump.

STORYBOARD OF PERFORMANCE PLOT

Drawing and storyboarding were essential aspects of the work with children. They provided a third or fourth language to communicate ideas, feelings, and events. On some days I would ask the students to draw their Rose and Thorn activity; at other times I would prompt them to draw what they did during the weekend. When they enjoyed drawing more, I would prompt them to draw about what they saw on the news or what they thought about what was going on in the media.

Once children became accustomed to drawing and acting, we began our storytelling and storyboarding activity with the goal of coming up with the final play we would perform for the entire school. The activity began with everyone sitting in a circle, and much like the game "Telephone" where a message is passed on by whispering to the other person one at a time, this version involved one child sharing one sentence aloud so that it would be part of the narrative of our play. Once the first person said an action and introduced the character, the next person would add to the story by saying aloud what happened next until we had a beginning, middle, and an end. We recorded the session, and by the end we had our final play where each person had contributed to the story we would perform.

After we had our story, we mapped out the plot and scenes. Students formed groups and worked on various drawings that represented what was happening in the play. Thus, we collaboratively created a story and once our storyboard was complete, children volunteered to play certain roles, came up with lines, but most of all, developed jokes and punch lines. For the final performance, we installed a large projector above the stage that showed the drawings children created; below that, children performed the same story. These projected drawings helped translate what children were performing in English in a way that helped their Spanish-speaking parents understand what was happening on stage. This provided a special relationship between the children acting and the "untraditional audience members" by expressing ideas, stories, and sharing laughs despite language barriers.

RESEARCH METHODS SPECIFIC TO THE CALIFORNIA STUDY

To do this work, I recorded each class, practice, and performance; then later professionally transcribed and translated each of the sessions. Typically, each class was one to two hours long, depending on how much extra time the teacher allowed us to take. I explored these questions through school and classroom observations (40 hours), carefully analyzing children's story drawings (n=136), and performances/classroom recordings (40 hours). I also conducted interviews with children, family members, and school officials (62 hours). Then, I collected pre- and post-tests in which children expressed their thoughts and feelings about a range of topics including art, class, neighborhood, family, future goals, love, cultural heritage, immigration, politics, and themselves.

The primary goal of this work is to expand our understanding of the most pressing needs of immigrant children in Los Angeles. It also fills the gaps in providing insight into the understudied population of pre-adolescent immigrant children. The second goal of this work is to center children's art as visual testimonies and material representations of their lives, concerns, and experiences. Since this project includes interviews, pre/post course assessments, and artwork from children, I used separate analytical strategies for each data set.

First, as mentioned above, I professionally transcribed and translated the interviews with children, parents, and teachers, then engaged in coding with the help of my research assistant through the online qualitative-analysis software Dedoose. My work with the undergraduate research assistant primarily focused on conducting an in-depth visual-content analysis of the images, which included pictures and drawings.[12] This analysis resulted in the creation of 60 codes divided into five categories, which include: Actors, Content/Actions, Emotions, Nationalities, and Aesthetic Qualities. Second, I comparatively analyzed the pre/post course assessments to see what variations occurred in students' thinking or feelings after taking the class. Finally, with the transcribed materials (class recordings from years 1 and 2 and interviews from year 2) we coded the students' creative products, which included performance recordings, storyboard drawings, and reflective drawings that provided unique insight into the lives of children.

Building on previous methods of visual coding, my committee and I developed a "Visual-Content Analysis" method to analyze children's artwork, which I employed for this project by teaching my research assistant this method for the purpose of reading the images as visual narratives and testimonies of children's experiences. This method of analysis comes from the work of Leo Chavez and Otto Santa Ana, who conduct narrative analysis.

To code the drawings, we combined inductive and deductive strategies as well as grounded theory.[13] The deductive strategy began with the broad organizational categories of (1) content (subject matter); (2) actors (people, characters, important players); (3) emotions; (4) nations; and (5) color choices. The inductive codes emerged directly from the data. The coding mechanism was to look at each drawing and go through the checklist of coding categories. To ensure that the process was standardized, my research assistant and I coded together for the first set of 20 images until we understood how to observe and code properly or calibrated in sync.

If a confusion arose, I would consult my committee and my research assistant again to ask for their feedback with the goal of maintaining transparency. The following step was to get a sense of the patterns and see how many children felt similarly, or to see if there was something unusual that stood out. Upon quantifying the codes, I grouped the various drawings by common themes to understand the narratives. Some of these topics emerged organically based on a numerical calculation of quantifying codes, and we also analyzed via Dedoose, which yielded unique reports based on the data. Together, this rich data set provided me with the crucial information to answer my research questions.

METHODOLOGICAL FINDINGS: INTERVIEWS VS. IMAGES

Perhaps one of the reasons this population is so understudied has to do with the challenges of engaging young children in traditional qualitative or quantitative methods of inquiry. Language, age, trauma, and other barriers make it difficult for children to express themselves. For this reason, I rely on creative and artistic methodologies. Through this work, I found that even when interviewing the child, the teacher, family member (parent or sibling, or all family), and the school administrator, nothing gave me more information as a researcher and teacher than the process of creating an art item or the art itself. Thus, this methodology has provided three important methodological findings: (1) creative methods lead to more rich and robust data; (2) children respond better to multiple methods of communication and interaction, especially those that include art; and (3) art is an important tool when working with children and/or vulnerable populations, particularly for its ability to provide reflection and opportunities for coping.

ARIZONA CODE DEFINITIONS

TABLE A.1. Content Codes.

Code	Definition
Deportation	Concerns with deportation, detention, and border issues. Includes the following content: detainment, ICE vehicles, the border, ICE facilities.
Family separation	Family members missing, children separated from parents.
Authorities	Police, sheriff car, helicopter, truck, highway patrol.
Protesting	A statement or action expressing disapproval of or objection to something.
Physical violence (hitting, beating)	Behavior involving physical force intended to hurt, damage, or kill someone or something.
Treated badly/humiliated (like animals)	To make someone feel ashamed and foolish by injuring their dignity and self-respect, especially publicly.
Xenophobia/racism/discrimination/ prejudice	Intense or irrational dislike or fear of people from other countries.
Rights (e.g., "We are like everyone else")	Rights that are believed to belong justifiably to every person.

TABLE A.2. Actor Codes.

Code	Definition
Arpaio	Sheriff Joe Arpaio of Maricopa County in Arizona. Infamous for his harsh policies toward undocumented immigrants.
Authority/ICE/Police/Highway Patrol/Sheriff's deputies	Any public-safety official.
Parents	Mother or father, including stepmother and/or stepfather.
Friends	Children/peers/friends.
Other family members	Extended family, aunts, uncles, cousins, grandparents, and siblings.
Other adults	Adults who are not part of one's family.
Unidentifiable	Person who is unidentifiable.

TABLE A.3. Emotion Codes.

Code	Definition
Fear	An unpleasant emotion caused by the belief that someone or something is dangerous, likely to cause pain, or a threat.
Sadness	The condition or quality of being sad (crying/tears).
Anger	A strong feeling of annoyance, displeasure, or hostility.
Unclear	Unclear.

CODES FOR CALIFORNIA DATA

TABLE A.4. Content (What is happening?)

Code	Definition
Deportation, detention, arrest, jail (family separation)	Concerns with deportation, detainment, and border issues. Includes the following content: detainment, ICE vehicles, the border, ICE facilities, apprehensions, disappearances.
State authorities	Police, sheriff car, helicopter, truck, Highway Patrol, sirens. Metaphorically, the law.
Protesting	A statement or action expressing disapproval of or objection to something. People holding signs; signs stating things.
Legal violence	(Menjívar &Abrego 2012) Legal violence is a lens that highlights the ways structural violence and the law intersect to create traumatic experiences for immigrant families.
Physical violence (hitting, beating, guns)	Behavior involving physical force intended to hurt, damage, or kill someone or something. Images of weapons, guns, knives, bombs, tanks, electrical fence.
Treated badly/Humiliated (like animals)	To make someone feel ashamed and foolish by injuring their dignity and self-respect, especially publicly. Also through the news/media or law.
Xenophobia/racism/ prejudice	An intense or irrational dislike or fear of people from other countries.
Rights (e.g., "We are like everyone else")	Rights that are believed to belong justifiably to every person.
Fighting for rights, advocacy	To combat institutions that do not allow for rights; advocate for oneself and others.
Plan in case of deportation/detention	Instructing children on what to do in case of deportation/ detention. Making plans with family members to take care of children, notarizing documents of legal guardianship.
Death	End of life; usually related to violence.
News, radio, media representation	How people gain information about current events.
Abuse, bullying	Intimidation and/or harm of another.
War	Conflict between nations, using violence including guns and other weaponry, intentionally or unintentionally harming another country. Could include verbal attack.
Election	To select a person based on a system of voting; presidential election.
Art/performance art	The production, expression, or creation of something aesthetically beautiful and meaningful.

TABLE A.5. Actors (Who is doing it?)

Code	Definition
Donald Trump	2016 presidential candidate and 45th president of the US.
Barack Obama	44th president of the US.
Hillary Clinton	Secretary of State and presidential nominee 2016.
El Chapo Guzmán	Narco-leader of Sinaloa Cartel.
Authority: ICE/Police/Highway Patrol/Sheriff's deputies/CIA/FBI	Any public law-enforcement official.
Parents	Mother or father, including stepmother and/or stepfather.
Friends	Children/peers/friends.
Other family members	Extended family aunts, uncles, cousins, grandparents, siblings, and caretakers.
Other adults	Adults who are not part of one's family.
Teacher	A person who instructs/educates as a profession.
Coyote	A person who helps immigrants cross the border, usually for a fee.
Immigrants	Someone who migrates to another country, usually for permanent stay; separated into legal and illegal categories.
Unclear	Unclear, stick figure/person/bystander.

TABLE A.6. Nation Sites (Countries/location represented)

Code	Definition
Border	Something that separates two areas of land; especially the US-Mexican border. Ideologically speaking, the borders we encounter. A journey from Central America to the US crossing multiple borders.
School	An institution where instruction is given; teachers, principal, students.
US	A country in the Western Hemisphere, with 50 states, associated with being "the land of the free," patriotism, Americans, English language; known as America, USA.
Mexico	A country south of the US; country of origin of many immigrants; Spanish language; Mexicans.
El Salvador	A country in Central America; country of origin of many immigrants; Spanish language; Salvadorans.
Guatemala	A country in Central America; country of origin of some immigrants; Spanish language; Guatemalans.
Honduras	A country in Central America; country of origin of some immigrants; Spanish language; Hondurans.
North Korea	A country in East Asia, associated with centralism and dictatorship, strict rule, nuclear threats; current "supreme leader" Kim Jong-un; Korean language.
Syria	A republic in southwest Asia, associated with US bombing, war; Arabic language.
Russia	A country in Eastern Europe/Northwest Asia, semipresidential republic; President Vladimir Putin; tensions with the US; associations with Trump; Russian language.

TABLE A.7. Emotions (Feelings evident)

Code	Definition
Fear	An unpleasant emotion caused by the belief that someone or something is dangerous, likely to cause pain, or a threat.
Sadness	The condition or quality of being sad (crying/tears).
Anger	A strong feeling of annoyance, displeasure, or hostility.
Shame	A painful feeling of disgrace/being improper.
Stress	A response feeling of intense worry, fatigue, or danger.
Nervousness	A feeling of uneasiness, worry.
Worry	An unpleasant emotion that causes one to suffer unease or anxiety.
Crying/tears	To weep or shed tears caused by overwhelming emotion(s).
Unsure	Unclear/miscellaneous.
Joy	An emotion of delight and happiness caused by something good or satisfying.
Relief	To be at ease, with something alleviated, a negative feeling removed.
Hope	A feeling and mentality of wishing for the best/positivity, no matter the circumstances.
Victory	To have success with regard to something, to win or accomplish.
Resilience	The ability to continue when challenges arise.
Self-hate/internalization	A dislike for oneself or for one's race, gender, sexuality, class status, nationality, etc.

TABLE A.8. Drawing Aesthetics.

Code	Notes
Black and white	Other materials available?
Lots of color	What colors?
Only pencil	Other materials available?
Lots of text, words, story	What does the text say?
Place of drawing on paper	Top left or right? Bottom left or right? Middle?

NOTES

INTRODUCTION

1 Abrego 2006; Enriquez 2017; Passel 2011.
2 Crivello et al. 2009; Driessnack 2005; Tumanyan & Huuki 2020.
3 I use the terms "immigrant children," "children of immigrants," "migrant children," and "children in mixed-status-families" interchangeably, given the various legal statuses that children I work with encompassed.
4 In April 2018 the Trump administration announced a so-called zero-tolerance policy on unauthorized immigration. Under this policy, each migrant—including asylum seekers—attempting to cross the US border anywhere other than at an official port of entry was to be detained and criminally prosecuted. This approach entailed the systematic separation of newly arriving adult migrants from children who had accompanied them if those migrants were crossing into the US without authorization (and outside of official ports of entry), and it led to thousands of family separations involving teens, children, and babies (Lind 2018).
5 Ayón 2018; Cohen et al. 2002.
6 Levin 2019; Mishori 2020.
7 Hennessy-Fiske 2019; Rappleye & Seville 2019.
8 "Lawyers Can't Find Parents of 545 Migrant Children Separated by the Trump Administration" 2020.
9 UN General Assembly Article 2, section e, cited in Briggs 2020.
10 Roberts 2002.
11 Briggs 2020.
12 Gordon 2001.
13 New York Foundling Hospital v. Gatti 1906, cited in Gordon 2001.
14 Briggs 2020, 12.
15 Shahani & Greene 2009; Vaughan 2006.
16 Menjívar & Abrego 2012.
17 Vaughan 2006.
18 Passel 2011.
19 Dreby & Adkins 2012; Yoshikawa 2011.
20 Yoshikawa et al. 2017.
21 Passel 2011.
22 Nava 2014; Szkupinski Quiroga et al. 2014.
23 Miroff 2017.

24 Pierce & Bolter 2020.

25 Stuart 2020.

26 Chaudry et al. 2010; Dickerson & Nixon 2017; Nava 2014.

27 Dickerson & Nixon 2017.

28 Lind 2018.

29 Dickerson & Nixon 2017; Hennessy-Fiske 2018.

30 Atkin 2018.

31 Dreby 2012a, 2015; Rodriguez Vega 2015, 2018a.

32 Dreby & Adkins 2012.

33 Ayers 2013; Cervantes et al. 2018.

34 Capps 2007.

35 Chaudry et al. 2010; Kirksey et al. 2020; Santillano et al. 2020.

36 Santos et al. 2017; Soto et al. 2020.

37 Abrego 2006; Ellis et al. 2019; Gonzales 2011.

38 Rendón García 2019; Suárez-Orozco et al. 2011.

39 Lachica Buenavista 2015; Lee 1994.

40 I use the term Latinx as gender expansive and inclusive language when speaking about people whose ancestry is from Latin America. As Adrienne Maree Brown states in her book *Pleasure Activism* "if this is being read in a future in which this language has evolved, then please know I would be evolving right along with you" (pg 18).

41 Suárez-Orozco & Suárez-Orozco 2000.

42 Suárez-Orozco et al. 2009; Suárez-Orozco & Quin 2006.

43 Barajas-Gonzalez et al. 2018.

44 Cloitre et al. 2005; Malchiodi 2008; McEwen 2017.

45 Malchiodi 2008.

46 Terr 1981.

47 Malchiodi 2008.

48 For more information, visit the National Child Traumatic Stress Network online.

49 Waddoups 2019.

50 The Center on the Developing Child at Harvard University posits that not all stress is bad. There are three types of stress. The first is a positive stress response where the heart rate is slightly elevated with a mild rise in certain hormones. Situations where this type of stress can happen include the first day of school or meeting someone new for the first time. The second type of stress is what is called a tolerable stress response, where a situation activates the body's alert systems to a greater degree as a result of more severe, longer-lasting difficulties, such as the loss of a loved one, a natural disaster, or a frightening injury. Importantly, "if the activation is time-limited and buffered by relationships with adults who help the child adapt, the brain and other organs recover from what might otherwise be damaging effects" (Center on the Developing Brain, https://developingchild.harvard.edu). The third and most dangerous type of stress is toxic stress. This type of stress can occur when a child experiences "strong, frequent, and/or pro-

longed adversity—such as physical or emotional abuse, chronic neglect, caregiver substance abuse or mental illness, exposure to violence, and/or the accumulated burdens of family economic hardship—without adequate adult support" (Center on the Developing Brain, https://developingchild.harvard.edu). This kind of prolonged activation of the stress response systems can be devastating for the child as it can disrupt the development of the brain's architecture and other organ systems, including an increased risk for stress-related disease and cognitive impairment well into the adult years.

When a person is experiencing stress, scholars have identified that "general adaptation syndrome" occurs (Selye 1956). This syndrome includes three stages. During the first stage, the stress causes the hypothalamus gland to secrete a biochemical product that causes the pituitary gland to create the adrenocorticotropic hormone. This hormone creates a rush of adrenaline and corticoids that has the effect of shrinking the thymus and accelerating the heart rate, elevating blood pressure, respiration rate, and more. These physical effects lead to the second stage popularly known as the "fight or flight" response (Cannon 1914; Malchiodi 2008). During the Paleolithic period, this process was helpful for humans at times of physical danger when confronting an enemy, hunting, or facing a ferocious animal. Now the body experiences the same process of stress, but rather than physical causes the stress is emotional and mental. The final stage is exhaustion, which occurs when there is continuous exposure to the same or similar stressors (Malchiodi 2008).

51 Landale et al. 2015.
52 Potochnick 2010.
53 Shonkoff et al. 2012, 236.
54 Shonkoff et al. 2012, 236.
55 Mallett 2017.
56 Allen et al. 2014; Bonstingl 2002; Giroux 2009.
57 Mallett 2017.
58 Benson 1975.
59 Malchiodi 2008.
60 Davidson et al. 2003.
61 Malchiodi 2008.
62 Michaesu & Baettig 1996.
63 Malchiodi 2008.
64 Kellermann & Hudgins 2000.
65 Pine & Cohen 2002.
66 Masten et al. 1990, 425.
67 Malchiodi 2008.
68 Above-average verbal communication skills, cognitive abilities and problem-solving abilities. Positive beliefs about self and the future. Stable, nurturing parent or caregiver and extended family and supportive, positive school experiences. Consistent family environment, such as family traditions, rituals, and/or struc-

tured routines. Strong cultural connections and cultural identity. In a way similar to resilience, children can harness posttraumatic growth. Some of the characteristics include feeling more compassion and empathy for others after trauma or loss; increased psychological and emotional maturity when compared to similar-age peers; increased resilience; a more complex appreciation of life when compared to similar-age peers; a deeper understanding of personal values, purpose, and meaning in life; and a greater value placed on interpersonal relationships (Cloitre et al. 2005; Rice & Groves, 2005; & Malchiodi 2008).

69 Masten et al. 2008.

70 Masten 2011 in Flores-Rojas 2017; Rutter 1979.

71 Center on the Developing Child 2018.

72 Kellogg 1969.

73 Johnson, Pfister, & Vindrola-Padros 2012.

74 Bermudez & Maat 2006; Dreby & Adkins 2011; Linesch, Aceves, Quezada, Trochez, & Zuniga 2012; Rousseau, Drapeau, Lacroix, Bagilishya, & Heusch 2005; Rousseau & Heusch 2000; Smokowski & Bacallao 2011.

75 Smokowski & Bacallao 2011.

76 Dreby & Adkins 2011.

77 Marsh 2017.

78 Hudson 2020.

79 Solorzano & Delgado-Bernal 2001.

80 Hannegan-Martinez et. al. 2022.

81 Shaw 2017.

82 Yosso 2005.

83 Delgado Bernal 1998; Ladson-Billings 2000.

84 *Rasquachismo* is "brash and hybrid, sending shudders through the ranks of the elite who seek solace in less exuberant, more muted and 'purer' traditions. . . . In an environment always on the edge of coming apart (the car, the job, the toilet) things are held together with spit, grit, and movidas. Movidas are whatever coping strategies you use to gain time, to make options to retain hope" (Ybarra-Frausto 1989, 5).

85 Shonkoff et al. 2012.

86 For more information, visit the Arizona Department of Education website.

87 Initially, the purpose of collecting these drawings was not to conduct research. It was not until graduate school in 2010 that I became academically interested in my work with the youth in the community centers and decided to utilize these documents (with the permission of the nonprofit) to conduct a secondary data analysis, which would eventually be available to the public and provide a glimpse into this overlooked but important aspect of immigrant life in Arizona.

88 Zhou 1997; Suarez-Orozco et al. 2009; Yoshikawa 2011.

89 Tseng 2004; Abrego 2006; Ziol-Guest & Kalil 2012.

90 Diver-Stamnes 1995.

91 Lewis et al. 2011.

92 Watts is also the site of the Watts Uprising in 1965 and one of the uprising sites in 1992 that stemmed from the police beating of Rodney King. Although the beating was caught on film, the police officers in the video were found not guilty, leading to massive fires and riots for a period of six days. It is estimated that over $1 billion in damages occurred during that week (Walker 2016). Over 2,000 people were injured, 12,000 were arrested, and 63 died. The chaos prompted the federal government to "restore order" by sending in the National Guard. The chief of the Los Angeles Police Department subsequently retired, but discriminatory and racist policies persisted (Walker 2016). Until this day, the problems that led to the riots have not been addressed or resolved and thus continue to affect children growing up in South Central Los Angeles.

93 Behrens 2011.

94 Mapping L.A. 2000.

95 Adair & Colegrove 2021.

96 Zhou 1997; Suárez-Orozco & Suárez-Orozco 2009; Yoshikawa 2011.

97 Abrego 2006; Tseng 2006; Ziol-Guest & Kalil 2012.

98 Du Bois 1903; Anzaldúa 1987; Chavez 1991; Zavella 2011; Lynn Stephen 2007.

99 Zavella 2011.

1. POLICIES

1 Chaudry et al. 2010.

2 Capps 2007.

3 Shahani & Greene 2009.

4 De Genova & Peutz 2010, 102.

5 De Genova & Peutz 2010.

6 De Genova & Peutz 2010.

7 Kandel & Massey 2002.

8 Guerin-Gonzales 1994.

9 Tichenor 2009.

10 Ngai 2014.

11 Ngai 2014, 132.

12 Ngai 2014, 143.

13 Bean et al. 1989.

14 Ngai 2014, 147.

15 Ngai 2014.

16 Ngai 2014, 155. In the first three months 170,000 people were apprehended and from 1953 to 1955, 801,069 Mexican migrants were deported.

17 Massey & Pren 2012.

18 Ngai 2014.

19 Massey & Pren 2012.

20 Ngai 2014, 266.

21 De Genova 2002, 2004; Kandel & Massey 2002; Ngai 1999, 2014.

22 Massey et al. 2002.

23 Cornelius 2001.

24 On March 1, 2003, INS (Immigration and Naturalization Services) became ICE (Immigration and Customs Enforcement).

25 Slack et al. 2013.

26 Motomura 2006.

27 Although there is an increasing use of the term crimmigration as put forth in the groundbreaking work of Stumpf (2006) to describe the way the criminal and immigration legal systems have become intertwined, I purposefully resist this term so as to not continue to normalize the linguistic linkage that continues to normalize the criminalization of immigrants. For more on this topic, see Abrego et al. 2017.

28 Hagan et al. 2009.

29 Kerwin 2018.

30 Kerwin 2018, 193.

31 Abrego et. al. 2017.

32 Eagly 2010.

33 Torres-Rivas 1998.

34 Another historical aspect of the US-Mexico border that is important to note is the way slavery and broken treaties factored into what we know today as California, Arizona, Texas, and the southwestern region of the US in general, which is the locus of this book. After Spanish and English colonists and their descendants settled in what is known today as Mexico and the US, the border between these lands shifted multiple times, especially during the first half of the 18th century. Native Americans who had always cared for these lands now were the primary threat to settlers, both Spanish Mexicans and Americans. With this in mind, Mexico made the northern territory available to American settlers in hopes that populating sparse northern lands would keep Natives from taking over. Yet this plan would eventually fail as exemplified in the many forms that Texas would take as a Mexican territory, an independent nation, and ultimately an American border state.

Aside from Native American retaliation, slavery was a majorly contested issue along what we now know as the US-Mexico border, particularly in Texas. In 1830 what was part of the Mexican territory of Coahuila y Tejas was a land previously open to American settlers on the conditions that they would learn to speak Spanish, convert to Catholicism, become Mexican citizens, and, perhaps most importantly, stop enslaving people. Yet, with so much land for profitable cotton fields and with the Mexican capital so far removed from this northern territory, Americans did not uphold the terms they agreed to, and in fact, continued to enslave Black people, remained Protestant, and spoke English.

Since Mexico abolished slavery before the Americans did, enslaved people used a southern escape route from American plantations into Mexican territory where they could find freedom. This created a community of Black Mexicans that would become integrated into communities of Afro-Tejanos who settled after arriving with Spanish conquistadors from Cuba. Later in 1830, when Mexico became aware of the outlawed slavery being practiced in Texas, it halted immigration by American settlers, eventually leading to the armed conflict of the US-Mexico war and the infamous battle of the Alamo won by the Mexican army. However, the war was lost when then-Mexican president Antonio Lopez de Santa Ana was captured and ceded almost half of the Mexican territory to the Americans including Texas, giving birth to the Treaty of Guadalupe Hidalgo in 1848. Yet, despite winning the war, Texas was ousted from what became the US because it refused to relinquish its ties to slavery, leading to a ten-year period where Texas was its own independent nation. Eventually, Texas was forced to abolish slavery after the Civil War.

It is important to have a historical lens when looking at the very contested, imagined, and reimagined terrain that is the US-Mexico border, as children and families who have long lived on this continent, even before the colonial invasion, continue to traverse these lands for purposes of survival. Even today this land is contested not only directly by people but also by the cementing of differences with walls and barbed wire.

35 McDowell & Wonders 2010; Summers Sandoval 2008.
36 Chavez et al. 2019; Dreby 2012b; Rodriguez Vega 2018a, 2019.
37 Michaud 2010.
38 Szkupinski Quiroga et al. 2014.
39 Campbell 2011.
40 Szkupinski Quiroga et al. 2014.
41 O'Leary & Sanchez 2011.
42 Berk & Schur 2001; Menjívar 2006; Menjívar & Abrego 2012.
43 Lacey 2011.
44 Brown 2018.
45 Gerstein 2020.
46 Lacey & Seelye 2011.
47 Welch 2019.
48 Lacayo 2011; Szkupinski Quiroga et al. 2014.
49 Gonzalez et al. 2020.
50 Nava 2014; Rumbaut et al. 2018.
51 G. Thompson & Cohen 2014.
52 Hing 2018.
53 Goodman 2020.
54 Hagan et al. 2009.
55 Hagan et al. 2009.
56 Shahani & Greene 2009.
57 Chacón & Davis 2006.
58 Doty & Wheatley 2013.
59 Menjivar et al. 2018.
60 Shahani & Greene 2009, 50.

61 Immigrant Detention Primer 2021.

62 Herrington & Llp 2009, 14.

63 The 72-hour limit comes from the Trafficking Victims Protection Reauthorization Act (TVPRA) of 2008. Referring to the detention of children in Customs and Border Protection (CBP) custody, it mandates their transfer to Office of Refugee Resettlement (ORR) shelters within that period. The Flores Settlement Agreement dates to 1997; it requires children to be released promptly to approved sponsors and held in the least restrictive setting, and sets forth detailed regulations on the humane treatment of children in custody.

64 Martin 2012.

65 Boehm & Terrio 2019; Heidbrink 2014, 2020; Terrio 2015; Zatz & Rodriguez 2015.

66 Provisions of the 2010 and 2017 Dream Acts and DACA 2017 see National Immigration Law Center. (2017).

67 Gonzales, Terriquez, & Ruszczyk 2014.

68 Abrego 2018.

69 Williams & Edelman 2020.

70 Pierce & Bolter 2020.

71 Miller & Nevins 2017.

72 BBC News 2021. Although at the start of his presidency Joe Biden halted border wall constructions, as of 2022, the Biden administration has decided that closing the gaps on the border wall in Yuma, Arizona, is a priority.

73 Bohmer & Shuman 2007.

74 Pierce, Bolter, & Selee 2018.

75 ACLU 2020.

76 Temporary Protected Status 2020.

77 Waters & Pineau 2016.

78 Aleinikoff 2018; Abrego 2018.

79 Ainsley 2019.

80 Asylum eligibility and procedural modifications 2019.

81 Cho, Cullen, & Long 2020.

82 American Immigration Lawyers Association 2020.

83 Muzaffar, Pierce, & O'Connor 2019.

84 Jordan 2019.

85 Levin 2019; Mishori 2020.

86 U.S. Immigration and Customs Enforcement 2020.

87 Cho 2020.

88 BBC News 2021; Alvarez 2021.

89 Marcelo & Herbert 2021.

90 Reilly & Carlisle 2019.

91 Long & Taxin 2019; Phippen 2016.

92 Jordan 2019.

93 Waddoups, Yoshikawa, & Strouf 2019.

94 Kandel 2018.

95 Da Silva 2019.

96 Ramkhelawan 2019.
97 Rotella et al. 2019.
98 Singh 2019.
99 Pierce & Bolter 2020.
100 Dalton 2019.
101 Nowlin 2020.
102 BBC News 2021.
103 Totenberg 2022.
104 Acevedo & Kaplan 2020.
105 Kanno-Young 2020.
106 Alamillo et al. 2019; Haynes & Sattler 2017.
107 BBC News 2021 Twitter Perm Suspends.
108 Saresma et. al. 2021.
109 Hodwitz & Massingale 2021.
110 Yam 2021.
111 Villarreal 2020.
112 Chavez et al. 2019; Menjivar et al. 2018; Sheehy 2016.
113 Gomez Cervantes et. al. 2018, 182.
114 Santa Ana 2002.
115 Adelman et al. 2017; Chavez et al. 2019; Gomez Cervantes et al. 2018.
116 Menjívar et al. 193.
117 Chavez 2013; Rivera 2014; Santa Ana 2002.
118 Silber Mohamed & Farris 2019.
119 Farris & Silber Mohamed 2018.
120 Chavez et. al. 2019.
121 Cacho 2012.
122 Morgane 1970.
123 Hansen 2015.

2. FEAR

1 Ayers 2013; Cervantes et al. 2018.
2 Dreby 2012c.
3 O'Leary & Sanchez, 2011.
4 Crenshaw & Peller 1992; Patton 1992.
5 Bornstein, Domingo, & Solis 2012.
6 Cervantes et al. 2018; Chaudry et al. 2010; Dreby 2012a.
7 Lacey 2011.
8 Rendón-García (2019).
9 Santos et al. 2017.
10 Bourdieu 1998; Menjívar & Abrego 2012.
11 Pavlakovich-Kochi 2006; Castañeda Pérez 2022; Vélez-Ibáñez & Szecsy 2014.
12 Abrego 2009, 2014.
13 Becerra et al. 2020; Becerra et al. 2017.
14 Hernandez 2010.

15 Passel & Taylor 2010.

16 Walters & Cornelisse 2010.

17 A coyote is a person undocumented immigrants hire to help them cross into the US. Coyotes are usually familiar with popular routes, dangers, and strategies for survival.

18 Theater of the Oppressed grew to become a powerful tool for community empowerment that both posed problems to be solved and blurred the lines between spectator and actor by creating what Boal called spect-actors. Everyone has been and is an actor in the issues facing the people. In the middle of the skits, a character known as the joker would freeze the play and invite the audience to offer another solution or to get on stage and embody their own character to act out their solutions to issues like illiteracy, governmental repression, labor abuses, and racism. Theater of the Oppressed has the following four goals: (1) to analyze the root causes of the situation, (2) to include both internal and external sources of oppression, (3) to explore group solutions for problems, and (4) through praxis—theory in action—to change the situation. Freire and Boal concur on the importance of dialogue and imagining a better outcome to current societal issues. Theater of the Oppressed encompasses six different types of theater, including: Image Theater, Forum Theater, Invisible Theater, Newspaper Theater, Rainbow of Desire, and Legislative Theater, all of which are influenced by solidarity, economy, philosophy, ethics, history, politics, and multiplication. Notably, Legislative Theater was created with the goal of working in communities to address important problems at the city level. Boal used didactic theater to talk about types of legislation that would benefit the community. The result was not only that policies were adopted to address public needs, but also that Boal was also elected to office as a legislator. Boal was an ARTivist who saw theater as a tool, a weapon of liberation. He visited communities experiencing an array of issues and gave them the tools to work through their own problems in a way that was sustainable and made sense to the particular community. After Boal's visits, the participants were fully versed in Theater of the Oppressed and continued to run workshops and forums. Years after his death in 2009, Theater of the Oppressed is still used by educators who work in a variety of settings and issues, such as healthcare, K–12 schools, and many college campuses around the world. Community organizers and local groups globally have created worldwide and regional conferences where people meet to talk about their experiences with Theater of the Oppressed and its applicability in multiple settings. See Boal, *Theatre of the Oppressed*.

19 Eschbach et al. 1999.

20 Bergmark et al. 2010; E. P. Macias & Morales 2001; Wallace, Mendez-Luck, & Castañeda 2009.

21 Dreby 2012c.

22 *Trompas* translated into English means horn, snout, mouth, lips, or blubber lips. Perhaps students had heard parents refer to Trump as Trompas, using this witty play on words. It calls attention to the lip movements and gestures that Trump

employs when he speaks, but it also importantly satirizes his statements as coming from an animal, as a snout indicates a body part of a pig or animalistic creature. Lastly, it connotes someone who is talking to just speak without having intelligible things to say, like a blabbermouth.

23 Image Theater is one of the styles of Theater of the Oppressed. It uses the body to create frozen images that can represent issues facing the participants or viewers. Through the molding of images, participants can gain depth and visual understanding of those issues. Images can also be made to represent solutions to problems people might be trying to solve. There is also a way to activate images by adding voice or sounds to each of the frozen participants. Those on the outside looking at the image can treat it like a gallery of sorts, where one can pay attention to the ways people create body positions, dynamics, facial expressions, and relationships between other images or frozen statues. In the end, the image looks like a photograph capturing an important message. This style of theater proved very useful in inspiring children's imaginations and brainstorming. (Boal, 1985/1979/2000, 137).

24 Leader of one of the most influential and powerful narcotrafficking organizations, the Sinaloa Cartel. The year before the start of data collection at the school, authorities raided El Chapo's home in Mazatlán Sinaloa, Mexico, and detained him in a high-security Mexican prison from which he escaped through the construction of a tunnel. Children were very enthralled by this news story and often talked about it.

25 Bouvier & Gardner 1986.

26 Armenta, From sheriff's deputies to immigration officers; Armenta, *Protect, serve, and deport*; Vitello, Path to deportation.

27 Foucault 2012; Piro 2008.

28 Foucault 1984; Reas 2009.

29 Cházaro 2015; Negrón-Gonzales, Abrego, & Coll 2015; Rodriguez Vega 2017.

3. RESPONSE

1 Lukinbeal & Sharp 2015.

2 See appendix for a full list of frequency codes and reports from Arizona.

3 Andrews 2017.

4 Carola Suárez-Orozco & Marcelo Suárez-Orozco 2009.

5 Robert F. Berkhofer 2011; Malhotra 2009.

6 Passed by the Arizona legislature in April 2010, SB1070 made it a state crime to be in the US illegally and empowered police officers engaged in a lawful stop, detention or arrest to ask about a person's legal status when reasonable suspicion existed that the person was in the US illegally; Aguirre 2012.

7 Enriquez 2015

8 Balderrama & Rodriguez 2006; Hoffman 1974.

9 Hernandez 2010; Lilian Jiménez 2011.

10 Greene 2013; Jiménez 2011.

11 Golash-Boza 2015; Robertson & Manta 2019; Wessler 2018.

12 hooks 2001; Virost 1986, 29. (hooks quotes Virost in *All About Love*.)

13 Rodríguez 2014, 35.

14 Burner 1993; Christle & Yell 2008.

15 Alexander 2012.

4. RESISTANCE

1 Barajas-Gonzalez et al. 2018.

2 Seifert 2003.

3 Forth et. al. 2003, in Grisso, Vincent, & Seagrave 2005; Hrynkiw-Augimeri 1998; Seifert 2006; Seifert & Ray 2012.

4 Chavez et al.2019; Roche et al. 2018.; Suárez-Orozco & Suárez-Orozco 2000.

5 Suárez-Orozco & Quin 2006.

6 Coe, Harmon, Verner, & Tonn 1993; Covey 2010; Flores 2016.

7 Anderson 1999.

8 Crenshaw & Peller 1992.

9 Bornstein et al. 2012.

10 Giroux 2018, 102.

11 Welch 2017, 105.

12 Cotton & Range 1990.

13 Seifert 2003.

14 Speece & Brent 1984.

15 Suárez-Orozco et al. 2009.

16 As noted in the introduction, Trump's social media accounts including Twitter have been deactivated as they were deemed a danger to others.

17 Giroux 2017.

18 Suárez-Orozco et al. 2009.

19 Abajian 2013.

20 Mariscal 2010.

21 Huerta 2016

22 Cook et al. 1996.

23 Abajian 2013.

24 Kort-Butler 2012.

25 Demjén 2016.

26 Portilla 1966; Broyles-González 1994.

27 El Teatro Campesino was founded by Luis Valdez in 1965 on the picket lines of the United Farm Workers movement and used theater to organize, inform, and empower farmworkers alongside Cesar Chavez, Dolores Huerta, and the UFW members.

28 *Actos* were short skits performed by UFW members on the picket lines and on the backs of trucks driving through farm working fields to inform and organize farm workers. Their goal was to: (1) inspire the audience to social action; (2) illuminate specific points about social problems; (3) satirize the opposition; (4) show or hint at a solution; and (5) express what people are feeling.

29 *Carpa* was a Mexican theater style popularized in the 1920s and 30s where comedy, satire, political commentary, and vaudeville-style acts were performed in large tents. The tradition of *carpa* theater was made popular by the great comedian Cantinflas; it also served as a counterhegemonic tool of the disenfranchised against the oppressor (Broyles-González 1994, 7).

30 Memory as a tool for theater is indeed the cultural storehouse; with the human body, it constitutes the central vehicle of cultural transmission for oral histories. Both cultural identity and cultural survival within oral culture depend on memory. See Broyles-González

31 Broyles-González 1994.

32 Huerta 1977.

33 Fielder 2014.

34 Hopkins 1994.

35 Cleaver 1970.

36 Belur 2010; Uildriks & Van Mastrigt 1991.

37 Becerra et al. 2020; Nava 2014; Szkupinski Quiroga et al. 2014.

38 Kandel & Massey 2002.

5. RESILIENCE

1 Freire (2018) believed that he needed to teach people how to read the world, first, before teaching them how to read words (Santos 2019). The goal of knowing how systems of oppression created the oppressive conditions is achieved through what he calls *conscientização* or conscientization. Conscientization is the process of developing critical awareness of society through reflection and action. The action component is an important part of what creates praxis. Praxis is at the nexus of action and theory/reflection, where knowledge for the sake of knowledge is not the goal but rather a call to change the situation.

2 Malchiodi 2008.

3 Toxic stress is defined as the extreme, frequent, or extended activation of the stress response that causes distress for the child and may lead to negative psychological and physical health outcomes (Cohen et al. 2002; Hornor 2015; Johnson et al. 2013; Porges 1995; Schaaf et al. 2003).

4 Hinnant & El-Sheikh 2009.

5 Fondren et al. 2020.

6 Southwick et al. 2005.

7 King 1963.

8 King 1968.

9 Albritton 2015; Broyles-González 1994; Espinosa 2007; Guerra 2016; Mendel-Reyes 1994.

10 Most notably, this is the place where uprisings occurred in the 1960s and '90s. Reminders of that era are painted in murals around the community, and police brutality is made ever visible as children grow up during the Black Lives Matter movement.

11 Felker-Kantor 2018.
12 Casillas 2014.
13 Giroux 2018; H. A. Giroux 2017; Gonzalez 2012; Love 2016, 2019; Tuck & Yang 2011; Valencia 2004; Valenzuela 2005; Welch 2017.
14 Hornor 2015.
15 Love 2019.
16 Orellana et al. 2001; Orellana 2001, 2009, 2015.
17 de los Rios 2017; Garcia 2009.
18 Navarro 1998.
19 Sandoval 2000.
20 In this space, Anzaldúa (1987) asserts, I challenge the collective cultural/religious male derived beliefs of Indo-Hispanics and Anglos; yet I am cultured because I am participating in the creation of yet another culture, a new story to explain the world and our participation in it, a new value system with images and symbols that connect us to each other and to the planet. See also Homi Bhabha (1994) and Rosaldo (1989).
21 Quoted in hooks 1996, 59.
22 Butler 2017; Brown 2017.
23 Appadurai 2000.
24 Appadurai 1996.
25 Appadurai 2000, 6.
26 hooks 2001, 20.

CONCLUSION

1 hooks & Mesa-Bains 2017, 54.
2 Yoshikawa 2011.
3 Passel, Cohn, & Lopez 2011; Rong & Preissle 1998.
4 Rodriguez Vega 2018b, 2019.
5 Massey et al. 2002.
6 Yoshikawa 2011.
7 Mehta & Fine 2019.
8 Cariaga 2018, 2019; Hannegan-Martinez, 2020.
9 See Pierce & Bolter 2020 for a fuller recent accounting of these policies.
10 Cervantes et al. 2018; MacLean et al. 2019.
11 Medina & Menjívar 2015.
12 Summarized in Durand & Massey 2019.
13 MacLean et al. 2019; Boehm & Terrio 2019; Heidbrink 2020; Mayers & Freedman 2019; Terrio 2015.
14 Bellows 2019.
15 Yoshikawa, Suárez-Orozco, & Gonzales 2017.

APPENDIX

1 Chavez 2001; Santa Ana 2002; Rodriguez Vega 2018 a & b.
2 Smith-Maddox & Solorzano 2002.

3 Boal 2005.

4 Bean et. al. 2015.

5 Greenberg & Harris 2012.

6 Frank & Schrobenhauser-Clonan 2014; Harnett & Dawe 2012.

7 Boal 1979, 137.

8 Huerta 1977.

9 Huerta 1977

10 Huerta 1977.

11 Valdez 1990.

12 Rodriguez Vega 2018 a & b.

13 Straus & Corbin 1998; Ryan & Bernard 2003.

BIBLIOGRAPHY

Abajian, S. M. (2013). Drill and ceremony: A case study of militarism, military recruitment and the pedagogy of enforcement in an urban school in southern California. UCLA, escholarship.org.

Abrego, L. (2006). I can't go to college because I don't have papers: Incorporation patterns of Latino undocumented youth. *Latino Studies, 4*(3), 212-231.

Abrego, L. (2009). Economic well-being in Salvadoran transnational families: How gender affects remittance practices. *Journal of Marriage and Family, 71*(4), 1070–1085.

Abrego, L. (2014). *Sacrificing families: Navigating laws, labor, and love across borders.* Stanford University Press.

Abrego, L. (2018). Renewed optimism and spatial mobility: Legal consciousness of Latino Deferred Action for Childhood Arrivals recipients and their families in Los Angeles. *Ethnicities, 18*(2), 192–207.

Abrego, L., Coleman, M., Martínez, D. E., Menjívar, C., & Slack, J. (2017). Making immigrants into criminals: Legal processes of criminalization in the post-IIRIRA era. *Journal on Migration and Human Security, 5*(3), 694–715.

Acevedo, N., & Kaplan, A. (2020, February 5). Hundreds deported from U.S. to El Salvador have been killed or abused, new report says. NBC News. https://www.nbcnews.com.

Adair, J. K., and Colegrove, K. S.-S. (2021). *Segregation by experience: Agency, racism, and learning in the early grades.* University of Chicago Press.

Adelman, R., Reid, L. W., Markle, G., Weiss, S., & Jaret, C. (2017). Urban crime rates and the changing face of immigration: Evidence across four decades. *Journal of Ethnicity in Criminal Justice, 15*(1), 52–77.

Aguirre, A. (2012). Arizona's SB1070, Latino immigrants and the framing of anti-immigrant policies. *Latino Studies, 10*(3), 385–394.

Ainsley, J. (2019). Miller wants border agents to screen migrants to lower asylum numbers. NBC News. https://www.nbcnews.com, July 30.

Alamillo, R., Haynes, C., & Madrid, R. (2019). Framing and immigration through the Trump era. *Sociology Compass, 13*(5), e12676.

Albritton, L. W. (2015). *"Que Viva la Virgen de Guadalupe!": Documenting Guadalupan devotion along the US-Mexico border.* University of Texas at Dallas.

Aleinikoff, D. M., & Faye Hipsman, T. Alexander. (2018). The U.S. asylum system in crisis: Charting a way forward. Migration Policy Institute.

Alexander, M. (2012). *The new Jim Crow: Mass incarceration in the age of colorblindness*. New Press.

Allen, Q., & White-Smith, K. A. (2014). "Just as Bad as Prisons": The Challenge of Dismantling the School-to-Prison Pipeline Through Teacher and Community Education. *Equity & Excellence in Education*, 47(4), 445–460.

Alvarez, P. (2021). Biden administration to close two immigration detention centers that came under scrutiny. CNN, https://www.cnn.com, May 20.

American Civil Liberties Union. (2020). International Refugee Assistance Project v. Trump—Supreme Court opinion. https://www.aclu.org/legal-document/international-refugee-assistance-project-v-trump-supreme-court-opinion

American Friends Service Committee. (2020). Trump has ended Temporary Protected Status for hundreds of thousands of immigrants. Here's what you need to know. [Blog]. https://www.afsc.org/blogs/news-and-commentary/trump-has-ended-temporary-protected-status-hundreds-thousands-immigrants

American Immigration Lawyers Association. (2020). Deaths in adult detention centers (AILA Doc. No. 16050900). https://www.aila.org/infonet/deaths-at-adult-detention-centers

Anderson, E. (1999). *Code of the street: Decency, violence, and the moral life of the inner city*. W. W. Norton.

Andrews, T. (2017). The Uncle Sam "I Want YOU" poster is 100 years old. Almost everything about it was borrowed. Washington Post, https://www.washingtonpost.com, April 3.

Anzaldúa, G. E. (1987). *Borderlands: La frontera* (Vol. 3). San Francisco, CA: Aunt Lute.

Appadurai, A. (1996). *Modernity Al Large: Cultural Dimensions of Globalization*. University of Minnesota Press.

Appadurai, A. (2000). Grassroots Globalization and the Research Imagination. *Public Culture*, 12(1), 1–19.

Armenta, A. (2012). From sheriff's deputies to immigration officers: Screening immigrant status in a Tennessee jail. *Law & Policy*, 34(2), 191–210.

Armenta, A. (2017). *Protect, serve, and deport: The rise of policing as immigration enforcement*. University of California Press.

Asylum eligibility and procedural modifications (2019, July 16). Federal Register, https://www.federalregister.gov.

Atkin, E. (2018, June 20). The uncertain fate of migrant children sent to foster care. New Republic, https://newrepublic.com.

Ayers, E. (2013, April 15). Is there trauma and resilience in adolescents who experienced immigration raids? An annotated bibliography of research. Digital Commons @ EMU, Senior Honors Theses & Projects, commons.emich.edu.

Ayón, C. (2018). Immigrants in the U.S.: Detention, discrimination, and intervention. *Race and Social Problems*, 10(4), 273–274.

Balderrama, F. E., & Rodriguez, R. (2006). *Decade of betrayal: Mexican repatriation in the 1930s*. University of New Mexico Press.

Barajas-Gonzalez, R. G., Ayón, C., & Torres, F. (2018). Applying a community violence framework to understand the impact of immigration enforcement threat on Latino children. *Social Policy Report, 31*(3), 1–24.

BBC News. (2021, November 17). What are President Biden's challenges at the border? https://www.bbc.com/news/world-us-canada-56255613

BBC News. (2021, January 9). Twitter "permanently suspends" Trump's account. https://www.bbc.com/news/world-us-canada-55597840

Bean, C. N., Kendellen, K., Halsall, T., & Forneris, T. (2015). Putting program evaluation into practice: Enhancing the Girls Just Wanna Have Fun program. *Evaluation and Program Planning, 49*, 31–40.

Bean, F. D., Schmandt, J., & Weintraub, S. (1989). Mexican and Central American population and US immigration policy. Center for Mexican American Studies, University of Texas.

Becerra, D., Hernandez, G., Porchas, F., Castillo, J., Nguyen, V., & González, R. P. (2020). Immigration policies and mental health: Examining the relationship between immigration enforcement and depression, anxiety, and stress among Latino immigrants. *Journal of Ethnic & Cultural Diversity in Social Work, 29*(1-3), 1–17.

Becerra, D., Wagaman, M. A., Androff, D., Messing, J., & Castillo, J. (2017). Policing immigrants: Fear of deportations and perceptions of law enforcement and criminal justice. *Journal of Social Work, 17*(6), 715–731.

Belur, J. (2010). *Permission to shoot? Police use of deadly force in democracies.* Springer.

Bellows, L. (2019). Immigration enforcement and student achievement in the wake of secure communities. *AERA Open, 5*(4), 1–20.

Benson, H. (1975). *The relaxation response: Psychophysiologic aspects and clinical applications.* New York: Morrow.

Bergmark, R., Barr, D., & Garcia, R. (2010). Mexican immigrants in the US living far from the border may return to Mexico for health services. *Journal of Immigrant and Minority Health, 12*(4), 610–614.

Berk, M. L., & Schur, C. L. (2001). The Effect of Fear on Access to Care Among Undocumented Latino Immigrants. *Journal of Immigrant Health, 3*(3), 151–156.

Berkhofer, R. F. (2011). *The white man's Indian: Images of the American Indian from Columbus to the present.* Vintage.

Bermudez, D. & Maat, M. (2006). Art therapy with Hispanic clients: Results of a survey
study. *Art Therapy, 23(4),* 165-171.

Bhabha, H. K. (1994). *The location of culture.* UK: Routledge.

Boal, A. (1985/1979/2000). *Theatre of the Oppressed* (C. A. & M.-O. Leal McBride, Trans.). Theatre Communications Group.

Boal, A. (2005). *Games for actors and non-actors.* Routledge.

Bohmer, C., & Shuman, A. (2007). *Rejecting refugees: Political asylum in the 21st century.* Routledge.

Boehm, D. A., & Terrio, S. J. (2019). *Illegal encounters: The effect of detention and deportation on young people.* NYU Press.

Bornstein, A., Charles, S., Domingo, J., & Solis, C. (2012). Critical race theory meets the NYPD: An assessment of anti-racist pedagogy for police in New York City. *Journal of Criminal Justice Education*, *23*(2), 174–204.

Bonstingl, J. J. (2002). Expanding Learning Potential for All Students. *Leadership*, *32*(2), 8–11.

Bourdieu, P. (1998). *Practical reason: On the theory of action.* Stanford University Press.

Bouvier, L. F., & Gardner, R. W. (1986). Immigration to the U.S.: The unfinished story. ERIC, Population Bulletin, https://eric.ed.gov/?id=ED278738, November.

Briggs, L. (2020). *Taking children: A history of American terror* (1st ed). University of California Press.

Broyles-González, Y. (1994). *El Teatro Campesino: Theater in the Chicano movement.* University of Texas Press.

Brown, A. M. (2017). *Emergent Strategy: Shaping change, Changing Worlds*, AK Press.

Brown, A. M. (2019). *Pleasure Activism: The politics of feeling good.* AK Press.

Brown, T. (2018). The court can't even handle me right now: The Arpaio pardon and its effect on the scope of presidential pardons notes & comments. *Pepperdine Law Review*, *46*(2), 331–366.

Brunner, M. S. (1993). Reduced recidivism and increased employment opportunity through research-based reading instruction. U.S. Department of Education.

Butler, O. E. (2017). *Kindred: A graphic novel adaptation.* Abrams.

Cacho, L. M. (2012). *Social death: Racialized rightlessness and the criminalization of the unprotected* (Vol. 7). NYU Press.

Campbell, K. M. (2011). The road to S.B. 1070: How Arizona became ground zero for the immigrants' rights movement and the continuing struggle for Latino civil rights in America. *Harvard Latino Law Review*, *14*(1), 1–22.

Cannon, W. B. (1914). The emergency function of the adrenal medulla in pain and the major emotions. *American Journal of Physiology-Legacy Content*, *33*(2), 356-372.

Capps, R. (2007). Paying the price: The impact of immigration raids on Americas Children. The Urban Institute, 1-109.

Cariaga, S. (2019). Towards Self-Recovery: Cultivating Love with Young Women of Color Through Pedagogies of Bodymindspirit. *The Urban Review*, *51*(1), 101–122.

Cariaga, S. M. (2018). *Pedagogies of wholeness: Cultivating critical healing literacies with students of color in an embodied English classroom* (Doctoral dissertation, UCLA).

Casillas, D. I. (2014). *Sounds of belonging: U.S. Spanish-language radio and public advocacy.* NYU Press.

Castañeda Pérez, E. (2022). Transborder (in) securities: transborder commuters' perceptions of US Customs and Border Protection policing at the Mexico–US border. *Politics, Groups, and Identities*, *10*(1), 1-20.

Center on the Developing Child. (2018). Resilience. Harvard University. Retrieved from https://developingchild.harvard.edu/science/key-concepts/resilience/

Cervantes, W., Ullrich, R., & Matthews, H. (2018). Our children's fear: Immigration policy's effects on young children. ERIC, Center for Law and Social Policy, https://eric.ed.gov.

Chacón, J. A., & Davis, M. (2006). *No one is illegal: Fighting violence and state repression on the U.S.-Mexico border*. Haymarket Books.

Chaudry, A., Capps, R., Pedroza, J. M., Castaneda, R. M., Santos, R., & Scott, M. M. (2010). Facing our future: Children in the aftermath of immigration enforcement. ERIC, Urban Institute, https://eric.ed.gov.

Chavez, L. R. (1991). Outside the imagined community: Undocumented settlers and experiences of incorporation. *American Ethnologist, 18*(2), 257–278.

Chavez, L. R. (2001). *Covering immigration: Popular images and the politics of the nation*. University of California Press.

Chavez, L. R. (2013). *The Latino Threat: Constructing Immigrants, Citizens, and the Nation, Second Edition*. Stanford University Press.

Chavez, L. R., Campos, B., Corona, K., Sanchez, D., & Ruiz, C. B. (2019). Words hurt: Political rhetoric, emotions/affect, and psychological well-being among Mexican-origin youth. *Social Science & Medicine, 228*, 240–251.

Cházaro, A. (2015). Beyond respectability: New principles for immigration reform. Social Science Research Network, https://papers.ssrn.com, September 27.

Christle, C. A., & Yell, M. L. (2008). Preventing youth incarceration through reading remediation: Issues and solutions. *Reading & Writing Quarterly, 24*(2), 148–176.

Cleaver, E. (1970). On the ideology of the Black Panther Party. Freedom Marches, https://www.freedomarchives.org.

Cloitre, M., Miranda, R., Stovall-McClough, K. C. & Han, H. (2005). Beyond PTSD: Emotion regulation and interpersonal problems as predictors of functional impairment in survivors of childhood abuse. *Behaviour Therapy, 36*(2), 119-124.

Cohen, J., Perel, J. M., Debellis, M. D., Friedman, M. J., & Putnam, F. W. (2002). Treating traumatized children: Clinical implications of the psychobiology of posttraumatic stress disorder. *Trauma, Violence, & Abuse, 3*(2), 91–108.

Cho, E. H. (2020, January 14). *The Trump administration weakens standards for ICE detention facilities*. American Civil Liberties Union. https://www.aclu.org/news/immigrants-rights/the-trump-administration-weakens-standards-for-ice-detention-facilities/

Cho, E. H., Cullen, T. T., & Long, C. (2020). *Justice-free zones: U.S. immigrant detention under the Trump administration*. American Civil Liberties Union.

Coe, K., Harmon, M. P., Verner, B., & Tonn, A. (1993). Tattoos and male alliances. *Human Nature, 4*(2), 199–204.

Cook, T. D., Church, M. B., Ajanaku, S., Shadish, W. R., Kim, J.-R., & Cohen, R. (1996). The development of occupational aspirations and expectations among inner-city boys. *Child Development, 67*(6), 3368–3385.

Cornelius, W. A. (2001). Death at the border: Efficacy and unintended consequences of US immigration control policy. *Population and Development Review, 27*(4), 661–685.

Cotton, C. R., & Range, L. M. (1990). Children's death concepts: Relationship to cognitive functioning, age, experience with death, fear of death, and hopelessness. *Journal of Clinical Child Psychology, 19*(2), 123–127.

Covey, H. C. (2010). *Street gangs throughout the world*. Charles C Thomas.

Crenshaw, K., & Peller, G. (1992). Reel time/real justice colloquy: Racism in the wake of the Los Angeles riots: Essay. *Denver University Law Review, 70*(2), 283–296.Crivello, G., Camfield, L., & Woodhead, M. (2009). How can children tell us about their wellbeing? Exploring the potential of participatory research approaches within young lives. *Social Indicators Research, 90*(1), 51–72.

Dalton, J. (2019, July 8). Trump's migrant camps on U.S. border 'undignified and damaging', says UN human rights chief. *The Independent.*

Da Silva, C. (2019, October 25). More than 5,400 children were separated from their parents by the Trump administration, "shocking" new tally shows. *Newsweek.*

Davidson, R. J., Kabat-Zinn, J., Schumacher, J., Rosenkranz, M., Muller, D., Santorelli, S. F., . . . & Sheridan, J. F. (2003). Alterations in brain and immune function produced by mindfulness meditation. *Psychosomatic Medicine, 65*(4), 564–570.

Delgado Bernal, D. (1998). Using a chicana feminist epistemology in educational research—ProQuest. *Harvard Educational Review.*

de los Ríos, C. V. (2017). Picturing ethnic studies: Photovoice and youth literacies of social action. *Journal of Adolescent & Adult Literacy, 61*(1), 15-24.

De Genova, N. (2002). Migrant "illegality" and deportability in everyday life. *Annual Review of Anthropology, 31*(1), 419–447.

De Genova, N. (2004). The legal production of Mexican/migrant "illegality." *Latino Studies, 2*(2), 160–185.

De Genova, N., & Peutz, N. (2010). *The deportation regime: Sovereignty, space, and the freedom of movement*. Duke University Press.

Demjén, Z. (2016). Laughing at cancer: Humour, empowerment, solidarity and coping online. *Journal of Pragmatics, 101*, 18–30.

Dickerson, C., & Nixon, R. (2017). Trump administration considers separating families to combat illegal immigration. *The New York Times*, December 21.

Diver-Stamnes, A. C. (1995). *Lives in the balance: Youth, poverty, and education in Watts*. SUNY Press.

Doty, R. L., & Wheatley, E. S. (2013). Private detention and the immigration industrial complex. *International Political Sociology, 7*(4), 426–443.

Dreby, J. (2012a). *How today's immigration enforcement policies impact children, families, and communities: A view from the ground*. Center for American Progress.

Dreby, J. (2012b). The burden of deportation on children in Mexican immigrant families. *Journal of Marriage and Family, 74*(4), 829–845.

Dreby, J., & Adkins, T. (2012). The strength of family ties: How US migration shapes children's ideas of family. *Childhood, 19*(2), 169–187.

Driessnack, M. (2005). Children's drawings as facilitators of communication: A meta-analysis. *Journal of Pediatric Nursing, 20*(6), 415–423.

Du Bois, W.E.B. (1903). *The souls of Black folk: Essays and sketches*. New York, NY: Fawcett.

Durand, J., & Massey, D. S. (2019). Evolution of the Mexico-U.S. migration system: Insights from the Mexican Migration Project. *Annals of the American Academy of Political and Social Science, 684*(1), 21–42.

Eagly, I. V. (2010). Prosecuting immigrating. *Northwestern University Law Review*, *104*(4), 1281–1360.

Ellis, B. D., Gonzales, R. G., & Rendón García, S. A. (2019). The Power of Inclusion: Theorizing "Abjectivity" and Agency Under DACA. *Cultural Studies — Critical Methodologies*, *19*(3), 161–172.

Enriquez, L. E. (2017). A "master status" or the "final straw"? Assessing the role of immigration status in Latino undocumented youths' pathways out of school. *Journal of Ethnic and Migration Studies*, *43*(9), 1526–1543.

Eschbach, K., Hagan, J., Rodriguez, N., Hernandez-Leon, R., & Bailey, S. (1999). Death at the Border. *International Migration Review*, *33*(2), 430–454.

Espinosa, G. (2007). "Today we act, tomorrow we vote": Latino religions, politics, and activism in contemporary US civil society. *Annals of the American Academy of Political and Social Science*, *612*(1), 152–171.

Felker-Kantor, M. (2018). "Kid thugs are spreading terror through the streets": Youth, crime, and the expansion of the juvenile justice system in Los Angeles, 1973–1980. *Journal of Urban History*, *44*(3), 476–500.

Farris, E. M., & Silber Mohamed, H. (2018). Picturing immigration: How the media criminalizes immigrants. *Politics, Groups, and Identities*, *6*(4), 814–824.

Fielder, E. R. (2014). On strike and on stage: Migration, mobilization, and the cultural work of El Teatro Campesino. *American Studies in Scandinavia*, *46*(1), 103–121.

Fondren, K., Lawson, M., Speidel, R., McDonnell, C. G., & Valentino, K. (2020). Buffering the effects of childhood trauma within the school setting: A systematic review of trauma-informed and trauma-responsive interventions among trauma-affected youth. *Children and Youth Services Review*, *109*.

Forth, A. E., Kosson, D. S., & Hare, R. D. (2003). *Hare psychopathy checklist: Youth version*. Multi-Health Systems.

Foucault, M. (1984). Docile bodies. In M. Foucault, *The Foucault reader* (P. Rabinow, Ed.) (Vol. 181). Pantheon.

Foucault, M. (2012). *Discipline and punish: The birth of the prison*. Knopf Doubleday.

Frank, B. B., & Schrobenhauser-Clonan, A. (2014). Effectiveness of a school-based yoga program on adolescent mental health, stress coping strategies, and attitudes toward violence: Findings from a high-risk sample. *Journal of Applied School Psychology*, *30*(1), 29–49.

Freire, P. (2000). *Pedagogy of the oppressed*. Continuum.

Freire, P. (2018). *Pedagogy of the Oppressed: 50th Anniversary Edition*. Bloomsbury Publishing USA.

García, O. (2009). Education, multilingualism and translanguaging in the 21st century. In *Social justice through multilingual education* (pp. 140–158). Multilingual Matters.

Gerstein, J. (2020). *Court won't let Trump pardon void guilty verdict against Arpaio*. POLITICO. https://www.politico.com/news/2020/02/27/trump-pardon-arpaio-117918

Giroux, H. A. (2017). *The public in peril: Trump and the menace of American authoritarianism*. Routledge.

———. (2018). *Pedagogy and the politics of hope: Theory, culture, and schooling: A critical reader*. Routledge.

———. (2009). *Youth in a Suspect Society: Democracy or Disposability?* Springer.

Golash-Boza, T. M. (2015). *Deported: Immigrant policing, disposable labor and global capitalism*. NYU Press.

Gomez Cervantes, A., Alvord, D., & Menjívar, C. (2018). "Bad hombres": The effects of criminalizing Latino immigrants through law and media in the rural Midwest. *Migration Letters, 15*(2), 182–196.

Gonzales, R. G. (2011). *Learning to Be Illegal: Undocumented Youth and Shifting Legal Contexts in the Transition to Adulthood.*

Gonzalez, T. (2012). Keeping kids in schools: Restorative justice, punitive discipline, and the school to prison pipeline. *Journal of Law & Education, 41*(2), 281–336.

Gonzalez, D., Hansen, R., & Wingett Sanchez, Y. (2020). How SB 1070 helped pave the way for Donald Trump's rise to the presidency. *USA TODAY.*

Gonzales, R. G., Terriquez, V., & Ruszczyk, S. P. (2014). Becoming DACAmented: Assessing the short-term benefits of Deferred Action for Childhood Arrivals (DACA). *American Behavioral Scientist, 58*(14), 1852–1872.

Goodman, A. (2020). *The deportation machine: America's long history of expelling immigrants*. Princeton University Press.

Gordon, L. (2001). *The great Arizona orphan abduction* (Rev. ed.). Harvard University Press.

Greenberg, M. T., & Harris, A. R. (2012). Nurturing mindfulness in children and youth: Current state of research. *Child Development Perspectives, 6*, 161–166.

Greene, J. A. (2013). Local democracy on ICE: The Arizona laboratory. In D. C. Brotherton, Daniel L. Stageman, & S. P. Leyro (Eds.), *Outside justice* (pp. 23–44). Springer.

Guerin-Gonzales, C. (1994). *Mexican workers and American dreams: Immigration, repatriation, and California farm labor, 1900–1939*. Rutgers University Press.

Guerra, L. F. (2016). *Beautified by the spirit: Community murals as a liberative source for constructive pneumatology*. Graduate Theological Union.

Hagan, J., Castro, B., & Rodriguez, N. (2009). The effects of U.S. deportation policies on immigrant families and communities: Cross-border perspectives Panel 3: Families and global migration. *North Carolina Law Review, 88*(5), 1799–1824.

Hannegan-Martinez, S. (2020). *Literacies of love: Trauma, healing, and pedagogical shifts in an English classroom*. University of California, Los Angeles.

Hannegan-Martinez, S., Mendoza Aviña, S., Delgado Bernal, D., & Solorzano, D. G. (2022) (Re)imagining transformational resistance: Seeds of resistance and pedagogical ruptures. *Urban Education.*

Hansen, N. (2015). Vivencias juveniles de la migración centroamericana—La película "La Jaula de Oro." FLACSO Andes, http://repositorio.flacsoandes.edu.ec, February.

Harnett, P. H., & Dawe, S. (2012). The contribution of mindfulness-based therapies for children and families and proposed conceptual integration. *Child and Adolescent Mental Health, 17*(4), 195–208.

Haynes, C., & Sattler, J. (2017). The Twitter effect: How Trump used social media to stamp his brand and shape the media narrative on immigration. *Digital Commons*, Political Science Faculty Publications, https://digitalcommons.newhaven.edu, November.

Heidbrink, L. (2014). *Migrant youth, transnational families, and the state: Care and contested interests.* University of Pennsylvania Press.

Heidbrink, L. (2020). *Migranthood: Youth in a new era of deportation.* Stanford University Press.

Hennessy-Fiske, M. (2019, May 24). Six migrant children have died in U.S. custody. Here's what we know about them. Los Angeles Times, https://www.latimes.com.

Hernandez, K. L. (2010). *Migra! A history of the U.S. Border Patrol.* University of California Press.

Herrington, O., & Llp, S. (2009). *HALFWAY HOME: Unaccompanied children in immigration custody.* Women's Refugee Commission.

Hing, B. O. (2018). *American presidents, deportations, and human rights violations: From Carter to Trump.* Cambridge University Press.

Hinnant, J. B., & El-Sheikh, M. (2009). Children's externalizing and internalizing symptoms over time: The role of individual differences in patterns of RSA responding. *Journal of Abnormal Child Psychology*, 37(8), 1049.

Hodwitz, O., & Massingale, K. (2021). Rhetoric and hate crimes: Examining the public response to the Trump narrative. *Behavioral Sciences of Terrorism and Political Aggression*, 0(0), 1–18.

Hoffman, A. (1974). *Unwanted Mexican Americans in the Great Depression: Repatriation pressures, 1929–1939.* University of Arizona Press.

hooks, B. (1996). Teaching to transgress: Education as the practice of freedom. *Journal of Leisure Research*, 28(4), 316.

hooks, b. (2001). *All about love: New visions.* Harper Perennial.

hooks, b. & Mesa-Bains, A. (2017). *Homegrown: Engaged cultural criticism.* Routledge.

Hopkins, N. (1994). School pupils' perceptions of the police that visit schools: Not all police are "pigs." *Journal of Community & Applied Social Psychology*, 4(3), 189–207.

Hornor, G. (2015). Childhood trauma exposure and toxic stress: What the PNP needs to know. *Journal of Pediatric Health Care*, 29(2), 191–198.

Hrynkiw-Augimeri, L. K. (1998). *Assessing risk for violence in boys: A preliminary risk assessment study using the Early Assessment Risk List for Boys (EARL-20B)* (Unpublished master's thesis). Ontario Institute for Studies in Education, University of Toronto, Ontario, Canada.

Huerta, J. A. (1977). Chicano agit-prop: The early actos of El Teatro Campesino. *Latin American Theatre Review*, 45–58.

Huerta, J. A. (2016). The Campesino's early actos as templates for today's students. *Latin American Theatre Review*, 50(1), 133–145.

Hudson, A. (2020). Learning From a Young Indigenous Artist: What Can Hip-Hop Teach Us? *Art Education*, 73(1), 18–22.

Immigrant Detention Primer. (2021). TRAC Immigration, Immigration Detention Quick Facts, https://trac.syr.edu.

Jiménez, L. (2011). America's legacy of xenophobia: The curious origins of Arizona Senate Bill 1070. *California Western Law Review, 48,* 279.

Johnson, S. B., Riley, A. W., Granger, D. A., & Riis, J. (2013). The science of early life toxic stress for pediatric practice and advocacy. *Pediatrics, 131*(2), 319–327.

Johnson, G. A., Pfister, A. E., & Vindrola-Padros, C. (2012). Drawings, photos, and performances: Using visual methods with children. *Visual Anthropology Review, 28*(2), 164-178.

Jordan, M. (2019, September 27). Judge blocks Trump administration plan to detain migrant children. *The New York Times.*

Kandel, W. A. (2018). *The Trump administration's "zero tolerance" immigration enforcement policy.* Congressional Research Service.

Kandel, W., & Massey, D. S. (2002). The culture of Mexican migration: A theoretical and empirical analysis. *Social Forces, 80*(3), 981–1004.

Kanno-Young, Z. (2020, March 6). Immigration officers say asylum deal with Guatemala is unlawful. *The New York Times.*

Kellermann, P. F., & Hudgins, K. (Eds.). (2000). *Psychodrama with trauma survivors: Acting out your pain.* Jessica Kingsley Publishers.

Kellogg, R. (1969). Analyzing Children's Art. *Palo Alto, California.* National Press Books.

Kerwin, D. (2018). From IIRIRA to Trump: Connecting the dots to the current us immigration policy crisis. *Journal on Migration and Human Security, 6*(3), 192–204.

King, M. L. (1963). *I have a dream.* Edizioni Mondadori.

King, M. L. (1968). *I have been to the mountaintop.* American Rhetoric.

Kirksey, J. J., Sattin-Bajaj, C., Gottfried, M. A., Freeman, J., & Ozuna, C. S. (2020). Deportations near the schoolyard: Examining immigration enforcement and racial/ethnic gaps in educational outcomes. *AERA Open, 6*(1).

Kort-Butler, L. (2012). Extracurricular activity involvement and adolescent self-esteem.

Lacayo, A. E. (2011). *One Year Later: A Look at SB 1070 and Copycat Legislation.* http://publications.nclr.org/handle/123456789/666

Lacey, M., & Seelye, K. Q. (2011, November 10). Recall Election Claims Arizona Anti-Immigration Champion. *The New York Times.*

Lacey, M. (2011). U.S. finds pervasive bias against Latinos by Arizona sheriff. New York Times, https://www.nytimes.com, December 15.

Ladson-Billings, G. (2000). Racialized discourses and ethnic epistemologies Handbook of qualitative research (pp. 257277). Thousand Oaks, CA: Sage Publications.

Landale, N. S., Hardie, J. H., Oropesa, R. S., & Hillemeier, M. M. (2015). Behavioral Functioning among Mexican-origin Children: Does Parental Legal Status Matter? *Journal of Health and Social Behavior 56*(1), 2–18.

Lechica Buenavista, T. (2015). Model (undocumented) minorities and "illegal" immigrants: Centering Asian Americans and US carcerality in undocumented student discourse: Race Ethnicity and Education: Vol 21, No 1. *Race and Ethnicity in Education.*

Lee, S. J. (1994). Behind the Model-Minority Stereotype: Voices of High- and Low-Achieving Asian American Students. *Anthropology & Education Quarterly, 25*(4), 413–429. JSTOR.

Lawyers can't find parents of 545 migrant children separated by the Trump administration. (2020, Oct. 20). MSNBC, https://www.msnbc.com.

Levin, S. (2019, Dec. 10). US immigration officials bar doctors from giving flu shots to detained kids. The Guardian, https://www.theguardian.com.

Lewis, L. B., Galloway-Gilliam, L., Flynn, G., Nomachi, J., Keener, L. C., & Sloane, D. C. (2011). Transforming the urban food desert from the grassroots up: A model for community change. *Family & Community Health, 34*, S92–S101.

Lind, D. (2018, July 5). The Trump administration just admitted it doesn't know how many kids are still separated from their parents. *Vox.*

Linesch, D., Aceves, H. C., Quezada, P., Trochez, M., & Zuniga, E. (2012). An art therapy exploration of immigration with Latino families. *Art Therapy, 29*(3), 120-126.

Long, C., & Taxin, A. (2019, August 21). Trump moves to end limits on detention of migrant children. AP News. https://apnews.com/b66e925bdda14877ba8edfeoec55a0cc

Love, B. L. (2016). Anti-Black state violence, classroom edition: The spirit murdering of Black children. *Journal of Curriculum and Pedagogy, 13*(1), 22–25.

Love, B. L. (2019). *We want to do more than survive: Abolitionist teaching and the pursuit of educational freedom.* Beacon Press.

Lukinbeal, C., & Sharp, L. (2015). Performing America's toughest sheriff: Media as practice in Joe Arpaio's Old West. *GeoJournal. 80*(6), 881–892.

Macias, E. P., & Morales, L. S. (2001). Crossing the border for health care. *Journal of Health Care for the Poor and Underserved, 12*(1), 77–87.

Macias, J. (2019, Nov. 29). "Our money was stolen": Braceros wait for wages owed from decades ago. Sonoma Index-Tribune, https://www.sonomanews.com.

MacLean, S. A., Agyeman, P. O., Walther, J., Singer, E. K., Baranowski, K. A., & Katz, C. L. (2019). Mental health of children held at a United States immigration detention center. *Social Science & Medicine, 230*, 303–308.

Malchiodi, C. A. (2008). *Creative interventions with traumatized children.* Guilford Press.

Malhotra, R. (2009). American exceptionalism and the myth of the frontiers. In R. K. Kanth (Ed.), *The challenge of Eurocentrism: Global perspectives, policy, and prospects* (pp. 171–215). Palgrave Macmillan.

Mallett, C. A. (2017). The school-to-prison pipeline: Disproportionate impact on vulnerable children and adolescents. *Education and Urban Society, 49*(6), 563-592.

Mapping L.A. is the Los Angeles Times' resource for maps, boundaries, demographics, schools and news in Los Angeles County. (2000). Los Angeles Times. http://maps.latimes.com/neighborhoods/neighborhood/watts/

Marcelo, P., & Herbert, G. (2021, August 5). Immigrant detentions soar despite Biden's campaign promises. AP NEWS, https://apnews.com.

Mariscal, J. (2010). Latin@s in the US military. In *Inside the Latin@ experience* (pp. 37–50). Springer.

Martin, L. L. (2012). "Catch and remove": Detention, deterrence, and discipline in US noncitizen family detention practice. *Geopolitics, 17*(2), 312–334.

Marsh, K. (2017). Creating bridges: Music, play and well-being in the lives of refugee and immigrant children and young people. *Music Education Research, 19*(1), 60–73.

Masten, A. S., Best, K. M., & Garmezy, N. (1990). Resilience and development: Contributions from the study of children who overcome adversity. *Development and Psychopathology, 2*(4), 425-444.

Masten, A. S., Herbers, J. E., Cutuli, J. J., & Lafavor, T. L. (2008). Promoting Competence and Resilience in the School Context. *Professional School Counseling.*

Masten, A. S. (2011). Resilience in children threatened by extreme adversity: Frameworks for research, practice, and translational synergy. *Development and Psychopathology, 23*(2), 493–506.

Massey, D. S., Durand, J., & Malone, N. J. (2002). *Beyond smoke and mirrors: Mexican immigration in an era of economic integration.* Russell Sage Foundation.

Massey, D. S., & Pren, K. A. (2012). Unintended consequences of US immigration policy: Explaining the post-1965 surge from Latin America. *Population and Development Review, 38*(1), 1–29.

Mayers, S., & Freedman, J. (2019). *Solito, solita: Crossing borders with youth refugees from Central America.* Haymarket Books.

McDowell, M. G., & Wonders, N. A. (2010). Keeping migrants in their place: Technologies of control and racialized public space in Arizona. *Social Justice, 36*(2), 54–72.

McEwen, B. S. (2017). Neurobiological and systemic effects of chronic stress. *Chronic Stress, 1,* 2470547017692328.

Medina, D., & Menjívar, C. (2015). The context of return migration: Challenges of mixed-status families in Mexico's schools. *Ethnic and Racial Studies, 38*(12), 2123–2139.

Mehta, J., & Fine, S. (2019). *In search of deeper learning: The quest to remake the American high school.* Harvard University Press.

Mendel-Reyes, M. (1994). Remembering Cesar. *Radical History Review, 58,* 143–150.

Menjívar, C. (2006). Family reorganization in a context of legal uncertainty: Guatemalan and Salvadoran immigrants in the United States. *International Journal of Sociology of the Family, 32*(2), 223–245. JSTOR.

Menjívar, C., & Abrego, L. J. (2012). Legal violence: Immigration law and the lives of Central American immigrants. *American Journal of Sociology, 117*(5), 1380–1421.

Menjívar, C., Simmons, W. P., Alvord, D., & Salerno Valdez, E. (2018, July 27). Immigration enforcement, the racialization of legal status, and perceptions of the police. *Du Bois Review: Social Science Research on Race.* Cambridge Core, https://www.cambridge.org.

Michaud, N. D. (2010). From 287(g) to SB1070: The decline of the federal immigration partnership and the rise of state-level immigration enforcement. *Arizona Law Review, 52*(4), 1083–1134.

Michaesu, G., & Baettig, D. (1996). An integrated model of posttraumatic stress disorder. *European Journal of Psychiatry, 10*(4), 243-245.

Miller, T., & Nevins, J. (2017). Beyond Trump's big, beautiful wall. *NACLA Report on the Americas, 49*(2), 145–151.

Miroff, N. (2017, Sept. 28). Deportations slow under Trump despite increase in arrests by ICE. *Washington Post.*

Mishori, R. (2020). U.S. policies and their effects on immigrant children's health. *American Family Physician, 101*(4), 202–204.

Morgane, B. (1970, January 1). *La jaula de Oro, canción interpretada por Los Tigres del norte.*

Motomura, H. (2006). *Americans in waiting: The lost story of immigration and citizenship in the United States.* Oxford University Press.

Muzaffar, C., Pierce, S., & O'Connor, A. (2019, April 24). *Despite flurry of actions, Trump administration faces constraints in achieving its immigration agenda.* Migration Policy Institute.

National Immigration Law Center. (2017). *Provisions of the 2010 and 2017 Dream Acts and DACA.*

Nava, E. J. (2014). Federal immigration reform would help New Jersey's striving immigrants and boost the state's economy. New Jersey Policy Perspective, https://www.njpp.org.

Navarro, F. (1998). A New Way of Thinking in Action: The Zapatistas in Mexico—A Postmodern Guerrilla Movement?. *Rethinking Marxism, 10*(4), 155-165.

Negrón-Gonzales, G., Abrego, L., & Coll, K. (2015). Introduction: Immigrant Latina/o youth and illegality: Challenging the politics of deservingness. *Association of Mexican American Educators Journal, 9*(3).

New York Foundling Hospital v. Gatti, 203 US 429 (Supreme Court 1906).

Ngai, M. M. (1998). *Illegal aliens and alien citizens: United States immigration policy and racial formation, 1924-1945.* Columbia University.

Ngai, M. M. (2014). *Impossible subjects: Illegal aliens and the making of Modern America* (Updated ed.). Princeton University Press.

Nowlin, S. (2020, February 12). Doctors without borders report shows "wait in Mexico" policy exposing asylum seekers to physical and mental harm. *San Antonio Current.*

O'Leary, A. O., & Sanchez, A. (2011). Anti-immigrant Arizona: Ripple effects and mixed immigration status households under "policies of attrition" considered. *Journal of Borderlands Studies, 26*(1), 115–133.

Orellana, M. F. (2001). The work kids do: Mexican and Central American immigrant children's contributions to households and schools in California. *Harvard Educational rReview, 71*(3), 366–390.

Orellana, M. F., Thorne, B., Chee, A., & Lam, W. S. E. (2001). Transnational childhoods: The participation of children in processes of family migration. *Social Problems, 48*(4), 572–591.

Orellana, M. F. (2009). Translating childhoods. In *Translating Childhoods.* Rutgers University Press.

Orellana, M. F. (2015). *Immigrant Children in Transcultural Spaces: Language, Learning, and Love.* Routledge.

Passel, J., & Taylor, P. (2010, August 11). Unauthorized immigrants and their U.S.-born children. Pew Research Center, https://www.pewresearch.org.

Passel, J. (2011). Demography of immigrant youth: Past, present, and future. *The Future of Children, 21*(1), 19–41.

Passel, J. S., Cohn, D. V., & Lopez, M. H. (2011). Hispanics account for more than half of nation's growth in past decade. *Washington, DC: Pew Hispanic Center*, 1–7.

Patton, A. L. (1992). The endless cycle of abuse: Why 42 U.S.C. 1983 is ineffective in deterring police brutality. *Hastings Law Journal*, 44(3), 753–808.

Pavlakovich-Kochi, V. (2006). The Arizona-Sonora region: A decade of transborder region building. *Estudios Sociales* (Hermosillo, Sonora), 14(27), 25–55.

Phippen, J. W. (2016, May 6). Is it an immigration detention facility or a child-care center? *The Atlantic*.

Pierce, S., Bolter, J., & Selee, A. (2018). *U.S. immigration policy under Trump: Deep changes and lasting impacts*. Migration Policy Institute.

Pierce, S., & Bolter, J. (2020). Dismantling and reconstructing the U.S. immigration system: A catalog of changes under the Trump presidency. MPI, https://www.migrationpolicy.org, July 30.

Pine, D., & Cohen, J. (2002). Trauma in children and adolescents: Risk and treatment of psychiatric sequelae. *Biological Psychiatry*, 51(7), 519-531.

Piro, J. M. (2008). Foucault and the architecture of surveillance: Creating regimes of power in schools, shrines, and society. *Educational Studies*, 44(1), 30–46.

Porges, S. W. (1995). Cardiac vagal tone: A physiological index of stress. *Neuroscience & Biobehavioral Reviews*, 19(2), 225–233.

Portilla, J. (1966). Fenomenología del relajo y otros ensayos. *México: CREA*.

Potochnick, S. R., & Perreira, K. M. (2010). Depression and Anxiety among First-Generation Immigrant Latino Youth: Key Correlates and Implications for Future Research. *The Journal of Nervous and Mental Disease*, 198(7), 470–477.

Ramkhelawan, D. (2019). The separation of migrant families at the border under the Trump administration's zero-tolerance policy: A critical analysis of the mistreatment of immigrant children held in U.S. custody. *Child and Family Law Journal*, 7(1).

Rappleye, H., & Seville, L. R. (2019, June 9). 24 immigrants have died in ICE custody during the Trump administration. NBC News, https://www.nbcnews.com.

Rice, K. F., & Groves, B. M. (2005). *Hope and healing: A caregiver's guide to helping young children affected by trauma*. Washington D.C.: Zero to Three.

Rivera, C. (2014). The brown threat: Post-9/11 conflations of Latina/os and Middle Eastern Muslims in the US American imagination. *Latino Studies*, 12(1), 44–64.

Reas, E. I. (2009). ICE raids: Compounding production, contradiction, and capitalism. *Berkeley Undergraduate Journal*, 22(1).

Reilly, K., & Carlisle, M. (2019, Sept. 30). The Trump administration's move to end rule limiting detention of migrant children rejected in court. Time, https://time.com.

Rendón García, S. A. (2019). "No vamos a tapar el sol con un dedo": Maternal communication concerning immigration status. *Journal of Latinx Psychology*, 7(4) 284.

Roberts, D. (2002). *Shattered bonds: The color of child welfare* (Repr. ed.). Civitas Books.

Robertson, C. B., & Manta, I. D. (2019). (Un)Civil denaturalization. *New York University Law Review*, 94(3), 402–471.

Roche, K. M., Vaquera, E., White, R. M. B., & Rivera, M. I. (2018). Impacts of Immigration Actions and News and the Psychological Distress of U.S. Latino Parents Raising Adolescents. *Journal of Adolescent Health*, 62(5), 525–531.

Rodríguez, J. M. (2014). *Sexual futures, queer gestures, and other Latina longings*. NYU Press.

Rodriguez Vega, S. (2015). From Barbies to Boycotts: How Immigration Raids in Arizona Created a Ten-Year Old Activist. *InterActions: UCLA Journal of Education and Information Studies*, 11(2).

Rodriguez Vega, S. (2017). Selfless selfie citizenship: Chupacabras selfie project. In A. Kuntsman (Ed.), *Selfie citizenship* (pp. 137–147). Springer.

Rodriguez Vega, S. (2018a). Borders and badges: Arizona's children confront detention and deportation through art. *Latino Studies*, 16 (2018), 310–340.

Rodriguez Vega, S. (2018b). Praxis of resilience & resistance: "We can STOP Donald Trump" and other messages from immigrant children. *Association of Mexican American Educators Journal*, 12(3), 122–147.

Rodriguez Vega, S. (2019). Teatro vs. Trump: Children in South Central Los Angeles fight back. *Aztlan: A Journal of Chicano Studies*, 44(1), 189–198.

Rong, X. L. , & Preissle, J. (1998). *Educating immigrant students: What we need to know to meet the challenge*. Thousand Oaks, CA: Corwin Press.

Rosaldo, R. (1989). Imperialist nostalgia. *Representations*, 26, 107–122.

Rotella, S., Golden, T., & ProPublica. (2019, Feb. 21). Human smugglers are thriving under Trump: The president's "zero tolerance" policy drains manpower and money from deeper probes that target criminal syndicates. *The Atlantic*.

Rousseau, C., Drapeau, A., Lacroix, L., Bagilishya, D., & Heusch, N. (2005). Evaluation of a classroom program of creative expression workshops for refugee and immigrant children. *Journal of Child Psychology and Psychiatry*, 46(2), 180–185.

Rousseau, C., & Heusch, N. (2000). The trip: A creative expression project for refugee and immigrant children. *Art Therapy*, 17(1), 31–40.

Rumbaut, R. G., Dingeman, K., & Robles, A. (2018, July 2). Immigration and crime and the criminalization of immigration. Social Science Research Network.

Rutter, M. (1979). Separation experiences: A new look at an old topic. *The Journal of Pediatrics*, 95(1), 147–154.

Ryan, G. W., & Bernard, H. R. (2003). Techniques to identify themes. *Field Methods*, 15(1), 85–109.

Salazar, A. (2020). *Land of the cranes*. Scholastic Inc.

Sandoval, C. (2000). *Methodology of the oppressed* (Vol. 18). University of Minnesota Press.

Santa Ana, O. (2002). *Brown tide rising: Metaphors of Latinos in contemporary American public discourse*. University of Texas Press.

Santillano, R., Potochnick, S., & Jenkins, J. (2020). Do immigration raids deter Head Start enrollment? *AEA Papers and Proceedings*, 110, 419–423.

Santos, B. (2019). *Theatre of the Oppressed—roots and wings: A theory of praxis*. Kuringa.

Santos, C. E., Menjívar, C., VanDaalen, R. A., Kornienko, O., Updegraff, K. A., & Cruz, S. (2017). Awareness of Arizona's immigration law SB1070 predicts classroom behavioural problems among Latino youths during early adolescence. *Ethnic and Racial Studies, 41*(9), 1672–1690.

Saresma, T., Karkulehto, S., & Varis, P. (2021). Gendered Violence Online: Hate Speech as an Intersection of Misogyny and Racism. In M. Husso, S. Karkulehto, T. Saresma, A. Laitila, J. Eilola, & H. Siltala (Eds.), *Violence, Gender and Affect: Interpersonal, Institutional and Ideological Practices* (pp. 221–243). Springer International Publishing.

Schaaf, R. C., Miller, L. J., Seawell, D., & O'Keefe, S. (2003). Children With Disturbances in Sensory Processing: A Pilot Study Examining the Role of the Parasympathetic Nervous System. *American Journal of Occupational Therapy, 57*(4), 442–449.

Seifert, K. (2003). Childhood trauma: Its relationship to behavioral and psychiatric disorders. *Forensic Examiner, 12*(9), 27–33.

Seifert, K. (2006). *How children become violent: Keeping your kids out of gangs, terrorist organizations, and cults.* Kathryn Seifert.

Seifert, K., & Ray, K. (2012). *Youth violence: Theory, prevention, and intervention.* Springer.

Selye, H. (1956). *The stress of life.* McGraw-Hill Education.

Shahani, A., & Greene, J. (2009). *Local democracy on ICE: Why state and local governments have no business in federal immigration law enforcement.* Justice Strategies.

Shaw, R. D. (2018). The vulnerability of urban elementary school arts programs: A case study. *Journal of Research in Music Education, 65*(4), 393–415.

Sheehy, G. (2016). America's therapists are worried about Trump's effect on your mental health. *Politico.*

Shonkoff, J. P., Garner, A. S., Siegel, B. S., Dobbins, M. I., Earls, M. F., McGuinn, L., . . . & Committee on Early Childhood, Adoption, and Dependent Care. (2012). The lifelong effects of early childhood adversity and toxic stress. *Pediatrics, 129*(1), e232–e246.

Shonkoff, J. P., Duncan, G. J., Fisher, P. A., Magnuson, K., & Raver, C. (2011). Building the brain's "air traffic control" system: How early experiences shape the development of executive function. *Contract, 11.*

Silber Mohamed, H., & Farris, E. M. (2019). 'Bad hombres'? An examination of identities in US media coverage of immigration. *Journal of Ethnic and Migration Studies,* 1–19.

Singh, M. (2019, September 26). Trump sets cap for refugee admission at an all-time low. *The Guardian.*

Slack, J., Martinez, D., Whiteford, S., & Lee, A. (2013). *Border militarization and health: Violence, death, and security.* Puentes Consortium, University of Arizona.

Smith-Maddox, R., & Solorzano, D. G. (2002). Using critical race theory, Paulo Freire's problem-posing method, and case study research to confront race and racism in education. *Qualitative Inquiry, 8*(1), 66–84.

Smokowski, P. R., & Bacallao, M. (2011). *Becoming bicultural: Risk, resilience, and Latino youth.* NYU Press.Solorzano, D., & Delgado Bernal, D. (2001). Critical race theory, transformational resistance and social justice: Chicana and Chicano students in an urban context. *Urban Education, 36*(3), 208–342.

Soto, R. C., Berger Cardoso, J., Brabeck, K., Fix, M., Ruiz, A. (2020). *Immigration Enforcement and the Mental Health of Latino High School Students*. Migrationpolicy.Org.

Southwick, S. M., Vythilingam, M., & Charney, D. S. (2005). The psychobiology of depression and resilience to stress: Implications for prevention and treatment. *Annual Review of Clinical Psychology, 1*(1), 255–291.

Speece, M. W., & Brent, S. B. (1984). Children's understanding of death: A review of three components of a death concept. *Child Development*, 1671–1686.

Stephen, L. (2007). Transborder lives. In *Transborder Lives*. Duke University Press.

Straus, A., & Corbin, J. (1998). *Basics of qualitative research: Techniques and procedures for developing grounded theory*. Sage.

Stuart, T. (2020, October 13). Why Trump's immigration policies will be so hard to undo. *Rolling Stone*.

Stumpf, J. (2006). The crimmigration crisis: Immigrants, crime, and sovereign power. *American University Law Review 56*, 367.

Suárez-Orozco, C., & Suárez-Orozco, M. M. (2009). *Children of immigration*. Harvard University Press.

Suárez-Orozco, C., Suárez-Orozco, M. M., & Todorova, I. (2009). *Learning a new land*. Harvard University Press.

Suárez-Orozco, M., & Suárez-Orozco, C. (2000). Some conceptual considerations in the interdisciplinary study of immigrant children. *Immigrant Voices: In Search of Educational Equity*, 17–36.

Suárez-Orozco, M. M., & Quin, D. B. (2006). Globalización: Cultura y educación en el milenio. *Globalización y justicia internacional, 2006, ISBN 978-968-16-8284-2, págs. 129-177*, 129–177.

Suárez-Orozco, C., Yoshikawa, H., Teranishi, R., & Suárez-Orozco, M. (2011). Growing Up in the Shadows: The Developmental Implications of Unauthorized Status. *Harvard Educational Review, 81*(3), 438–473.

Summers Sandoval, T. F. (2008). Disobedient bodies: Racialization, resistance, and the mass (re)articulation of the Mexican immigrant body. *American Behavioral Scientist, 52*(4), 580–597.

Szkupinski Quiroga, S., Medina, D. M., & Glick, J. (2014). In the belly of the beast: Effects of anti-immigration policy on Latino community members. *American Behavioral Scientist, 58*(13), 1723–1742.

Taylor, D. (2003). *The archive and the repertoire: Performing cultural memory in the Americas*. Duke University Press.

Terr, L. C. (1981). Psychic trauma in children: Observations following the Chowchilla school-bus kidnapping. *The American Journal of Psychiatry, 138*(1), 14–19.

Terrio, S. J. (2015). *Whose child am I?: Unaccompanied, undocumented children in U.S. immigration custody*. University of California Press.

Thompson, G., & Cohen, S. (2014, April 6). More deportations follow minor crimes, records show. *New York Times*.

Tichenor, D. J. (2009). *Dividing lines: The politics of immigration control in America.* Princeton University Press.

Torres-Rivas, E. (1998). Sobre el terror y la violencia política en América Latina. In *Violencia en una Sociedad en Transición: Ponencias.* San Salvador, El Salvador: PNUD.

Totenberg, N. (2022). Supreme Court's conservatives divided over "Remain in Mexico" policy. *NPR.*

Tuck, E., & Yang, K. W. (2011). Youth resistance revisited: New theories of youth negotiations of educational injustices. *International Journal of Qualitative Studies in Education, 24*(5), 521–530.

Tumanyan, M., & Huuki, T. (2020). Arts in working with youth on sensitive topics: A qualitative systematic review. *International Journal of Education Through Art, 16*(3), 381–397.

Uildriks, N. A., & Van Mastrigt, H. (1991). *Policing police violence.* Aberdeen University Press.U.S. Immigration and Customs Enforcement. (2020). *ICE guidance on COVID-19.* https://www.ice.gov/coronavirus

Valdez, L. (1990). *Luis Valdez—early works: Actos, bernabe and pensamiento serpentino.* Arte Publico Press.

Valencia, R. R. (2004). *Chicano school failure and success: Past, present, and future.* Routledge.

Valenzuela, A. (2005). Subtractive schooling, caring relations, and social capital in the schooling of US-Mexican youth. In L. Weis & M. Fine (Eds.), *Beyond silenced voices: Class, race, and gender in United States schools* (83–94). SUNY Press.

Vaughan, J. (2006). *Attrition through enforcement: A cost-effective strategy to shrink the illegal population.* Center for Immigration Studies.

Vélez-Ibáñez, C. G., & Szecsy, E. (2014). Politics, process, culture and human folly: Life among Arizonans and the reality of a transborder world. *Journal of Borderlands Studies, 29*(4), 405–417.

Villarreal, D. (2020). Hate crimes under Trump surged nearly 20 percent says FBI report. Newsweek, https://www.newsweek.com, November 16.

Viorst, J. (1986). *Necessary losses: The loves, illusions, dependencies, and impossible expectations that all of us have to give up in order to grow.* Simon & Schuster.

Vitello, P. (2006). Path to deportation can start with a traffic stop. New York Times, nytimes.com, April 4.

Waddoups, A. B., Yoshikawa, H., & Strouf, K. (2019). Developmental effects of parent–child separation. *Annual Review of Developmental Psychology, 1*(1), 387–410.

Walker, M. (2016). 50 years of static: The consistent injustices facing African Americans in Los Angeles from the Watts Rebellion to the present. *Toro Historical Review, 1*(1). https://journals.calstate.edu/tthr/article/view/2597/2284

Walters, W., & Cornelius, N. (2010). *The Deportation Regime: Sovereignty, Space, and the Freedom of Movement.* Duke University Press.

Waters, M., & Pineau, M. G. (2016). *The integration of immigrants into American society.* National Academies Press.

Wallace, S. P., Mendez-Luck, C., & Castañeda, X. (2009). Heading south: Why Mexican immigrants in California seek health services in Mexico. *Medical Care, 47*(6), 662.

Welch, K. (2017). School-to-prison pipeline. In (Schreck C. J. Ed.), *Encyclopedia of juvenile delinquency and justice*. John Wiley & Sons, Inc.

Welch, D. (2019). Pearce says blood may need to be spilled to protect the country. *AZFamily*.

Wessler, S. F. (2018, December 19). Is denaturalization the next front in the Trump administration's war on immigration? New York Times Magazine.

Williams, P., & Edelman, A. (2020, June 18). *Supreme Court blocks Trump from ending DACA in big win for Dreamers*. NBC News.

Yam, K. (2021, March 9). Anti-Asian hate crimes increased by nearly 150% in 2020, mostly in N.Y. and L.A., new report says. NBC News, https://www.nbcnews.com.

Ybarra-Frausto, T. (1989). *Rasquachismo: A Chicano sensibility*. School by the River Press.

Yoshikawa, H. (2011). *Immigrants raising citizens: Undocumented parents and their children*. Russell Sage Foundation.

Yoshikawa, H., Suárez-Orozco, C., & Gonzales, R. G. (2017). Unauthorized Status and Youth Development in the United States: Consensus Statement of the Society for Research on Adolescence. *Journal of Research on Adolescence*, 27(1), 4–19.

Yosso, T. J. (2005). Whose culture has capital? A critical race theory discussion of community cultural wealth. *Race Ethnicity and Education*, 8(1), 69–91.

Zavella, P. (2011). *I'm neither here nor there: Mexicans' quotidian struggles with migration and poverty*. Durham, NC: Duke University Press.

Zatz, M. S., & Rodriguez, N. (2015). *Dreams and nightmares: Immigration policy, youth, and families*. University of California Press.

Zhou, M. (1997). Growing up American: The challenge confronting immigrant children and children of immigrants. *Annual Review of Sociology*, 23(1), 63–95.

INDEX

Page numbers in *italics* indicate Figures and Tables.
Plates are indicated by plate number.

ABOUT THE AUTHOR

SILVIA RODRIGUEZ VEGA is an Assistant Professor of Chicana and Chicano Studies at the University of California, Santa Barbara.